HIGH CRIMES

HIGH CRIMES

William Deverell

McCLELLAND AND STEWART

The Canadian Publishers
McClelland and Stewart Limited
25 Hollinger Road
Toronto M4B 3G2

CANADIAN CATALOGUING IN PUBLICATION DATA

Deverell, William, 1937-
   High crimes

ISBN 0-7710-2732-X

I. Title.

PS8557.E92H53   C813'.54   C81-094705-6
PR9199.3.D477H53

Printed and bound in Canada
by T. H. Best Company Limited

To Tekla, who keeps me afloat

AUTHOR'S NOTE

After much inner debate, I decided not to single out for acknowledgement any of the persons who aided in my research. To name a few risks offence to many. (On the other hand, some of my informants will be much relieved to learn they have gone nameless.)

But I must mention one source of inspiration, the writer Harold Horwood. He remains innocent of any conscious effort to assist me, but the short piece of history entitled "Rum-Runners and Masterless Men" in his engaging book *Newfoundland* introduced me to the original Peter Kerrivan.

Peter Kerrivan was an Irish boy who in the mid-1700s had been impressed into the English navy, where he was treated as cruelly as a slave. He jumped ship in Newfoundland and became leader of a band of Irish outlaws, themselves either victims of press gangs or indentured servants who had been abducted from Ireland and sold like animals to the wealthy English fishing merchants of the Newfoundland coast.

They became known as the Masterless Men, and they learned to live like Indians in the wilderness, hunting caribou, raiding the stores of the rich merchants, and trading goods with poor settlers in remote villages. The English sent many expeditions of marines against these men, but inevitably their forays ended in bog or bush, along blind trails prepared for them by Kerrivan's men. Only four of his band were ever captured, and these boys were taken on board an English frigate, quickly tried and quickly hanged.

But in their main camp atop a flat hill known as the Butter Pot, Kerrivan and his followers reigned for fifty years. Ultimately he and others of the Masterless Men married Irish girls from the coastal villages and raised families. Peter Kerrivan lived to a ripe age.

"There are hundreds of Kerrivans living in the small fishing settlements today," Horwood writes. "Some of them, at least, are proud to trace their ancestry to the Robin Hood of the Butter Pot who defied the King of England in the eighteenth century."*

*From *Newfoundland,* by Harold Horwood (Toronto: Macmillan, 1969).

HIGH CRIMES

Johnny Nighthawk

Testing. One, two, three, testing. Hello, this is the voice of Johnny Nighthawk, who is known as The Hawk. Testing.

This is Tape One. I will mail you more cassettes as I complete them. Do not try to contact me, please. I mean no offence, but my meeting with you gave me the impression you are unskilled when it comes to such matters as the police. You might bring heat on me, especially if they know you are researching a book about Pete Kerrivan.

If in the end you get it published: fine. I will be in touch with you and you can buy me a drink. I don't want money. Just tell my end of it to the world. There are gaps in what I know, but you told me you have an excellent Deep Throat who has given you the cloak and dagger of it from the other side. The other side being the good guys. While I am with the bad guys. So to speak.

I am, as I dictate, sitting on a wobble-leg chair in my cabana, watching a tropical sun melt into the Pacific sea. I am in a little village that the world has never heard of, in a little country that the world has happily forgotten. I have a cold beer in my hand. And that is all you need to know about me, a minor character.

Pete Kerrivan is the major character. He is an all-time

major character. Pete Kerrivan, who treated me like a brother, not a Tonto. He was the Rocket Richard of reefer, the Pavarotti of pot. He had style and balls and an endless supply of jam.

And he had luck. So much luck that Pete began to suffer delusions of his own invincibility. The cops had not krypton enough to stop the mighty Smuggleman. Or so Pete thought. Then they pinched him and Kevin Kelly with eight tons last year.

But until that time, Pete enjoyed his own myth, and he liked to trade on it, to eke each sweet drop of romance from it. He worked his ancestral legend, too, for Pete believed he carried in his chromosomes the seed of another Peter Kerrivan, the hero of the Masterless Men of Newfoundland two centuries ago. They were poor Irish boys, kidnapped by English press gangs or sold to English fish-plant owners in Newfoundland. Peter Kerrivan led them to freedom, and they lived like rebel-outlaws, raiding the rich, helping the poor, defying the muskets of the Englishmen who tried to hunt them down.

In the fishing villages of the southern shore of New-foundland, the old uncles still recount the stories passed down to them about that bygone Peter Kerrivan. Just as I now recount the story of this twentieth-century reproduc-tion, a somewhat flawed replica of the original, I must admit. But if we give Pete's legend time and sustenance enough, it will grow, and his failings will be edited away.

I intend to tell you of Pete like it is, as the sports announ-cers say. With all the rough edges. His main fault was he insisted on trying to enhance his own legend, and ended up watering it down. Like the trip before the trip before the last one, when we brought up three tons in an old tug, right up the snout of Judas Bight while some of our boys were getting the fellows from the police launch drunk at a wedding party. The wedding never happened, of course, but we kept the law happy and out of our way, and Pete made a nice dollar. He distributed to the crew our usual paltry shares, then donated the rest to build a doctors' clinic in his home town. There has never been a patient in that bright and modern and empty little building. No doctor cares to practise in O'Donoghue's Nose, Province of Newfoundland.

But that's Pete. It was better he wasted his money on foolish projects than on the tables in Vegas or Nassau. If he wasn't giving to the poor, he was giving to the rich casino owners. He was a high roller, Pete. We used to call him Captain Jackpot.

Okay, let's get started here. A date to start – how about April the first, last year? The Day of the Fool in the early, bitchy days of spring. It was the final day of the eight-ton trial of Pete Kerrivan and Kevin Kelly in St. John's, Newfoundland.

To give you some perspective, I should tell you it happens also to be the time when the *punta roja* begins to flower. *Roja*: red. *Punta*: small leaf. I am talking about the mindfuck pot that grows at four thousand feet in the Sierra Nevada of northern Colombia. . . .

PART ONE
Operation Crackpot

CHAPTER ONE

April the first. *El primero de abril*. A high mountain valley where the air is sharp and pungent.

The cutters were walking the rows of the cannabis bushes, looking at the freshly-sprung buds. The male plants, betrayed by the white and purple flowers which are the sign of their sex, fell swiftly to the whistling machetes. They were waste, and would be heaped and burned. Now the female plants would begin to weep a rich and intoxicating resin, red as blood.

The female of this plant, this plant of the red leaf, has power and mystery.

April the first. A villa on the Caribbean coast near the old walled city of Cartagena. Senator Publio Victor Paez was presiding over a family meeting while his cutters in the Sierra Nevada were toiling in the late-day sun.

The harvest was only weeks away. Senator Paez had angrily rejected all proposals made by his own people, and now entreated Rudy Meyers, formerly of the Central Intelligence Agency, to find him a ship and crew.

"Bring me gringos," he said, "and a gringo ship. A *norteamericano* who knows the ocean, a man we can trust." His voice was a whiskey growl. He was an old Colombian bull.

"But we have our own ships," said his brother, who was

an army general. "We have our own people who are sailors."

Senator Paez slammed the flat of his hand on the table and spat his words. "My countrymen are *sapos*, diseased with cheating and thievery. Colombia, my country, is dying under the crush of its own rot. *Por Dios*, I could weep."

The senator reached across the table and roughly took the shoulders of Rudy Meyers between his hands. "Rudy," he said, "bring me a gringo, a great ocean sailor. An honest man and an honest ship. I will make him rich."

Meyers could feel the old man's hot and rancid breath but he didn't show his disgust.

"And I will make you rich, too."

Meyers pulled away from the senator, who was known as El Patron, and brushed at his shirt where Paez had wrinkled it. He sat upright in his chair. Meyers was as proud and hard as an ancient warrior king.

"What is the crop worth, senator?" Meyers' voice was soft and without inflection.

"Rudy, my good friend, you will see with your own eyes, and even then your eyes will not believe. An entire hectare. Ten thousand square metres. The man you bring us will command a ship that will be richer than all the galleons that sailed from here with pillaged gold five centuries ago." He wet his throat with a swallow of whiskey. "*Sinsemilla*. The female flower of *punta roja* marijuana." His voice rose. "Twelve billion pesos, Rudy. Twelve *billion* pesos!"

Meyers didn't flinch. But he thought: three hundred million U.S. dollars. Christ!

"Find me an honest gringo," Paez said.

"*A la orden*," Meyers said. "At your service." He snapped his briefcase shut and stood up to go.

April the first. Billy Lee Tinker, born and raised in the second to last house of a dead-end road in a village known as

Turkey Neck Creek, Alabama, was also in Colombia, waiting for his own small crop to arrive.

His restored B-26 bomber, well-loved, well-preserved, sat hidden in the shade of a palm-frond canopy. In three days, or five, or eight, or twelve – time is elastic in this country – a barge would come down the river from the dry hills of the Guajira, and Tinker would load his plane and goad and curse it into the air for the long flight home.

In the meantime he was spending the gentle hours under a cypress tree, his John Deere peaked cap pulled over his eyes, his hands behind his head, his ankles crossed, a wooden matchstick working between his teeth. It was how he liked it. Fairly stoned.

April the first at half-past three. Marianne Larochelle, stewardess on a layover, danced slowly to the inner rhythms of Tai-Chi on a quiet but not deserted section of Paradise Beach near Nassau. Her cat eyes shone green and hinted of mysteries. She was topless.

Marianne Larochelle cared not whether people looked at her, or whether she offended them or turned them on. Her body was classic. She knew it. She liked it.

The man who would meet her here, a new connection with three ounces of virgin mother-of-pearl cocaine, had asked on the phone how to recognize her. "You will notice me," she had said.

April the first. Miami. The end of Jessica Flaherty's working day. She could smell her armpits. At the age of thirty, she had begun to think of herself as a wilting flower, soon going to seed. Waiting for her tonight was a late-cut outfielder from the Red Sox. A jerk. There had been one after another.

The CIA liaison man phoned just as she was about to leave the office.

"I've got someone for you," he said. "Big."

"They're all big when they make contact," she said. "They usually end up being small and shrivelled and useless."

"Take a chance. Is this a safe phone?"

"We're wired to the intelligence room."

"Cut it. This is strict confidence."

Flaherty switched off the recording line. "Okay, just you and me. I suppose you've wrung him dry. What has he got? Does he want money?"

"He couldn't give us anything we didn't know already," the CIA man said. "I don't think he wants money. He's into the April Seventeen Movement—he's a Cuban—but we have hard orders not to touch those guys. That comes right from the State Department."

"Sucking up to the *fascisti*. The new Ronnie Reagan style of politics."

"I'll ignore that," said the CIA man.

"What's the drug connection? Why does he want to talk to us?"

"I don't know. He won't tell me. He asked who the drug police were in this country. I said Drug Enforcement Administration. He asked me who the top man was here. I said you."

"I'm only *acting* top man," she said. "If I agree to do a sex change, they'll let me run Caribbean operations full time. I work for male hypocrites. Has he got any samples?"

"The name of a Colombian Mafia named Senator Publio Paez. Does that ring any bells for you?"

"It does. That's good for starters. We have a safe establishment back of Gadabout Tours. You know it; you've borrowed it. Set up a meeting for tomorrow night. What name does he use?"

"We have him coded. Alfredo J. He speaks English."

April the first in the Ottawa Valley. March had gone out neither a lion nor a lamb. More like a dirty, sad creature of the mud. Central Canada was emerging from its cold winter torpor into the annual slop of the spring melt.

Trudging through the slush along the path by the Rideau Canal, Sergeant Theophile O'Doull, suit pants rumpled into galoshes, daydreamed his way home from work. (He was tracking footprints left in the snow by a psychotic killer who even now was tearing the clothes off a beautiful woman behind the far clump of birch trees. He would have to move fast. . . .)

O'Doull was the miscast wizard of electronics at the RCMP central crime detection laboratory. Winter had sapped the energy of this sad, young Walter Mitty. He hungered for action in the field, but was held prisoner in a lab.

And finally to Newfoundland. A gaunt and flat and jagged rock that seems to have been flung casually into the Atlantic when the continents were formed. Its shape is a gnarled, closed hand, with an index finger pointing defiantly to the Labrador Sea. Soon the icebergs will start to move like battle cruisers down the eastern coast, carried by the cold waters of the Labrador Current, a current which collides with the tepid flow of the Gulf Stream and causes explosions of fog. The people of Newfoundland have learned to live with this. Fog, rain, and storm have made them seamen of prowess.

On this day, the fog was sitting like a mattress on top of the historied capital city of St. John's, enshrouding the buildings of Duckworth Street, sending fingers of cold into the corridors of the squat fortress which was the courthouse.

In that building the players in a long trial were wearily moving towards a verdict, an ending. The two men accused were sons of Newfoundland through many generations, and during their years they had carried on honoured pursuits. They were sailors. And fishermen. And smugglers.

CHAPTER TWO

"I don't know what kind of behaviour it is that you're allowed in other courtrooms, Mr. Peddigrew, but you're in a Newfoundland courtroom now. It happens to be *my* courtroom."

A fact that Judge Tilley kept reminding the young lawyer, who was from Toronto and who was quick of both mind and tongue but rarely in control of his arrogance.

Peddigrew attempted to interrupt but the judge held up two meaty hands, waved him off, and continued: "We may be lacking in wit and subtlety of mind in this poor, simple part of the world. We may lack in great learning when it comes to the law. But, Mr. Peddigrew, we *do* try to be polite."

"Your Honour, I am saying this with the greatest respect, and I mean it, the *greatest* respect: you are dead wrong. Whether we're in Newfoundland or Nairobi or New South Wales, the right to cross-examine is basic to British justice."

"I don't know what the courts do in New South Wales, Mr. Peddigrew—"

"The kangaroos run them, too." That was a passing shot from Kerrivan, *sotto voce*, but heard quite clearly by Inspector Mitchell on the witness stand. Let him lip off, the inspector thought. Kerrivan was about to go to jail for the next dozen years of his life. He was entitled to take minor liberties.

Kerrivan's comment had also been heard in the gallery, and laughter from Kerrivan's people caused Judge Tilley to break stride for a moment. He glared towards the prisoner's box. Kerrivan returned an innocent smile.

The judge resumed. "I was going to say there isn't a court in the world that doesn't protect witnesses from bullies with law degrees."

But Mitchell didn't want the judge shielding him. He wasn't afraid of Peddigrew. He had seen him before, in Toronto, playing to the galleries, bear-baiting the cops. Peddigrew had achieved recent stardom in publicity-laden cases, and in a few years had blossomed forth near the top of the list of the country's high-flying drug lawyers. To the inspector, though, this was just another confrontation in a twenty-year career of dodging verbal bullets in the courtroom. As Canada's chief narcotics man, he was the target for every potshot-happy defence lawyer in the country. They liked to make him the heavy. He didn't mind. He was good at this.

He wasn't so good at following the workings of the legal mind, and he soon tired of listening to Peddigrew's lecture to the judge. Mitchell was trained in more lucid forms of logic. He was, in fact, impatient with the courtroom, with the law's delay, its waste. This was a trial which should have ended the day it began – sensibly, with guilty pleas. Behind his impatience this day, there was some anxiety, some nervousness over the possibility of a last-minute ballup, some technicality that Peddigrew might slip into the gears of justice.

This was a big one for Harold Evans Mitchell. At forty-one, already an inspector, he was driving hard for superintendent and keeping his eye on the long chance – the commissioner's desk in Ottawa. Head cop of the country.

He was taking the hard route there, through narcotics, a dead end for most officers. But there were many who believed he would make it all the way. He now had a string of nine straight big ones, none easy, all high-class stuff: international action, million-dollar seizures. Heroin. Coke. Big-scale pot. And the Americans, the DEA, had agreed to let him head up Project Seawall, the two-government effort covering the Atlantic coast south to the 40th parallel. All of which made Mitchell a very upwardly mobile policeman.

Mitchell was intrigued by the classic confrontation of opposite personalities in the courtroom. Judge Tilley was a tireless slugger, Peddigrew a fancy and quick-stepping boxer. There *was* a prosecutor, but he had been sent reeling in the early rounds, and now seemed out of it, slumped in his robes as if hiding. Tilley obviously considered Peddigrew a mainland dandy, an ostentatious poppy with his hand-tailored silk shirt, his golden watch, and rings and emblems.

The local guys had briefed Mitchell on Tilley before the trial. The judge was old Newfoundland, resentful of non-islanders, a fact that Mitchell, a mainlander, kept well in mind. The locals claimed as well that the judge had a bent and unpredictable mind.

Peddigrew now had his index finger cocked at the judge like a gun, and was jabbing his points home.

"Attersly versus the Director of Public Prosecutions. Your Honour is undoubtedly acquainted with the famous words of Mr. Justice Wandsworth."

"I have never heard of that case, Mr. Pedigree."

"Peddigrew."

"Read it aloud if you wish. Educate me."

The words droned on. From the witness stand, Mitchell was able to scan the whole expanse of the court. Judge Tilley was sitting back with eyes closed beneath his high canopy of oak. To Mitchell's left was the prisoner's dock, where Peter Kerrivan and Kevin Kelly sat under police guard. Kelly was a little man with a fringe of long, red hair surrounding a bald top. His eyes at times would dart about the courtroom in wonder and disbelief. At other times he seemed to be in a calm and almost meditative state. Too much drugs, thought Mitchell. Causes permanent brain injury.

Beside him was Captain Peter Kerrivan, Kelly's pal, his guru, his sultan. Eight months in prison awaiting trial had smoothed the scars of the sea, but there were permanent lines. His hair was auburn, short, rough-cut. He wore glasses with metal frames.

Mitchell became aware that Kerrivan was staring back at him. Their eyes locked in an unfriendly embrace. Mitchell could not hold; he looked away, pretending to be distracted. When he looked back, Kerrivan was smiling.

Kerrivan—the notorious prince of the North Atlantic drug routes. He had been the hole in Seawall.

That hole was now plugged, after a year and a half of intense, driving work. Kerrivan and Kelly and their pal John Nighthawk had somehow wiggled an old scallop dragger through the police net and had landed the pot with the help of a shore crew. But ultimately Mitchell had won the day, arresting Kelly at his home, then working on him during two tiring twelve-hour sessions in a small room. Not once had Mitchell raised either his voice or his hand. He had employed all the techniques of a skilled and trained interrogator.

And that was what the issue was about this day. His techniques.

The point, to Mitchell, was that little Kevin Kelly had crumbled like dry pastry and had sung a long confession implicating Peter Kerrivan.

The point, to Peddigrew, was that Mitchell had somehow tricked the confession from the lips of his gullible client.

It was Peddigrew's argument that a police officer must not lie to a person accused of a crime. Mitchell indeed had lied, and Peddigrew was trying to colour the deed black and get the confession thrown out.

Mitchell chafed at the proposition that criminals may properly lie to the courts and to the police in the pursuit of crime – a practice well-honoured – while policemen may not lie to the criminals in pursuit of justice. He wondered what kind of fuzzy concept of civil rights was behind such thinking. But then, the idea was typical of the whimsical conceit of a system contrived and fostered by lawyers.

Mitchell's thoughts were drifting, and Peddigrew arrested them, mentioning his name.

"Inspector Mitchell, with a zeal misplaced, is himself guilty – of an obstruction of justice, an abuse of the criminal process. For all these reasons, I submit I should be allowed to question him without restriction."

Then a time of silence, magnified. The judge looked at Peddigrew, expressionless, his eyes half-lidded, a somnolent bear upon the bench.

"That is my submission," said Peddigrew.

"Are you *sure* you have nothing more to say?"

"That is my submission," Peddigrew repeated.

Judge Tilley had played with the lawyer as a cat would a mouse. A better analogy: he had played him as one would a fat salmon, letting him run, adding a little tension to the line, letting him run again, then quietly reeling him in.

"I'm against you, Mr. Peddigrew," he said.

Peddigrew got hot. "Is that your *ruling*?" His voice was pitched high. "Do you have reasons? For the record? In case I take this higher, will the court do the courtesy of giving me some reasons?"

"I do not allow lawyers to badger police witnesses. Those are my reasons. Now let's get on with this. We have a jury. They have been in a stifling room for six hours. Please finish your cross-examination so we can have them back. But you are *not* to threaten the witness. And if you can avoid the tedium of repetition, please do that as well."

Peddigrew's stiff, ungracious bow to the court was like a middle finger raised. "I *thank* Your Honour for the indulgence." The tone was extravagant.

"Sure, and you're welcome," said Tilley. His speech bore a touch of the local brogue.

Mitchell looked at Kerrivan, searching for a signal of surrender in his eyes. But there was just the smile. And, as Kerrivan caught Mitchell's eye, there was a soft wink.

Peddigrew, a hired gun in a strange and hostile land, stood quietly, breathing slowly, seeming to summon his strength for another go at Mitchell.

"All right, inspector, it appears that I am allowed to ask a few more questions," Peddigrew said, "as long as they don't embarrass you. Let us summarize: you told Kelly that if he did not assist you, he would be, quote, stamping out licence plates for the rest of his life."

"Something like that."

Kelly sat hunched, listening. Mitchell thought he looked comical with his circular fringe of hair. He had heard that Kerrivan's troupe referred to him as Friar Toke.

"And you also mentioned to him something about the duty he owed his wife and baby son."

"I told him that if he had thought very much about his family, he wouldn't be where he was, in jail. I said he owed them a duty to stay out of trouble."

"Let's get to the meat of it," Peddigrew said. "What you told him was this: 'Tell me where the marijuana was off-loaded, tell me where it's stored, and you can go home.' That's what you said, yes? That's true?"

"Yes."

"And after twenty-four hours of questioning, he told you where the two hundred and forty bales of marijuana were hidden, even took you down to the warehouse here in St. John's. And you *didn't* drop the charges, did you?"

"Well, I'd like to say something about that."

"I'm sure you would, but right now you're answering my questions."

The judge, predictably, cut Peddigrew off. "I would like to hear what the officer has to say."

"He's here to answer my questions, sir, not the court's. With respect."

The judge was calm. "I have a little interest in this case."

"This is an adversary system, Your Honour, and although traditions of justice seem a little out of place here, it is customary that the prosecutor, not the court, plays adversary to the defence."

"Unfortunately," said Tilley, "the prosecutor seems not to be playing much of a role at all." He sent a heavy look at the crown attorney, who jumped to his feet.

"Your Honour," he said, "the witness should be allowed to give an explanation of his answer."

Tilley smiled. "Thank you, mister prosecutor. I find in your favour." He turned to Mitchell. "Tell us, inspector, what you want to tell us. You made a promise to Kelly that he would go free if he co-operated. But here he is, still a prisoner, if I am not mistaken. Unless he wandered into this courtroom by mistake."

"I offered him immunity from prosecution if he assisted us. On that basis he disclosed that he and Kerrivan and certain other individuals he did not name had delivered the drugs to a warehouse. But when I asked him to give evidence against Kerrivan, he refused. So I simply took it that he was withdrawing his offer of co-operation. I, of course, withdrew my offer of immunity." Mitchell, his foot in the door, decided to try to open it all the way. "And may I say something else? Your Honour, we're dealing here with a drug shipment ultimately destined for the mainland which, even wholesale, was worth fifteen million dollars . . ."

Peddigrew angrily wheeled to his feet. "He's giving a little self-serving speech. It has nothing to do with whether the confession is improperly induced."

"But you see, Mr. Peddigrew," the judge said, "I am *interested* in this business. I'm really an innocent when it comes to drugs and such, and the more I learn, well, the better a judge I will be, don't you think?"

"It's improper, irrelevant, and prejudicial. I object. I want my objection recorded."

Tilley leaned down to the official court reporter. "Will you *record* the objection, mister reporter? And would you be sure to get Mr. Peddigrew's words down correct? Improper, he said, irrelevant, and prejudicial. Now, inspector, would you carry on?"

Mitchell could hear Kerrivan's voice, growling low in the direction of the gallery: "Lord, living Jesus, and it's the Spanish Inquisition."

"Mr. Kerrivan," said the judge, "the proper attitude for a judge when he overhears an accused person make a derogatory comment is to pretend he did not hear. I *am* pretending I did not hear you. Don't push your luck, boy. You'll have time enough to talk in your own defence. Inspector Mitchell?"

"As I was saying, Your Honour, drugs is a multi-million-dollar business along the Atlantic coast, especially in these waters now, with the U.S. southern coast being so well-patrolled. The big operators, the syndicates, are moving big loads into the Atlantic and north, then west, into the little coves and bays out here, where nobody lives any more. What they generally do is off-load from the mother ship into smaller boats, then truck it to central Canada and back down over the U.S. border."

"Syndicates, did you say?" asked Tilley.

"Your Honour!" It was Peddigrew.

"Sit *down!*"

"Well, as you know," Mitchell continued, "when there's a lot of money to be made, it's our experience that the mobs come in, and they run these operations like any big corporation. They hire local fellows, sailors like Kerrivan and Kelly, to make the runs from Colombia."

"A tool of the mobs," said Kerrivan, softer this time. "Ah, will the Lord have mercy on my soul."

"The syndicates are run out of New York and Miami," Mitchell added.

"Being that these local boys aren't smart enough to run their own show?" said the judge.

"Oh, they're smart enough, but not . . . " There was a warning bell in Mitchell's head. Be careful, he told himself. Avoid the Newfie putdown.

Tilley completed Mitchell's sentence: "Not as sophisticated as these big operators from the mainland, you might be wanting to say. That's where the *smart* criminals come from, I guess. And the smart lawyers . . . and, for that matter, the smart police, too."

Mitchell was wary. "I'm sorry, sir?"

"Don't be sorry, inspector. But I think sometimes it's a shame our local police haven't mastered all the clever tricks that a fellow like you uses to trap the wary criminal." The judge was having sport, Mitchell realized. "Like getting Mr. Kelly there to reveal all of his secrets. Now, some of our local boys wouldn't be bright enough for that."

Mitchell wished he were not lacking in the light, self-effacing wit that the occasion seemed to demand. Instead, to his discomfort, he found himself carrying on in ponderous police fashion.

"What I'm trying to say, Your Honour, is that I can't apologize for the manner in which I took Kelly's statement. We have to use every legitimate device to stop the flow. If we couldn't stop Kerrivan, the police would be laughed at. He's the number-one smuggler on this coast –"

"Peter Kerrivan there?" the judge interrupted. "A local lad from out of Bay D'Espoir?" He gently mimicked the brogue: "And how is it a b'y from Bay Despair l'arns the foine art o' smugglin', inspector?" He got laughs.

"I'm talking about narcotics, Your Honour. Not rum-running."

"Marijuana," said the judge. "Can it be as terrible as the stuff that comes in the casks from St. Pierre?"

Mitchell sought a funny line that did not come. All that was in his head was the tired old speech about the war on drugs. So he said nothing, and sensed the judge was giving up the sport.

"It's getting late," said Tilley, "and while it's always interesting to engage ourselves in such discussions, we do have a jury waiting outside, and they *are* entitled to know what has been happening in here." He turned to the court crier. "Bring them back."

Peddigrew, as if shot through with a bolt of lightning, almost knocked over a chair as he rose. "I have more questions. I have an argument to make. I'm not through."

Tilley looked at him wearily. "You *are* through. I do not need or want to hear any more cross-examination from you. As to your argument, my poor brain is sodden with argument and bored with words. No, Mr. Peddigrew, please sit and remain silent like the gentleman I know you to be."

"This is an outrage!" Peddigrew's voice cracked. Mitchell began to fear that the judge, in the pleasure he enjoyed at putting the lawyer down, might commit appealable error.

"Now, my son, calm yourself," said Tilley. "It is very unprofessional for a member of the bar to have a fit in court. You are not back in Toronto, where no doubt such things go on."

"I don't *believe* this." Peddigrew turned to the crown counsel, who did not meet his eyes. "Can *you* believe this?"

"Mister prosecutor," said the judge, "you have been generous with your silence. I suppose I am bound to call upon you, as a reward, for any submissions you have to make. Unlike your learned friend, you have not used your full quota of words."

"I leave the issue to you, Your Honour."

"Thank you for that excellent submission. Let us have the jury."

Peddigrew slumped to his seat, turning his head to the people in the back, as if seeking aid. "I have a right to be *heard*," he said.

And the jury was filing in. Mitchell relaxed.

This was finally it, the culmination of the last and best chapter of Project Seawall. Eighteen months of watching, waiting, hiding, running back and forth between Toronto and St. John's, between Washington and Miami and Bogota, compiling a file on Kerrivan that now was four feet deep.

He remembered the tension when Kerrivan's trawler was on the high seas – no one knew exactly where – out on the great expanse of ocean. The police had almost blown it. Newfoundland was a smuggler's paradise, with thousands of deserted bays and inlets, and Kerrivan seemed to know them all.

Now, with the convictions, Mitchell could return to Toronto, mission accomplished, future paved. He was not afraid to admit to himself that he enjoyed the spotlight of success. There would be newspaper and television interviews, talk shows.

Intruding annoyingly into Mitchell's thoughts, was a feeling of some distress. The judge was addressing the jury. Mitchell knew he should be listening. A part of him was refusing to listen, as if there were some barrier, a quarantine protecting him from the words of the judge. His mind seemed to be working selectively, censoring. But messages penetrated through . . .

". . . tactics you might wonder at . . . so lacking in fairness . . . those who purport to enforce our laws . . ."

Then everything clarified with a cold, sudden brilliance. Judge Tilley was looking dead at him. And the words came rushing to Mitchell's ears, as if a dam had burst.

". . . that frankly I am embarrassed, embarrassed *for*

Inspector Mitchell, since he does not seem embarrassed for himself. The blame rests at a high level in his case, for he is a senior officer of our federal police force. And he has involved himself in a flagrant intrusion upon individual rights."

Mitchell's brain was wrenched into full attention.

"The evidence convinces me that this officer undertook the studied and deliberate course of deceiving an accused person in order to elicit a confession. He offered a clear inducement to speak, an inducement which was inherent in the promise not to prosecute, and it renders the so-called confession inadmissible in any form. That being so, and there being no further evidence upon which you can reasonably connect the two accused with the cache of drugs, I am directing you to enter a verdict of Not Guilty with respect to each of these two men."

And Mitchell was staring hotly into the eyes of the judge, who smiled at him like a satisfied cat.

The mouse, after all, had not been Peddigrew.

"I make this further comment," the judge continued. "The probity of a high officer of the RCMP is in question here, and I would expect that his conduct will be the subject of the most careful scrutiny by the minister of the crown to whom he is ultimately responsible."

The muscles of Mitchell's face had contracted like a white, balled fist.

"Inspector Mitchell, you may now be excused from the witness stand. And Mr. Kerrivan and Mr. Kelly, you are free to go as well." He paused. "But no credit to either of you. Had you been convicted, I would have given each of you fifteen years in the penitentiary."

The judge rose.

The courtroom exploded.

CHAPTER THREE

Johnny Nighthawk

April the first in St. John's, Newfoundland, was a day as cold as a magistrate's heart. It was one of those afternoons that cannot decide whether to snow, sleet, or slop. A "mausey" day, they would call it there.

But it was one of the best days, too. It was the day that Pete Kerrivan and Kevin Kelly walked. When I say walked, I mean walked: out the front door of the old courthouse right onto Duckworth Street and out of the arms of the horsemen, as they call the redcoats up in Canada. These horsemen were very dumbfounded. Stupefied. Another word I like when I think of these police.

Forgive me if my jaundice towards that profession seems to poison my account. While I am not without bias, I am not narrow of spirit. Inspector Mitchell, to give him his due, is in fact a very shrewd civil servant, but on that afternoon he had the expression of one who had discovered he had been marching all day at the head of the Shriner's Day parade with his fly open and his cock hanging out. But Mitchell is Super Narc. We'll come to him more, later.

In court, this is the picture: I am standing up, and I am crying. I am not ashamed to say it. At first, like Mitchell, I am stupefied. Then in a few seconds, the whole wave and backwash drowns me. What really does it to me is watching Kevin Kelly.

I guess he had been in deep meditation, and at first all he seems to have heard is the phrase "fifteen years in the penitentiary." Those are gut-clenching words that will drive the most devoted swami, whatever his state of satori, back into this world. Kelly missed the "I find you Not Guilty" part.

"Fifteen years in the penitentiary." Follow this: you are in a state of inner tranquillity, alone with God and creation and nature, enclosed by all your pranic energy, then, *crash*, it's fifteen years in the big yard, Kevin Kelly. March him out, delouse him, give him a toothbrush and a bar of lye soap and a bedroll, and you eat dried beef and boiled turnip and shit from the screws, every day of every week of every month, and . . . okay, it's not important.

Kelly is wondering, I guess, why is there all this shouting and cheering? He does not understand that the judge's fifteen years is just a throwaway line to show the judge does not take the importing of eight tons of marijuana very lightly. "I know you did it," he is saying, "but the cops screwed up so badly I have to let you off, even though it breaks my heart to do it. But if you ever come back, boys, it's fifteen years in the slam."

Now you have to understand that the courtroom is full of Kerrivan's people. Not blood, but his family. I am one of them by now, although I come from Oregon. Being an Indian I understand the concept of tribe. And we are all smiling, laughing, hooting.

Kelly stares back at us, as if we are crazy. And then the dawn comes up like thunder. As he twigs, he evokes a foolish smile and cranes his short neck as he looks for Merrie, his lady, and the two babies: Raja, a redhead just like him, and Estrella, which is Spanish for star. She had been born five months before, while her father was in the joint, in jail.

Kelly starts moving through the crowd, people grabbing

at him, slapping him on the back. They open for him like the Red Sea, and then he is with Merrie, and he has little Estrella, and is touching her gently, her face, her little fingers that curl around his hair. This is the first time that he has ever held her. He is crying. And that is when I start crying, too.

Very mellow drama.

Pete Kerrivan, unlike Kelly and me, takes it all in stride. This is a moment of theatre for the Errol Flynn of Bay D'Espoir, and he vaults with one hand out of the prisoner's dock, blowing a goodbye kiss to the pretty court clerk, and plunges into the crowd.

Pete Kerrivan. You have to know him.

Let me describe him, first of all. You may have seen pictures; they do nothing. He is six feet, not quite as tall as me, not built like me at all, not heavy around the chest. Your first impression is that he is lean as a flagpole, but he is made with metal-reinforced whips – long muscles as taut as stays. The only thing weak about him are his eyes, which are about as strong as the average mole's, and so he sees the world through plastic lenses in skinny metal frames. He suffers astigmatism, but the point is not how well he sees with his eyes, but what others see *in* them. Women, I refer to particularly. He has these grey eyes that can freeze, melt, and undress a girl all in, say, five or six seconds. They are luminous eyes that can be soft and smiling one moment, clear and burning the next. They are eyes that never inquire. They always seem to know.

If you are with a woman, do not let Pete Kerrivan come within radar range. He does not mean any harm, but he will innocently disrupt your relationship. Especially if you are like me, not handsome, and with a nose broken so many times it looks like a hairpin road.

In court Pete Kerrivan is surrounded by three or four pretty groupies. I don't think Pete even knows any of these girls. They are new, from the mainland, maybe secretaries with the oil companies, but they look like dope-smoking girls, and dope-smoking girls have all heard of Pete Kerrivan, and dope-smoking girls tend to be very romantic. In my limited experience. (My history is one of swinging at third strikes.) Anyway: exit Pete Kerrivan from the courtroom, arms around two of the girls, through the big turret doors that go out onto the street.

I am slow to leave the court, savouring the scene, quaffing it like draft beer in August. In a way, I was jealous of Kelly and Pete; I envied them for their high. I *could* have been with them, getting myself acquitted, feeling that great surge of joy. (Johnny Nighthawk, by the way, no one has ever acquitted. Of anything.) You see, I was on the boat with them all the way up from Riohacha, helped land the bales on the beach and truck them into town. But when Pete and Kelly got busted, I became the Roadrunner, spun my legs like propellers, and wheeled back home to visit my stepdad in Oregon, returning when the heat died.

Back to the courtroom. Almost everyone has gone now: judge, jury, most of the police. A few reporters are still there, talking to the lawyer, Mr. James Ramsay Peddigrew. I cannot hear the words Peddigrew is speaking to the reporters, but no doubt they are about himself.

There is one other important person left in court, Inspector Mitchell. He is a stern, unsmiling man, not exactly a standup comic, and his head is as bare as a bullet. Ergo: The Bullet. That is how we know him. He is legend. A cross between Wyatt Earp and the High Sheriff of Nottingham. When we become stoned, we make anxious jokes about him coming to the door. This is not healthy humour, but it is unavoidable. You have to understand the world of the dope dealer; we enclose ourselves in a cocoon of paranoia. In this business a little paranoia is a healthy thing. Unless you are Kerrivan. To him fear is a stranger.

Mitchell, still on the stand, has a sad, faraway look. It is as if he has just been sentenced to life in the witness box. The thing is, the judge has just wiped his face in it, literally made him eat it.

One of the reporters, from the *Telegram* or somewhere, comes up to him with pencil and pad. Mitchell ignores him, steps down from the stand, and starts to walk away, past me. The reporter calls after him. "Sir, just a few words."

And Mitchell whirls around, and he shouts. I do not know if I have his voice right; it is heavy, the voice of a man used to giving orders.

"All right, I *have* a comment! If this is justice, you can shove it up your ass. The law, the lawyers, the judges, you can shove the whole thing up your little red rosy." Yep, that's what he says. And he walks out.

I say to the reporter, "You got that?"

"Yeah, but I don't know if I can spell all them big words."

I run outside. I don't want to miss any of this. Everyone is grouped around Peddigrew's fat little XJ12 Series III Jaguar four-door sedan, except Peddigrew, who goes running after Mitchell. I can smell Peddigrew's – what do you call male perfume? Cologne? Anyway, I catch a whiff of it as he runs past me, puts his hand friendly on The Bullet's shoulder, and makes him stop. Mitchell turns around, cold, and the lawyer starts talking in this jerky, intense voice of his.

"We're professionals, inspector," he says. "I don't like to lose; neither do you. You did a hell of a job, whatever the judge said." And he goes on, blah, blah. Magnanimous in victory, I think is the expression. "I get paid for defending guys like this," he says. "That doesn't mean I like what they do, but I will give my personal guarantee that these boys are going straight from now on." His clients have learned their lesson, and so forth. Lawyers always say that. Nobody ever believes them.

Mitchell comes back with, "It's all a game, isn't it?" And he carries on down the stairs to Water Street.

I like The Bullet for that. He does not mince words. I mean it *is* a game, and everybody knows it except the lawyers and judges. Of course when you are on the wrong end of a serious beef, you want someone who can *win* the game. I have seen lawyers who do not even know the rules. Peddigrew is good at the game. But do not let him draw up your rich aunt's will.

The smugness disappears from Peddigrew's face and is. replaced by dismay as he sees Pete smiling at him from behind the steering wheel of the Jaguar. Pete is inviting friends in. "Can I borrow your machine, boy?" he says, having done so already. "Would ye mind at all to take a taxi to your hotel?" I am not good at accents, but that is the idea.

Peddigrew is choked. He complains that Pete doesn't have a licence, it having expired. "Don't you worry about it at all, me darlin' man," Pete says. The car takes off like a stung horse, spewing slush and gravel.

Pete is yelling: "Free at last! Thank God a'mighty, we're free at last!"

I take Kevin, Merrie, and the kids to their home in my pickup. I can see that Merrie really wants Kevin to stick around – but she knows that this is celebration night, and in the end she sends him back out to the pickup with me. We head for the Blue Boar Lounge. That is where we celebrate. It is the local of Pete and his Masterless Men.

When we arrive, it is already rocking. Most of the folk from a local band called Stingo have got together for Pete and Kelly, and the amps are turned up to a level that threatens ear damage. The music is a kind of rock and reel: oldtime Newfoundland jigs and dances electrified and rocked up.

The evening is what they call there a "shockin' good toime." The management, which is Jimmy Arthur, one of the boys, has sprung for the first five rounds. I do not need drink to get loaded, because I am loaded on the vibrations.

As a student of highs, I can tell you that a contact high is among the best. You are looking into people's eyes, and you have to smile with them. No choice is offered. Such highs are rare now, although common fifteen years ago when everyone thought the world was going to get better. Business has now taken over the production of highs. Rednecks are dealing marijuana. Car salesmen are snorting cocaine. Cops sneak home with their purloined stashes and toke to Johnny Cash on their eight-tracks. You would not believe how everything has begun to suck.

After a while the good time at the Blue Boar has begun to peak, and there comes into the air a restlessness that forebodes an ill wind. Pete has been bouncing around like a pinball, a glass of rye whiskey in each hand, a half-smoked reefer hanging from his lower lip. His eyes have that ultimate glazed look, the kind you get before your lights go out for the night. He wears a crooked grin that is a warning beacon to anyone who knows him well.

Pete Kerrivan has just entered a marginal, unpredictable state of loadedness. And that is when the Phantom Riders make their grand entrance.

Midge Tobin and about ten or twelve of them push in past the lineup outside. By the way, there is nothing Jimmy Arthur or his doorman are going to do about Midge Tobin and the Phantom Riders. If these fellows want to come into a crowded bar, despite fire marshal's regulations, they come into that crowded bar. Tobin's expressed excuse for being there is to give Pete and Kelly a slap on the back, but there is another reason for this visit, which is that Midge Tobin has to show off Julie McIver, sweetly smiling in her new boots and leather.

Julie is Pete's most recent ex-lady, who after a while stopped visiting him in the joint and took up with Tobin, for whom she was a status symbol, with her arms around him sitting on the back of his hog, a Harley 74. She was a status symbol in that she used to go with Kerrivan.

" 'Tis a fine grand night for a party, Pete," Tobin calls out. His eyes are pinned, and to me he looks to have been doing white crosses, some of which were around then. They look like aspirin, hit you like speed, and I have known some laboratory maniacs to stretch them with strychnine. Anyway, Midge's hand is on Julie's bottom, on the starboard cheek. He is wearing her like an expensive jewel.

Pete stops dancing about, and he says to him: "Are you still riding bike, Tobin? And do you like to feel that big ugly machine up between your legs, old son? Are you still riding that dirty old vibrator, and does it get your rocks off?" This is the picture: Pete is just standing there, bellowing at Tobin above the music. "I didn't hear if you said something, boy," he goes on. "I asked if you're still riding the old love machine? Is it a great feeling, that dirty big roaring machine thundering between your legs?" Pete is eyeing Julie McIver all the while.

I do not catch all the lines in the exchange that follows, but Tobin's best one was, "You think you're God, don't you, you four-eyed finger-knuckle fucker." A fuck-knuckles, or a knuckle-fucker, is a Newfoundland rude phrase, and custom demands satisfaction and redress. I recall being in awe that Tobin, who is never straight, rarely sober, is able to get the words out without Peter-Pipering them.

Pete answers back, but muffs it. "How would you like to go outside and call me a four-eyed fingle-knucker-fucker? Let's see if you got the nuts to repeat it outside."

Midge's eyes narrow down to little slits, and almost disappear into the beef around them. "Sure," he says. "Sure, I'll see you outside." He leads his boys out; Julie stays. It would not be proper for her to watch the two combatants duel over her honour.

We all get up to go with Pete. Kelly is there, plus me, and we have thirty other good boys who could be counted on to look after the rest of the Riders. But Pete waves us all down.

"Easy, boys," he calls out. "There is no call for violence. I am a man of peace and love." He does not go outside.

After a few minutes Tobin opens the door and peeks in, and of course sees Julie caught in a lingering embrace with the man of peace and love. Tobin comes back to the bar, spitting like a jealous cat.

Pete is very casual, his arm around Julie, and he says, with a surprised look, "Tobin, old son, and what're you doing back here then? I told you to go outside and call me a four-eyed fuckle-knucker."

I don't see Tobin throw the mug of beer, but I assume he does, because there it is whirling through the air, gushing froth, beer pouring from it like a fat, wet rainbow over Pete's face. I am, so far, restraining myself. It is lucky I have had only a few beers because when I get smashed I tend to become King Kong. And I will back Pete up all the way, as he will me.

Anyway, Pete is standing there, his mouth open in a kind of joy as opposed to hurt or anger, and his glasses have slipped down and are hanging from one ear, and Tobin is thundering towards him like a diesel locomotive. When Pete is drunk his instincts seem to work better. Basically, that is because instinct is all he has going for himself on such occasions. As Midge's great hairy belly comes flying at him – like a fat black panther in one of the old Johnny Weissmuller movies – Pete lifts his right knee, a very hard and knobby item, and the onrushing groin of Midge Tobin makes a one-point landing on that knee. You would have to say that this has the effect on Tobin's groin of a steel wrecking ball.

There is a great grunt from Tobin. He bends double and carries on past Pete, powered by his own momentum, and as he goes by Pete gives him a crack with the reinforced toe of his workboot, and Tobin is a beached whale, flailing through the slosh on the floor, roaring, scrambling, temporarily out of action.

The rest of the Riders are pouring inside now, moving towards Pete, and people are getting up, chairs falling over, and the band is rocking like crazy on the stage.

But suddenly Pete has his arms high in the air and he is

yelling. Everyone stops moving and shouting. The lead guitar stops dead in the middle of a riff.

"Hold it, boys, hold it," Pete says. "I can't see without my glasses."

It is like stop-action on the televised hockey game, a frozen frame that lasts five or six seconds. Only Pete moves. He is slowly wiping the beer from his lenses with the tail of his shirt, and carefully fitting the glasses back on.

"I thank you," he says, "for your patience."

Then he picks up a chair and wings it right at Crazy Dewey Fitzgerald, who is second bike of the Riders.

Let me not dwell upon the carnage. I do not see it all, anyway, because I am no innocent bystander. I will say it was a good one; I hear they still talk about it.

When the Royal Newfoundland Constabulary comes by, everyone splits except for a few of the staff and Kelly and me and Pete and Midge Tobin, who has been decked to the floor and is just woozily coming to.

Pete is slumped in a chair studying his broken spectacles, uttering blasphemies. Kelly is holding some ice to Pete's jaw which, along with cheeks and fists, has begun to purple up. Constable Charlie Johnston is standing there, just shaking his head.

"I suppose this rings-around was your piece of work, Tobin," he says, as the two-wheel man climbs ponderously to his feet.

"No, Charlie," Pete says, "Midge just got in the way of somebody's fist. I think I may have started it, I'm not sure."

"I'm an innocent bystander," Tobin mumbles.

"Okay, get out of here," says Charlie.

Tobin limps out the front door.

Constable Johnston has brought his first-aid kit with him and begins brushing iodine on a beer glass cut on Pete's arm.

"Use your great wonderful brain, Pete," he says. "For

41

sure, you'll end up in the slammer again." He then includes Kelly and me in a wide sweep of his arm. "You too," he says, "both of you."

"I do no evil," says Pete. "My role on earth is to make people happy. I buy a little weed for my friends; I spread joy. Jesus, look at this," he says, and he is wiggling the frames of his glasses, which are broken apart at the middle where they go over the nose.

Charlie passes him a role of adhesive. "That'll hold them together until you get to an optimist," he says.

"An optimist is what I need," says Pete. "I am broke, ill-provided, and in straitened circumstances."

Charlie raises an eyebrow at this. "The Mounties think you should be a millionaire, Pete."

"It is a dream."

Captain Jackpot's dream. Whenever he got near it, he blew it. Pete was a great believer in our free enterprise system. He really believed a man could parlay his successes and come out at the end a millionaire. He bought the whole myth. (As for me, I was one of Pete's employees, the exploited working class, and this allowed me to feel righteous.) But with Pete the Capitalist it was always boom and bust. He never knew how to put any profits away. Whenever his ship came in, there were suddenly a hundred old friends who had had a bad year fishing, or somebody's house burned down, or his home town needed a clinic so they could persuade a doctor to work there. And if he had anything left after the handouts, that got scooped up by the croupiers in Vegas or Atlantic City.

Pete came close a couple of times. Once he was coming in with five tons and started celebrating a little too early, got stoned, and dropped a match into the bales in the hold of his old herring seiner. The bales smouldered for a while, then caught, and everything went down, and there we were, rowing ashore in a dinghy.

He was years recouping, and finally put together enough

money to buy a heavy, wooden-hulled dragger from a Lunenburg scallop company, and he persuaded the Ugarte family in Bogota to front him eight tons on a small down-payment. Pete had buyers lined up in Boston and after making his nut he figured to clear one and a half million. But, as you know, fate in the form of Inspector H.E. Mitchell intervened, and popped Pete's bubble.

And now Pete was back to square one. Worse. The square root of minus zip.

"I am busted," he moans to us.

"And busted you will be if you try to drive a car tonight," says Constable Charlie Johnston. "Why don't you try to earn a legal living, Pete? Would it be too terrible a shock to the system? Take your master's ticket and fly straight like a goose out of here, down to the States, away from the drug boys. The Mounties are after your blood – Mitchell, and that crowd."

"To be sure," says Pete, "there is no rest for the wicked."

"Now don't you be driving, me son, or I'll take you in for sure."

Charlie and his partner hang around for a while helping Jimmy Arthur clean up; then they go off.

Pete is slipping into a funk.

"I am a poor man without my boat," he mumbles. "They have seized and auctioned off my boat, boys." He looks at us with an expression that suggests he has been the victim of a great unfairness. "And they burned my pot. They're worse than arseholes, they're arsonholes. No boat, no pot, and I owe that greasy Mafioso my last coin."

I assume he is talking about Ugarte. Ugarte is head of one of the twelve big Colombian dope families. They are called Mafia down there, although there is no Sicilian connection.

Now Pete's expression slowly comes alive. He looks up at us with sly eyes and a puffy smile. I know this look.

"Well, boys," he says, "we need to earn some bread quick. *Muy pronto.* So what are we going to do?"

He wants the answer to come from us.

Kelly, who has stated his position many times before, states it again this night. "I am out of it, Pete," he says. "We did the one too many. The thirteenth." Kelly is superstitious in the extreme. I have seen him panic if somebody whistles on a boat.

Pete says, "Ah, but Kevin, me darling man, the next trip will be number fourteen."

"I don't count the last one," says Kelly.

"Kevin, me dear son, one final, last, and never-to-be-repeated journey to the land of the Guajira is the very bottom line. As well, it is a necessity of life. The Bullet having put the torch to sixteen thousand pounds of Colombian gold, we are in hock to Ugarte a couple of million, and it may as well be a trillion dollars."

"*You* are in hock, Pete," says Kelly. "Johnny and me, we are just crew members, persuaded against our will for the *last* never-to-be-repeated trip."

"One more trip," says Pete. "It gets us just dead even keel, and then we retire to a life of dissipation."

Kelly just shakes his head. He is one of the best marine mechanics you will find, a good man from anchor to anchor, as they say, and over the years he has kept many of Pete's broken-down tubs afloat with gum and old bolts.

Pete tries a different approach, aimed at Kelly's compassionate heart. "My dear man, I am going to need your help on one more trip just to save myself from some *asesino* they send up here who wants to put a knife in my back. Ugarte, you pay him in hard dollars, or you pay him *en sangre fria.*" Which is to say, in cold blood.

"He won't send anyone up here," Kelly says.

"You bet your biff he will," says Pete.

"You have no boat, anyway."

Pete slumps in his chair, realizing this is a good argument. His trawler had been auctioned off for a song.

"Ah, God," he says. "Lard Jasus, b'ys." His brogue is pronounced when he has been drinking. "It's a terrible hard life running a small business." He pulls himself together, gets up on his feet. "Just the same, I'm going down one more time." And he looks down at Kelly through his puffy eyes. "You *certain* you don't want to come?"

"My dear man," says Kelly, "I am as certain as the stars."

Pete does not bother to ask me. He knows me well, and he understands that I am a smuggling junkie. I will go with him even if I have to row the pot back up in a ten-foot dory. But Kelly, I could not blame him, with his kids and wife.

We all get into the Jaguar. Pete stamps on the pedal and the car rears into the air. We go off to the Grand Ballroom, which stayed open until four A.M.

CHAPTER FOUR

James Peddigrew's first thought, as he struggled to wake from a dream in which he was being pursued, was that a lynch mob was at the door. He looked at his watch: six-thirty in the morning. The sound from outside his hotel-room suite was the sound of Peter Kerrivan, drunken and raucous.

"All right, all right," Peddigrew called, and he crawled from his bed, put a robe on, and unlocked the door. Kerrivan looked like the wrath of God and smelled like an alehouse bum. Leaning against him, half asleep, was an attractive young woman.

"I thought I'd return your car, James, boy. Sorry about the left door, but the poor fellow in the truck wouldn't stop for the green light. He must have been drunk."

Peddigrew muttered a weary oath.

"I thought if you were checking out today, we'd use your room to crash for the rest o' the mornin'." The words came with a south Newfoundland lilt.

"It's six-thirty, for Christ's sake," said Peddigrew.

"Yes, an unholy hour, for certain. This, my dear man, is Belinda. Belinda, darling, I'd like you to meet my mouth-piece, Mr. Peddigrew."

"Hi," she murmured.

"You're a mess," Peddigrew told Kerrivan. "What happened to you?"

Kerrivan led Belinda into the room, squeezing past Peddigrew. "I was set upon by some unruly men," he said. He found Peddigrew's bottle of single malt scotch on the bureau, and splashed a few ounces into a glass.

"Can we talk alone?" Peddigrew's voice had a hushed, conspiratorial edge.

"We've got no secrets," said Kerrivan. "I owe you money, no getting around that. I'll pay you as soon as I get my affairs in order."

"How are you going to do that? You don't have a pot to pee in."

"Pot. Ah, my dear man, pot is the answer. The Sierra Nevada is abloom with flowers at this season. It's a wonderful grand sight."

"You're going back down?" Peddigrew looked nervously at Belinda, who was in the middle of the room, swaying drunkenly.

"Why, sure, and I'm going to put together the biggest damn smuggle of the century. I'm aiming to pick myself up twenty tons of Colombian gold. So I thought you could lend me a little cash to get me going. Enough to buy a couple of trawlers and a bit of diesel fuel, and a little spending money."

"That's crazy." Peddigrew emitted a nervous snort. He went to the door of the bathroom, and motioned for Kerrivan to follow. "Come in here for a few minutes. I want to talk to you."

"Keep the bed warm, Belinda, love, and I'll be joining you in a minute." Kerrivan eased her towards the bed, gave her a nudge, and she toppled onto it.

In the bathroom, Peddigrew turned the faucet on, a precaution against listening devices. He knew it was silly, but one never knew. He closed the door behind Kerrivan. "I am pissed right off," he said.

"Well, I thought you'd be up, because you told me you were taking an early flight back."

"Never mind. Forget it. And how are you going to go back down? You're broke; you have no boat."

"There *is* a negative cash flow situation, as they say."

Peddigrew looked at him, as if measuring him. "I may have some ideas." He pulled a small bindle packet of coke from his shaving kit. "Like a toot?"

Kerrivan closed the toilet seat and slumped onto it. "My sinuses get stuffed. Maybe a little. A pick-me-up."

"This is like silk. I don't have to chop it." He dipped the point of a nail file into the packet, and took a hit up his nostril, then passed it to Kerrivan.

"It adds a bright edge to a dreary day," Peddigrew said. "I'm almost out. I'm getting another half-ounce flown in."

Hip Toronto lawyer syndrome, thought Kerrivan. "Altogether very too, too much," he mumbled.

"Ninety-seven per cent pure."

Bullshit, Kerrivan thought to himself. It might register about forty per cent. But he didn't want to destroy his lawyer's illusions. "You said you had some ideas."

Peddigrew started to search his face in the mirror for blemishes, drawing the skin taut by stretching it between two fingers. Kerrivan assumed it was a morning ritual.

"There is a company in Halifax," Peddigrew said. "A marine wreckers. I happen to know the principals. I have an ex-client in Colombia, in Barranquilla, who has a marine works. Every once in a while he comes upon an old coastal freighter that might have one more long trip left in her."

"Yeah?"

"He's got one now."

"And the Halifax company will buy it for scrap," Kerrivan said. "Hey, that's a pretty good scam. Who's the Halifax company? You?"

Peddigrew looked at him with an expression of shock that Kerrivan guessed was feigned. He remembered it from the courtroom. "I am a signing officer, of course," Peddigrew said. "A paper director. That's common in the law business."

"How big is it? How many tons will she carry?"

"I'm going to have breakfast, then catch my plane, Peter. Why don't you visit me in Toronto?"

"Toronto? I can't afford to get my shoes shined."

"Look, we have an order from the judge releasing to me in trust all the equipment that was on your trawler: the navigational devices, which are worth something, the radios, radar, scuba gear, life vests, the camping stuff, the dinghies even. You'll get three, four thousand dollars on a quick sale."

"That won't get me into a poker game."

"It will get you to Toronto."

"And then what?"

"I'm going to give you a chance to help earn your fee," said Peddigrew. "It's going to be high."

The final leg of the Eastern Provincial Airways flight had been cancelled at midnight because of an obdurate fog at St. John's airport, so Superintendent Milton Edwards had to lay over in Halifax. Even now, at seven A.M., thick fingers of mist ribbed the landing field, and Edwards stiffened in his seat until the 737 grunted onto the runway, bounced, then settled.

The Kerrivan debacle, Edwards feared, would further damage the image of his beloved police force, already beset by a circling wolf pack: journalists, politicians, and civil rights activists making forays from ivory towers. They made an unholy and unsavoury combination. But as superintendent in charge of external relationships for the RCMP – image polisher and flak catcher – Edwards had learned to become thick of skin and patient.

Defusing the bomb the judge had tried to drop on Mitchell was going to require all of Edwards' skills.

As the taxi he'd taken from the airport slowed to a stop in front of the RCMP building, Edwards saw that the lights were already on in Mitchell's offices. Give him credit, Edwards thought. He gets up early.

But the Mitchell that Edwards observed, sitting behind his desk making notes from a tall pile of file folders, was a Mitchell who seemed not to have gone to bed at all. Edwards had opened the door without knocking and was watching the inspector's deep concentration. The man's clothing was rumpled, there was a stubble of beard over his rough, meaty face, and a shine of perspiration on his head.

"It's seven-thirty," Edwards said. "Did you get any sleep at all?"

Mitchell's eyes did not seem to focus on him. They looked diseased, raw.

"I should have guessed you'd be the first they'd send to jump on my ass," Mitchell said.

Edwards suddenly felt all of Mitchell's pain. "The nature of the business," he said, "is that sometimes they don't convict." He went to the coffee machine and poured a fresh cup for Mitchell, one for himself.

"You can stuff the soft soap," Mitchell said.

"You're on the front pages."

"Yeah? Did I make 'The National,' too? 'Good evening, here is the CBC news. RCMP Inspector Harold Mitchell today was accused of enforcing the law. Parliament has ordered a royal commission.' God." He paused. Then he brought his fist down hard on the table. "Why the *Christ* didn't I get any support on this case?"

"What do you mean?" Edwards asked.

"Just for example, that jerk they sent to identify Kerrivan's voice on the tapes. He's supposed to be an expert at identifying voices from wiretap. After we bust Kerrivan, this guy talks to him in an interview room for *half an hour*. About fishing and the weather and God knows what. And he *still* can't identify Captain Jackpot's voice when the wiretap is played in court. 'I couldn't swear to it, Your Honour,' he says. Right in front of the jury. God spare me. Everyone *else* knew who it was."

Edwards sipped his coffee, waiting for Mitchell to let go, to blow out the steam.

"I don't mind the shit in my face so much," Mitchell said, "it's Kerrivan laughing – that's what I can't stand."

Mitchell gave a long, wheezing sigh, and pulled one of the files from the pile.

"This was him in 1973. Jamaica." The photograph showed Kerrivan walking down a dock with a black man. "He was doing ganja then, kind of small time, while he was working on his master's ticket."

Another file. "We almost had him in 1975. This is Kerrivan and Kelly on the ketch they rented." The picture showed the two men in yachting whites, looking like wealthy kids on a summer holiday. "The Puffin II, they called it. Cute, hey? Sixteen hundred pounds of Colombian gold down below." Mitchell shuffled through other files. "He got bigger and bigger. Three tons, five, eight. How does he finance it? Who's his bankroller? The guy wastes every dime he makes on blackjack and women."

"Why don't you take a week or two, Harold? Get a little sun."

"Uh-uh. How'd you like to help me prepare a budget, Milt?" It sounded like an order, and Edwards felt irritation.

"A budget? I should be working on your obituary."

"Milt, you've got to get me into the minister's office. I've got to get a budget approved. I'm talking about a couple of million dollars."

"Come on, Harold, you can't get that kind of money for pot."

"You can sell it for me, Milt. You got the grease with the minister."

"They're cutting back. It's a year of fiscal restraint."

Mitchell exploded. *"Restraint? Restraint?* Kerrivan and his snot of a lawyer have made the whole fucking force look like clowns with putty noses. Restraint—bullshit! We went penny wise and pound foolish this time. The guy in charge of Project Seawall—me—is looking like Inspector Clouseau walking backwards into a swimming pool."

"They'll think you wasted your money on this last one."

"Well, I've got some news for you. Kerrivan has already started to get the next one together. If we're going to do this right, we start yesterday. I'm putting some eyes on Kerrivan and his buddies right now. And ears. Our lawyers better get me a judge who'll give me some decent wiretap. I'm going to cover this town with wire. Every place Kerrivan has stayed over the last five years. Friends. Relatives. Old girlfriends. There are about two hundred of them. Every pay phone these guys use. I want a blanket authorization. I don't want to have to keep coming back kissing ass for extensions."

"They use a guy named Judge King out here."

"Let's get him. God, I wish I'd had him in court yesterday. And I've got to have someone who can identify their goddamn voices on tape. It's got to be somebody we trust. Half the dumb Newfs around here think Kerrivan stands on the right hand of God." Mitchell was drumming his fingers on the table. "Look, Milt, when you're working on the budget, remember we may have to pay out some money to people here and there."

"Yes." Edwards, somehow, had now clearly been assigned the budget job.

"One other little tiny detail," Mitchell said. "I want an undercover operation. It's got to be someone with Caribbean connections."

"We can borrow someone from Washington."

"No goddamn way! This is *my* show." A short, strained

smile. "Okay, *our* show. I want someone *we* control, not the Yanks."

"Harold, we do happen to work with the Americans on these things."

"Piss on them. If we use a DEA agent, the DEA will grab all the credit."

"Suit yourself. We don't have anyone in Colombia."

"The Americans have a list of private entrepreneurs. Maybe we can find someone who could cut a few corners."

Edwards didn't say anything.

"Do you want to know how we're going to sell this to Ottawa?" Mitchell asked.

"Tell me."

"Come with me." Mitchell took Edwards into the phone room. No one else was on duty, but some machines were recording. Mitchell pressed reverse on a Uher reel-to-reel and waited until the tape had rewound, then pushed the play button.

There was a sound like quiet breathing, possibly a snore. Mitchell moved the tape ahead a few feet.

"This morning, about an hour ago," he said.

There was a sound of knocking. Mitchell turned up the volume. The knocking became heavy, incessant. A groan. A voice. "*All right, all right.*"

The sound of feet shuffling, a door being opened. A voice distant but loud enough to make out: "*I thought I'd return your car, James, boy. Sorry about the left door —*"

Mitchell pressed fast forward. "Let me just spin this ahead. The scene is Peddigrew's hotel room, by the way."

"*You're going back down?*"

"*Why, sure, and I'm going to put together the biggest damn smuggle of the century. I'm aiming to pick myself up twenty tons of Colombian gold.*"

Mitchell pushed the stop button. "There's some other chit chat. Kerrivan had a dame with him, so there's half an hour of fucking. If that turns you on."

Edwards wasn't saying anything.

"Well?" said Mitchell. "Twenty tons of dope. Do you know what that's worth on the street? Figure it out. Colombian gold goes for a hundred and twenty an ounce and up."

Edwards snorted. "You know he's bullshitting."

"Sure, but the minister isn't going to know that." He was smiling. "This tape buys me a lot of electronic hardware, some high-class undercover, and maybe a witness or two."

"Tell me, Harold, how long have you had a bug in the lawyer's room?"

Mitchell looked past him, his expression benign. "Oh, a few weeks."

"You know you don't have a court order to intercept from a lawyer's room."

"Aw, come on, Milt, don't play the pansy with me. This isn't public. It's not for court."

"You can't replay it for the minister."

Mitchell had the look of a truant schoolboy. "We can tell him we have information. We wouldn't be lying." He doodled on a pad for a few seconds, then looked up squarely into Edwards' eyes. "You know what, Milt? I was too honest in that court. I didn't have to say I promised Kelly immunity. I didn't have to say I promised him a damn thing. There was nothing in writing. I got nailed because I was too honest in there. Yeah, I come out smelling like shit pie and Kerrivan and his merry men are out all night having a howl, busting up a bar with a bunch of bikers. Jesus, Milt, *come on*. We're doing a *job*. You know what it's all about."

Mitchell slowly sank back into a chair. His face seemed to collapse, lines radiating inward. "He's *got* to make just one more run." He was breathing slowly, trying to beat back the tiredness. "If I can get the hardware ... if I can get top-quality undercover, and I mean the *cream*, Milt, the best there is, I don't care what it costs – I'm going to sting Kerri-van. I'm going to pull off the biggest goddamn operation since the Normandy invasion."

"*You're* going to?"

"*We're* going to, Milt. You and me and the RCMP. With a little help from our friends."

CHAPTER FIVE

Jessica Flaherty wiggled an index finger into her loose pack of menthols, fishing out one of the last two cigarettes. She stroked a wooden match up the zipper of her jeans and it seemed to burn like a flare in the late-night gloom of the Miami waterfront park. She snapped a quick mental picture of her new informant, Alfredo J., a man who wished to meet only in darkness. He had said no to the DEA house.

His manner was professional, although he seemed over-dressed for the role of unobtrusive spy: a loose tunic, belted at the waist, a scarlet feather in his hatband. He spoke clear English.

"As you come to know me and trust me, we will work closer together," he said.

Having had a good glimpse of him, Flaherty decided she wouldn't mind that at all. She hoped he wasn't gay.

"It is even more important that I learn to trust you," he went on. "Are you interested in politics?"

"Sure."

"Maybe we will discuss politics some day. Paez's people seek, I believe, to avoid the Florida coastline, where there are too many patrol boats. I have seen them studying maps—New England, the Maine coast, where there are quiet bays. Ultimately, the cargo will go to New York City. There is a large Colombian community there, and Senator

Paez has cousins in the Borough of Queens."

"How will they move it?"

"They do not tell me everything, because I am too new to them. Obviously they are looking for experts, experienced *contrabandistas*. Gringos. They believe gringos are more efficient, smarter, braver." He sounded sorrowful. "There is a great lack of pride among Latin people." He amended: "Among certain Latin people. They want a ship that cannot be connected to them."

"What do you want out of this?"

"Perhaps, some day, a favour. One day we will talk politics."

Flaherty shrugged, and snubbed her cigarette on the bench. It died with a soft sputter of sparks.

"I'll be your only friend in there," Edwards had told Mitchell.

"In there" meant in the office of Jean-Louis Lessard, Her Majesty's minister in charge of the Department of the Solicitor General, the man at whose desk the RCMP buck stopped.

On that desk now sat Mitchell's two-million-dollar budget.

But the minister was ignoring it. Instead, he was pounding a stubby forefinger at the front page of the Toronto *Globe and Mail*.

"Quote," he said, "Shove Law, Shove Judges, Says RCMP Inspector. Unquote." His eyes peered up at Mitchell under beetle brows. Mitchell was sitting on a leather-covered chair, trying to strike a relaxed pose.

"That's the headline," Lessard said. "Unfortunately, they didn't bury your earthy prose behind the classifieds."

"I've read it, sir," Mitchell said. He looked out of the corner of his eye at Edwards, who was standing near the desk, sipping coffee, looking out the window. Edwards had told Mitchell to keep his mouth shut, to let him do the talking.

Otherwise, he had said, Mitchell would have *no* friends in there.

Lessard seemed to relish reading the article aloud. "'St. John's, Newfoundland. By The Canadian Press. A senior officer of the RCMP told a reporter Thursday he could shove the Canadian system of justice up his A-dash-dash. The comment was made after a judge ordered two men acquitted of marijuana importing charges. "If this is justice, you can shove it," Inspector H.E. Mitchell said after the verdict. "You can shove the lawyers, the law, and the judges up your red, rosy A-dash-dash H-dash-dash-dash."'"

Lessard raised his hands in a gesture of Gallic supplication. "The article tells us how this particular judge shoved the law up *yours,* inspector. 'The honesty of a high officer of the RCMP is in doubt.' That's the judge talking. 'His conduct should be the subject of close scrutiny by the minister to whom he is responsible.' *C'est moi,* inspector."

Lessard turned to the deputy minister, who was seated in a far corner of the room. "Who is this judge?" he yelled. "Where in God's name do we get these jerks?" He didn't wait for an answer, turning back to Mitchell, his eyes blazing.

"So you're the hotshot narcotics man the commissioner has been bragging about. Well, I want to tell you something, hotshot: you just delivered a load of hotshot shit to my front door. Who's going to clean it up? *You're* not going to clean it up. *I'm* going to clean it up. *I'm* the guy who has to stand in front of the TV cameras explaining how RCMP inspectors are only human beings."

Mitchell hoped someone else would say something. But the others, Edwards, the deputy minister, the department counsel, were arranged in a circle like spectators at a one-sided cock fight.

Lessard picked up the budget proposal. "It's an expensive cleaning bill. *Two million bucks?* You're serious?"

"That's not far above average for a big narcotics operation, Mister Minister," the deputy said.

"A couple of dumb Newfoundland pot pushers?" Lessard said. "It *can't* be worth it. And if it's the price of revenge, inspector, I can't afford it."

Just as Mitchell was beginning to feel deserted by Edwards, the superintendent turned away from the window, and began speaking in a quiet voice.

"Mister Minister, Harold Mitchell got axed in that courtroom. He got axed brutally. And without fair reason. And by a judge whose appointment you once personally okayed."

"You cops stick together, don't you?" Lessard said. "Well, okay, Milt, you've prepared a little lecture for me. You're my liaison officer, so liaise. Tell me about police morale, Milt. Tell me about how the government is going to have to back up its cops or we're going to have mass resignations. Tell me how the evil dope traffickers are going to take over the country. Tell me, Milt, why it should cost two million dollars to put this monster Kerrivan away. Tell me about the evils of marijuana."

Edwards paced to the centre of the room.

"Mister Minister, you have a law on the books about marijuana," he said. "If you do not want to pay the money to enforce it, then repeal it." He paused. "That's not the speech. And the speech is not about Kerrivan. One of the few things in this country we shouldn't be ashamed of is the RCMP. Name one other country in the world where tourists go just to look at the policemen. I *am* proud of the RCMP, goddamnit, even though I know that such things as pride in uniformed men are a little corny and old hat these days. Sure there are bad apples – human mistakes walking around in uniform. And maybe some guys try too hard, and maybe that's Harold's problem. He *tries*. But you know this, Mister Minister, there has been no police force in the history of the entire world which has had to work so hard to maintain the reputation that has been claimed for it. It's hard, damn it. It's hard!"

59

Edwards pressed the palms of his hands on the minister's desk and leaned towards him as if daring him to throw the first punch. "We have had our good name dragged, battered and bleeding, up and down this country by royal commissions that are so busy prying into our affairs that we don't dare turn our back. Add to that the yahoos on hotline shows. Left-wing ding-a-lings writing magazine columns. Nutty lawyers screaming police brutality every time some snot nose punk gets a boot in the pants. How do you run a police force when it's worrying all the time about between which ribs the next knife is going to be stuck?" His voice had risen, and he was shaking.

"Easy, Milt," Lessard said. "On this issue, I am the converted."

"What I am saying is I think we're entitled to the respect of your government, and its support."

"Then earn it."

"Give us the tools."

"Two million dollars buys a lot of tools."

"Two million dollars doesn't buy nose pickings. You can't make a decent high-level buy with a quarter of that. We're not talking about some back alley bootlegger. We're talking about narcotics. Maybe close to thirty million dollars' worth, and I'm not talking street prices. That's what Kerrivan's group is getting together right now." He paused. "We have information."

"Information?" Lessard had relaxed a little. "A little bird tell you that?"

"A little bug." Edwards folded his arms. "Take my word for it."

The minister looked from man to man in the room.

Edwards continued. "We can smash that operation if you give Inspector Mitchell the green light. We'll get Kerrivan, even if it's on the rebound from the last case, and when we do we'll have earned the respect we are talking about. Then people might forget about this crap." He picked up the newspaper and tossed it roughly back onto Lessard's desk.

Lessard smiled. "You should be in politics, Milt."

"A thirty-million-dollar dope bust will give the royal commissions something to chew on," Edwards said. "Something, for a change, other than our ass."

Lessard picked up the budget and frowned at the figures. "Maybe it would be cheaper just to legalize pot completely. Half the damn civil service smokes the stuff."

"Is that the kind of country we want to live in, sir?" It was Mitchell, and his question was followed by an awkward silence.

Edwards glared at Mitchell, then, leaning towards Lessard, he spoke slowly and emphatically: "We want this one, Mister Minister. I think you *owe* this one to us."

The only sound for several seconds was that made by Lessard, who seemed to be trying to clear his throat.

"I see," he said finally, again glancing over the budget. "Are any of these figures flexible? Your undercover costs, can they go that high—hundreds of thousands of dollars?" Then he held up his hands as if to discourage response. "Maybe I shouldn't hear any more about it." He pointed to one of the three marble monkeys on his paperweight, the one holding its hands over its ears. "I'm this guy," he said.

Then he turned to Mitchell. "Inspector, if this doesn't come off, I will personally stick *you* up *your* red, rosy A-dash-dash H-dash-dash-dash."

Outside the office, Mitchell drew Edwards aside. "He *owes* us one? What was that all about?"

"You'd be surprised what the morality boys get on some of the local wiretap."

CHAPTER SIX

Mitchell was in a cocktail lounge at Montreal's Dorval Airport, waiting for a change of planes to Miami, when he heard a familiar voice, loud and defiant. Mitchell groaned. There, at the door to the lounge, were Peter Kerrivan and Johnny Nighthawk, and Kerrivan was berating one of Mitchell's undercover men.

"For the sake of the Lord, b'y, would you be so kind as to stop walking on my heels. Why is it an innocent man can't go about in a free country without being followed everywhere? You're dressed like a working man, but I know you're not a working man at all because you're soft and pudgy." He put on a heavy Newfoundland accent. "The truth of it be y'er a policeman, and a pore crayture of one, t'be sure." Then he dropped the accent. "Look, fella, get your nose out of my ass, or I'm going to sue. I know my rights."

The undercover constable strode angrily into the bar, almost bumping into Mitchell's table. He blushed when he saw Mitchell. "I followed them from St. John's," he mumbled. "They narked me. It wasn't my fault."

"Get out of here," Mitchell hissed. "Phone someone else to pick them up."

"Well, if it isn't himself," said Kerrivan, coming up to Mitchell's table. "What's the matter, inspector, you look like you just swallowed a chili pepper." He swung his head in the direction of the retreating constable. "I get it—he follows us to Montreal, and you take over from here."

"Good morning, inspector," Nighthawk said with a sour smile. Native Indians whom Mitchell had known usually had flat voices, but Nighthawk's was soft and expressive. Mitchell assumed he was there as Kerrivan's bodyguard. He was a huge man with a large gut and broad shoulders. An ex-con. His hair was in two braids at the back.

"What are you doing here?" Mitchell asked.

"Why, we thought we'd stop over in Montreal, check out the old city, and celebrate the victory," Kerrivan said. "Do you want to know our hotel, inspector, or can your boys find it out for themselves?"

Kerrivan was carrying a small leather bag. "What's in that, Peter?" Mitchell asked. "Anything I should know about?"

"I'm doing a heroin delivery for the Chinese Chow Chew, inspector. I've gone into the hard stuff."

Mitchell laughed politely.

It was slim pickings at the agent shop in Miami. Mitchell knew the Drug Enforcement Administration kept a Caribbean file of private operators who do the kind of work that doesn't have to be recorded in triplicate.

He explained that he wanted someone who would not be bothered by technicalities. Someone efficient and fast. The best man he could get in the business.

"The best man I can get," was, unfortunately, the phrase he had used after introducing himself to Special Agent Jessica Flaherty, acting head of the DEA's Caribbean desk.

"The best man, huh?" she said. "Any other requirements? White? Anglo-Saxon? Blue eyes? Royal bloodlines?"

"It may be dangerous. I would feel better with a man, that's all."

Flaherty's look told him the excuse was lame and old. "Dangerous? What are you looking for, a hit man? Try the CIA, down the street."

Mitchell knew her reputation. Tough in the field. First woman team leader in the DEA. Mitchell suspected her brittle, sneering feminism covered up for an anti-RCMP bias. She had worked undercover on loan to the RCMP, and it was known she held her Canadian colleagues in low esteem.

Flaherty unlocked a sliding metal file and drew out about six cards. She held them away from his eyes as if guarding a poker hand. "George Singleton," she said. "Ex-DEA. Now heads up security for a hotel chain. But he won't do drug ops any more. I don't know what his problem is. I should move him to the dead file."

She laid the card face down so he could not read it, and picked up another one. "Keffler. Very classy, very knowledgeable. Unfortunately he's already out on a big job for us. Can't free him up for another three months." Another card. "Susan Marques. A really hot number. Wrong sex, though, hey?"

Mitchell wasn't liking this. For one thing, he hated to come begging to the Americans. For another, he didn't like snideness.

"Martinez," she continued. "On the bottle. McAuley. Don't think his Spanish is good enough for what you want." She shrugged. "Billings. Too much of a wimp. No Wild Bill Hickoks in here, inspector. The rest of our regulars are all in use." She gave him a mock sad look. "Want me to go down to B-grade?"

"I need number-one material, Miss Flaherty." He wondered if she had really gone through all the names. He had understood there were at least twenty. He was about to get his hat.

"Hang on," Flaherty said brightly. "You say you want a corner cutter?"

"I said I want someone quick and smart. If it means being a little elastic when it comes to getting the job done, I won't worry about it."

"How much bread can you lay out?"

"A lot."

"What's a lot?"

"Maybe a hundred and fifty, two hundred. For the right . . . man."

"Two hundred? As in thousands? Jesus, you guys are loaded for this one. What's Kerrivan planning to do this time, blow up Parliament? He must have stuck it up your ass real hard."

Mitchell remained silent.

"I gather this is separate from Project Seawall. Otherwise we'd be working on it with you. What do you call it again – Operation Potshot?"

"Potship."

"That's very original and Canadian. Why don't you call it Operation Shitpot? Just joking." Mitchell supposed that the DEA secretly enjoyed much humour at the expense of their naïve northern cousins.

Flaherty went on to another file. "Okay, for two hundred thousand dollars – what's two hundred thousand, anyway? A baseball player gets that – for two hundred Gs, maybe you are up in Rudy Meyers' range."

She pulled out two red cards, stapled together. There was typing on each side of both cards.

"We call this the flashing-red file. You stop and look around before you enter. We don't go into here very often. For various reasons. And Meyers, we don't use *at all* any more. For various reasons. You'll have to make a strong pitch if you want him. He is the very cream, inspector. Ice cream, you could say."

"What's wrong with him?"

"What do you mean?"

"Why don't you use him?"

Flaherty ran her hands through her closely cropped hair and shook it out. She was attractive, Mitchell decided, but that was lost in her hard, free-wheeling style. Very American, he supposed.

"I don't know why we don't use him," she said. "Some desk jockey's decision, who's never been in the field. The CIA let him go several years ago. He went into private business, contracting with us. Then we grounded him, stopped giving him contracts." She spread her arms in an expansive gesture. "Well, I'll tell you. You hear things. Maybe he was *too* effective. He has a very . . . *loose* way of working. Also, he's kind of political."

"What does that mean?"

She had a sly grin. "Got himself involved in something dicey during a presidential campaign. He has pretty conservative views. Mind you, they're in vogue these days." She lit a cigarette. Mitchell noticed she held it between the balls of her fingers like a joint, an undercover cop's habit.

Flaherty looked to the side, as if to see if anyone were listening from the open doorway of her office, then leaned towards Mitchell. "He's a fucking Nazi, if you want my opinion. Right now his main scam is training a bunch of Cuban so-called refugees – and he's welding them, he thinks, into a mighty fighting force. Arms training, commando karate, explosives, maybe even assassination. Meyers worked with Howard Hunt. He remembers the Bay of Pigs like some people remember the Alamo. The April Seventeen Movement, his group is called. In 1961, on that date, Castro put the boots to that bunch of losers Hunt and the CIA helped to organize."

She wrinkled her nose when she mentioned the CIA, as if there were an uncomfortable smell in the room.

"Anyway, so what?" she continued. "We got right-wing crazies like him working all over the place. Ex-Nam people who couldn't stomach the defeat. If they do their job, who cares? But Meyers is too hot for us, right? Too hot for Ronnie Reagan even, if you can believe it. So the CIA tells us not to touch Meyers. He's a potential embarrassment. Or maybe they want him to concentrate on his army, not waste time busting druggies. Who knows with those guys? Anyway, we laid off him. We buy information from him, but that's all. In a way, it's too bad we can't use him—he's got first-class Colombian connections."

Mitchell shrugged. "Politics doesn't interest me. My job is drugs. What are these connections?"

"Meyers has infiltrated some of the biggest Colombian families, inspector. He's got them eating out of his hands like he's some kind of *consigliaro*. He sets up smugglers for us, or used to. We got them when they showed up stateside. But the bodies he sold us were pricey. He costs a bundle."

"What else can you tell me?"

"Like I say, he is very rich cream. A brilliant tracker dog, in case you lose the target's scent. Knows the routes of all the big drug movers. Speaks six or seven languages—not that you're likely to need Afrikaans or Somali. You guessed, he did the standard African mercenary number. Also, he can handle himself pretty good, maybe too good. Black belt in karate, fourth dan."

She flipped a glowing cigarette butt end over end into an empty wastebasket.

"Which means, I guess, he could be pretty effective at killing. If that's part of the operation."

Mitchell blanched. "As I said, Miss Flaherty, my job is drugs." There was ice in his voice.

"Yeah, well, two hundred thousand dollars—that's a lot of money. Operation Pisspot, that's what you should call it. Or Operation Jackpot. Isn't that what they call Kerrivan—Captain Jackpot? No, that wouldn't work. People would start calling it Operation Crackpot."

Mitchell felt her smile was smarmy.

After the mixed review, Meyers turned out to be surprisingly urbane, not the wild-eyed redneck that Mitchell had expected. Meyers' Miami headquarters was in a modern air-conditioned building. The sign on the door said "Rudy W. Meyers. Private Investigations. Licensed. Offices in Miami, Bogota, and Mexico City." The motif was Oriental, the furnishings fragile, tasteful. Mitchell saw into the back offices where professional-looking men were working on files. Meyers was not fly-by-night.

He offered Mitchell a choice of coffee, tea, scotch, or bourbon. Mitchell took coffee. Meyers poured himself some kind of pungent herbal tea.

When Mitchell mentioned Kerrivan's name, Meyers nodded.

"Yes, 1975," he said. "West Indian Club on Grand Cayman. Kerrivan wouldn't remember me. I had worked my way inside the Ugarte family, a Bogota family. They were to receive a considerable amount of cash from him. A considerable figure, yes. I could have sold Kerrivan to you back then. Perhaps I *should* have called you."

"Ugarte family. Who are they?"

"Yes, it was a Mafia family. The Colombian Mafia, not the real thing, of course. The cheap imitation. Although they *are* getting better. Yes, indeed. I have excellent lines into some of these people. I suspect that is where I can become invaluable to you, Inspector Mitchell. May I call you Harold?"

"Yes."

"Frankly, I am surprised that Jessica Flaherty gave you my name. I suspect she is unfriendly to me. A liberal snob, that woman. She comes from Brooklyn – perhaps that explains it. At any rate, Harold, to the task at hand. You are seeking my services because I will do a job that cannot be done by one whose moves are dictated by the heavy hand of the public bureaucracy."

Mitchell was fascinated by the man's mouth. There was little movement as he talked. Words seemed to seep from between his lips, which formed a thin smile that was enduring, fixed. Above the upper lip there was a trimmed military bristle moustache. Mitchell wondered how this man could work effectively undercover in the world of narcotics.

"Let me tell you something about myself," Meyers said. "I am a mercenary. That is true. I am that. I have even stooped so low as to hire myself out to a government of a once-great nation which is busily selling off the world to the Kremlin, one little country at a time. It hasn't stopped with Reagan, although some of us had hoped it would. We are led by a sheep in wolf's clothing, Harold, a sheep in wolf's clothing. You will find me a strange mercenary. I toil for dollars and earn a great deal of them. But I have no use of money for myself. My needs are simple, my life is spartan. I walk while others ride limousines. I read books while others surround themselves with stereophonic noise-makers, junk-food restaurants, and pornography. I seek the pleasures of the mind as others do the flesh."

Throughout this monologue, Meyers' eyes were pinned coldly on Mitchell's. They were set close together in the middle of a large, round head.

"I will charge you a fancy fee, Harold, if you wish to retain me. It will go to a good cause. Not a weak cause, a strong one." He stopped short. "Forgive me my little sermon. I tend to preach, although I am not religious. I pay homage first to my ideal of man, then to my ideal of God." Then, abruptly: "I guarantee my work. If I fail, I charge nothing, not even expenses. At those rates, I dare not fail." The lips opened to shape the sound of laughter, but none came.

"And what exactly will you guarantee?" Mitchell asked.

"Do you understand the concept of a controlled delivery, Harold?"

"Yes, of course."

"That is what I guarantee. If you retain me to deliver goods, I will deliver the goods. The goods consist of Mr.

Peter Kerrivan, his crew, his ship, his cargo. I will deliver all these to you."

"Where?"

"In Canada, of course." Again the smile fractionally widened. "You would not achieve much satisfaction if Kerrivan were somehow to decide to land his cargo in the United States. I understand that. When I have completed my work, you will be able to tie a pink ribbon around this package and present it to any judge or jury. I guarantee a case that will convict – with the co-operation, of course, of your police force, and that of our own beloved Drug Enforcement Administration. You *do* have their assistance, of course? And that of the U.S. Coast Guard?"

"They will work with us," Mitchell said. "I'm in charge of Project Seawall."

"Yes, your reputation is well known, Harold. I will need, through you, the co-operation of the DEA and Coast Guard. We will require clear passage to Canada. Please impress upon these agencies that this is a Canadian operation. Otherwise they will try to grab the ship. They are hungry for big busts, too, Harold, because everyone likes a promotion."

"If this doesn't work, we owe you nothing?"

"Yes."

"And if you succeed?"

"You understand that these matters are expensive. I have my own staff, of course. I run my own agents. There is no extra fee for them. Everything is included, even the *mordida*."

"The *mordida*?"

"The bite, in Spanish. Often, in Colombia, there are people who have to be paid to make the way smooth. When there is a big shipment of drugs, there is often much *mordida* involved. Everyone likes to take a little bite."

"And what is your . . . bite, Rudy?"

"You would, of course, be circumspect. The essence of all

70

good operations, as you know, is a very tight lid. There is a maxim by La Rochefoucauld: 'If you cannot keep your own secrets, do not expect anyone else to keep them for you.' At the outset, I ask for one thing: not your confidence – I will earn that – your confidentiality."

"Of course. And what will you charge?"

"Five hundred thousand dollars."

Mitchell's throat went dry.

"You will pay only if I succeed, of course. Only if I succeed."

The starboard engine of the government surplus B-26 argued and sputtered as Billy Lee Tinker gave it throttle and urged it up, up towards the banks of dry cloud that sat squat upon the hills of the Serriana de Jarara, cloud banks moving like a slug high over the red-dirt airstrip.

"Git up, sweet baby, git up. Git up, you rotten fart!" His words were lost in the lament of ancient engines.

Tinker's body was aflame with the itch of the tiny floating hemp fibres that infested the aircraft. One of the twenty-eight pillow bags of marijuana had broken open and the odour in the cockpit was suffocating and sweet.

The plane grunted into the clouds and Tinker began to count – his altimeter had died many months ago. "One thousand and one, one thousand and two, one thousand and three. Git up. Git up."

Fifteen seconds. The clouds broke, and the scrubby trees on the peaks of the Jarara *cerros* were fifty feet below the tip of the starboard wing. Tinker went into a furious straining bank and pulled the plane over the hills towards the Caribbean Sea. The snowy crest of the Sierra Nevada shone in the distance far to the west.

In Viet Nam, the F-14s had flown themselves. But his Second World War bomber was a wobbly old lady who needed care and patience and the right instincts.

Tinker made a course adjustment to the Yucatan Channel

to avoid Cuban air space, and watched the Guajira coast fall away behind him. When he entered the Gulf Air Defence Identification Zone, he descended beneath radar level, pulled out a fat joint of Santa Marta gold, and lit it.

It was harvest time in the Guajira. He would be flying like crazy for the next three weeks. If his plane held out.

CHAPTER SEVEN

Johnny Nighthawk

We could have used the navigational hardware – the
Omega, the Loran, the radar – for our next expedition, but
Pete needed a fast injection of capital, so we sold everything
from his dragger, right down to the dinghies and lifejackets,
for three thousand bucks. A thief's price.

It was a matter of speed. We were right into the spring
crop season, it being April, and we were going to have to
hop quick to get down there on time. You would not believe
the amount of hassle that is involved in running an import-
export business. The romantic end of things is much exaggerated. The truth is that a major smuggle usually involves
months of meticulous preparation, lots of bucks, excellent
timing.

We had neither time nor bucks, and also making it
difficult was The Bullet, who had his people on our ass
every waking minute. You buy a pair of socks; there's a guy
on the other side of the counter examining jock straps. You
take a piss in the public john; there's a guy at the next urinal
studying his pecker. They never look you in the eye.

For instance, we had to stop over in Montreal to make the
stateside border arrangements. We were tailed all the way
on the plane from St. John's. At the Montreal airport the

undercover man was replaced by no less a personage than The Bullet himself, who acted stunned as if we were not supposed to know him. Words were bandied. Mitchell is a humourless man.

We rented a car at the airport, and it took us an hour and a half to shake the bulls. Then we slipped across to the south shore, down to the border. Pete has an old friend in southern Quebec who got out of the trade at the right time and put his savings into a farm which straddles the Canada-Vermont border. He has gone back to the land, as they say, but that does not mean he is not a shrewd businessman. He always charges a big toll for us to truck our goods across his property into the States. We spent the day with him, smoking his musty home-grown, and setting up communications for later in the spring.

Back in Montreal, we decide to stop over for the night to fortify ourselves before braving the rigours of Toronto and James Peddigrew.

We start about Atwater Street and work our way slowly, by foot and taxi, east along St. Catherine Street. The narcs have by this time caught up to us again. They had all the Hertz offices staked out, I guess, and spotted us when we dropped off the car. Pete kept sending drinks over to them.

Later, we are in a bistro, hanging around with some low-lifers. Pete, who is dressed in black Stetson, leather vest, and cowboy boots – it is the year of the cowboy and Pete is into it – has managed to surround himself with a gaggle of hustlers, and has them wide-eyed with far-fetched tales and fictitious exploits. Then suddenly he is no longer with us. I do not mean physically, because he is there in the flesh. His spirit has, however, drifted across the bar to a little round table in the corner.

The table is covered by a linen cloth. There is a candle in the centre. One chair is empty. Upon the other sits – what can I say? You know the rock singer Debby Harry, from Blondie? Colour the hair a touch more sand, thin her out a tender fraction, maybe lift the cheekbones a nibble. Somehow work in a note of unsuppressed vanity. You have her. She is excellent.

She is looking directly into Pete's eyes. You may say bullshit as you listen to this, but across the room, in the dancing glow of that candle, I can see the colour of her eyes. They are as green, if I might be allowed, as the winter sea.

Suddenly, Pete is no longer with us in spirit *or* in flesh.

His conversation with this lady, later described to me by the great romantic himself, is as follows:

"Hello," he said he said. "*Bonjour*. You are beautiful. *Tu es belle*." That's about all the French he knows.

She says, "*Merci*. Thank you. And before you ask—no, you cannot buy me a drink. I am sorry I was staring at you."

"I didn't think you were staring at me," Pete says. (This is *his* version.) "I thought we were looking into each other's eyes."

She smiles. I see a flash of whiteness as her lips part. She is very tanned.

Pete goes on. "You are a madonna."

"Thank you. And you are a cowboy. But where is your horse?"

"Can I buy you *one* drink?"

She tosses her hair lightly. There is a fleeting whisper of a smile. "It is, I am afraid, impossible."

And that is when her escort, with a gruff "*Excusez-moi*," shoulders past Pete, sets a carafe of wine and two glasses on the table, and sits on the empty chair.

Pete touches his hand to the brim of his Stetson and retreats.

Pete is dour now, and he depresses everyone at our table.

We continue down the street, visiting a jazz club, a strip joint, a high-class blind pig.

"That lady has laid me in ruins," Pete says. "I am haunted."

He is poor company.

"There was an eye flash," he tells me. "You know the thing that happens – a connection, a message, a conversation of eyes."

I have never had any such conversation with women. I am unsympathetic.

Later, as we get drunk, events become clouded. We find ourselves in a party in someone's swish apartment.

"I don't believe this," Pete says. I follow his eyes. There she is, the same girl. Talking gaily to a group of friends. She sees Pete and their eyes lock again.

Her friend does not like the vibrations and soon brings her coat and takes her down the stairs to the street.

Drunken Pete Kerrivan goes stumbling down after them, trips on the middle step, and bounces on his ass to the landing below, stopping just at her feet.

"I've fallen for you," he says. "What is your name?"

"Marianne."

"Phone number?"

"So many questions." She blows him a kiss, shatters him with a wink of a sea-green eye. "*Bonjour*, cowboy."

Pete stumbles to his feet and follows her outside. But her escort tugs at her, and they climb into a taxi. From the top of the staircase I look down at Pete. He seems destroyed. We go to our hotel. We crash.

Once you have done fairly big time, as I have on a couple of rough beefs, you are sucked against your will into a low-life network. You meet guys you have known on the inside, and it is considered polite to sit around with such people and catch up.

This underground meshwork had already spread the fact of my presence in Montreal, so I am not particularly surprised, although not happy, when Joe the Fish and another gentleman sidle up to me and Pete in the coffee shop of our hotel, where we are having breakfast at two o'clock in the afternoon.

Joe the Fish is Joey Bart, a numbers man who had been in the joint with me over a racetrack thing.

"Hello, Hawk," he says. "Mind if we have a coffee?"

I give Pete a quick look to let him know that this is unsavoury company. Joey Bart introduces his friend. "This is Hymie Solomon," he says. I say to myself: Oh-oh. I know of this man. He is known as Cut-'Em-Up Hymie. He is a captain for a very heavy, and I do not mean corpulent, operator in Montreal. These men are dressed as if they have come from a funeral, which is as likely as not.

"I have heard about you, Mr. Kerrivan," Hymie says. "I am told you and Mr. Nighthawk are in town."

They order coffees, and there is a half-hour of social intercourse. How long are you in Montreal? Can we be of any help? That sort of thing. You want tickets to the Canadiens-L.A. Kings series? You want ringside at the Steve Martin show? Girls? Some real lookers? Just ask. Also, there are funny stories. Hymie turns out to be lots of laughs when he gets going.

Ultimately, he slides into the business part of it. "I hear you might be a little short of cash."

"I'm not looking for partners," says Pete.

Hymie smiles, pats Pete on the shoulder. "No, no, no," he says with a big chortle. "You like to run your own show. I understand that. I appreciate that. I *like* that." Real smarmy. "Nobody ain't talking about partners; nobody ain't talking about dealing theirselves in. Where do you think we are? Chicago? Nineteen-twenty?" He and Joe the Fish are laughing. I am smiling to be friendly. Pete is cleaning his teeth with a toothpick.

Hymie says, "We can work one of three ways. We can bankroll for a cut of the product. You get a fair cut – the fat, naturally. Or, second way, we can just loan you, repayable say two, t'ree months."

These will not be Royal Bank rates. Figure ten per cent a week.

Pete looks Hymie in the eye and shakes his head.

"Do you want to know the third way, schmuck?" Hymie is smiling like a Mexican. "The third way is we break your spine."

Pete is still working at his toothpick, engrossed. He finally dislodges something, probably bacon rind, and flicks it. It lands on Solomon's lapel and sticks there.

"Let's get some fresh air, Johnny," Pete says, and stands up. The Fish and Hymie get up, too, blocking our route to the aisle.

"Get out of my way or I'll drive you," Pete says. Calmly, not loud.

The *capos* stand there for a minute, then step back a bit.

"You a hard guy, eh?" hisses Joey Bart. "Get out of Montreal. Or we'll send you home by river express."

We brush past these guys. My asshole is clenched tight as Aunt Milly's change purse.

When we return to our room, I suggest: "Let us make hasty retreat from this city."

"Yes," says Pete. "Leave us fold our tents like the Arabs and get the fuck out of here."

But as luck would have it there is half a bottle of tequila left on the dresser, not worth the trouble to pack. After finishing that, we have room service send some more rounds up and, thus emboldened, venture down to the bar, thence to the street. Ultimately, as if drawn by a magnetic force, Pete Kerrivan and his faithful Indian companion find themselves in the little east-end bar where Pete first saw Marianne of the Emerald Eyes, as he calls her.

And by God, she is there. And when she sees Pete, she bolts, out the door, into a cab, before Pete can say anything.

I run outside with Pete, whose mouth is hanging open. "Does she think I've got leprosy?" he mumbles.

We are about to go back into the bar when we are greeted by four messengers from Hymie and Joe. Where are the police when you really need them? We have accidentally slipped our tail.

Anyway, it did not matter much. The Fish and Cut-'Em-Up Hymie must have felt it was beneath them to wrinkle their dacron suits over us, because they sent some really inexperienced fellows. The worst I got out of it was a sprained knee and a dislocated toe in exchange, I believe, for some cracked ribs. Pete tore his shirt and broke the damn frames of his glasses once again, but three of those boys checked out fast after a few seconds, and the fourth, we just left him on the sidewalk spitting out teeth.

The message from Hymie is, however, clear. He is not going to give us tickets to the Canadiens-L.A. Kings series after all. He is a man whose good humour cannot be stretched too far.

Anyway, we have girded our loins and we are ready for James Peddigrew.

CHAPTER EIGHT

There was a rush of excitement from Potship headquarters when Mitchell returned from Miami. Constable Bechard, who had been in Montreal, provided the good news.

"Kerrivan's made the connection," he told Mitchell. "Angelo Peritti. Kerrivan and The Hawk met with a couple of his *capos* yesterday, Joe Bartolucci and Hymie Solomon. Looks like Peritti is trying to set up a Colombian operation."

"How close did you get?"

"Nobody could hear nothing. It was in a hotel coffee shop. They split up and must have met later to work out the details. Next time we picked up on the targets they looked pretty beat up."

"That's how Peritti puts a deal together," Mitchell said. "If the other guy doesn't like the terms, he gets his teeth kicked in."

"Assuming a deal *was* put together," came the voice of Sergeant Theophile O'Doull.

"The deal was put together," Mitchell said. "Kerrivan isn't floating down the St. Lawrence River, is he? Peritti gets his way." He studied O'Doull for a long moment. "What's eating your ass, anyway?"

"I didn't expect that," O'Doull said. "I never thought Pete would get involved with that kind of people."

"What kind of people?"

"Organized crime."

"*Organized crime?*" Mitchell snorted hard. "What do you think this is all about, Theo? Kerrivan *is* organized crime. Get with it. You're not playing cap-pistol cowboys with this guy any more. People change. Kerrivan is into dope and money. Dope and money have this weird way of fucking you up, right?"

"Yeah," O'Doull said softly. "But it's just pot."

"Pot, shmot. It's organized crime and it's big bucks, and if the bucks are there it doesn't matter whether the shit goes in your arms or your lungs or up your asshole. Stop mooning."

Mitchell wished that O'Doull would act more like a cop. If the man had not made himself invaluable, Mitchell would have given him the can.

Theophile O'Doull, Thewf the Newf, had come, magically, out of the bowels of the central crime detection laboratory in Ottawa, dug out of there like a long-entombed mummy. He had been flown to Newfoundland – where he had been born and raised – and showed up in Mitchell's office in a lumpy off-the-rack suit, pale and stammering and apologizing. He told Mitchell he had been up all night worrying. Kerrivan and Kelly had been his boyhood friends. He was too close to them. Mitchell gruffly explained that a professional puts emotion aside.

That did not seem to content O'Doull, but he became Mitchell's voice man, anyway.

Mitchell could not quite bring into the focus of his mind a picture of O'Doull playing right wing on a line with Peter Kerrivan. But that's what his talent scout had said: O'Doull and Kerrivan played hockey for St. Joseph's Secondary in St. John's. Along with Kelly, they shared a dormitory for four years, shot pool, and dated girls together, worked together one summer on the same fishing boat.

Mitchell's mind, not given to fantasy, composed these 1960s pictures with blurred images. O'Doull *was* given to fantasy, and seemed to daydream through his shifts while still managing, in a manner not understood by Mitchell, to do the work of ten.

The experienced drug team which Mitchell had assembled for Operation Potship – even before the budget was approved – would describe O'Doull as straight. The streetwise undercover experts ranged from mod to longhair. The wiretap people and the surveillance group were, at worst, contemporary in their choice of grooming. O'Doull, on the other hand, looked like a throwback to the 1950s – not a hint of sideburns, basic cowlick hairdo. He was sallow, yet rangy, and there was a boyishness about him, a quick, nervous manner of speaking. Bob Newhart, with a St. John's brogue.

Although seemingly beset with a faint heart, O'Doull was a find. He had local knowledge. He had an ear for voices, and after listening to a bugged phone for a few minutes he could tell what part of Newfoundland the speakers came from. He could pick out Kerrivan's voice from fifty others who might have used the same coin telephone on the same day.

But more than that, O'Doull, Mitchell thought, might be an electronic genius. He was, of all things, a Ph.D., who, for reasons inexplicable, had joined the RCMP. The Mounties, always short of good scientists, had grabbed him quick.

At Potship headquarters in St. John's, O'Doull had taken charge of the scientific end of things, and was running the wiretap centre, which he had set up in two days of furious activity on the second floor of a downtown building next to Mitchell's makeshift office. The other teams worked out of the ground floor, back of a camera shop. O'Doull had organized the security people from Newfoundland Telephone to run pairs from twenty-seven different phone locations: houses, flats, apartments, pay phones in bars that the targets frequented.

And so, with Meyers already in action down south, Potship was on course, Mitchell's firm hand at the helm.

"What's on the tapes?" he asked O'Doull.

"Kevin Kelly won't be going on this trip," O'Doull said. "He told his wife he's going to stay home. He'll help Pete put the Canadian end together, that's all."

Mitchell was disappointed. He would have liked to have Kelly in the bag, too.

"He's small potatoes, anyway," Mitchell said. He turned back to Bechard. "What else from Montreal?"

"Just a lot of boozing, beating about. Captain Jackpot and The Hawk are in Toronto now."

"And?"

"Kerrivan went up to his lawyer's office. I don't know what he's doing there."

"Peddigrew, that cunt," Mitchell said. "I'd like to nail him and his three-piece suit to the wall. Kerrivan's probably getting illegal advice. How to beat the revenuers." Something hanging around O'Doull's neck caught his eye. "What the hell is that?"

"This? A magnifying eyepiece. I've been working on some recorders."

Mitchell glanced at the solid-state circuitry scattered about O'Doull's work table. Patch cords, adapters, recorder preamplifiers.

"When I get this thing together," O'Doull said, "it will pick up voices up to twenty metres. Transmits to a receiver about an inch in diameter. If we can borrow Pete's watch, we can replace the workings and fit this in with them."

"How are we going to do that, Theo?"

Mitchell tried to follow O'Doull's discussion about an electronic pulse that could deactivate a self-winding watch. "He'll have to take it in to get it fixed," O'Doull said.

"Kerrivan doesn't wear a watch," Mitchell said. He showed him some of Bechard's surveillance pictures from Montreal. Blow-ups. No watch on either wrist.

O'Doull cleared his throat. "I'm working on something

else." He pointed to a tiny metal object about a quarter of an inch square. "It's an all solid-state crystal-controlled transmitter that sends to a total power degenerate interferometer receiver with a pair of quadraloop antennas. The sort of thing they use in rocket-launching systems. We can stick it anywhere in his car. We can even wire it to a twelve-volt battery and set it to activate whenever the ignition is turned on. With a relative direction meter, we can sit two or three miles behind his car and follow him without his ever seeing anyone behind him."

Mitchell was getting a headache. "Kerrivan doesn't own a car," he said. "He takes taxis."

O'Doull's problem was these lapses. He should know better, Mitchell thought. All the surveillance data were available to him.

"Since Kerrivan isn't going to be bringing a car up from South America," Mitchell said, "I'd be happier if you could get something onto his ship."

"He doesn't have a ship. Yet."

"He will. You see, Theo, that's the number-one problem in this operation." Mitchell played the patient school teacher. "When they start to come north, we're going to lose them. Unless we find out exactly where they plan to land. Can't we get something onto the ship?"

"We can put a bird-dog transmitter by the step of the mast, but we're not going to get much distance. The ocean is a lot bigger than it looks on the map, inspector." He thought for a moment. "We could bounce something off the ionosphere. Some kind of bumper-beeper pulse. Why don't we talk to NASA? Borrow one of their satellites?"

"Yeah? That's possible? Work on it, Theo. Because if we don't get something on board so we can track the ship, I can see this whole operation going to . . ."

"Going to pot," said O'Doull with a smile.

"Yeah. Unless Meyers comes up with some brilliant ideas."

Mitchell turned around to the others. "Okay, the targets should be going back to Montreal. Let's get something happening. Let's get some wire going. Taps on Peritti and his people. We'll get the whole Montreal Mafia in our net along with Kerrivan. Let's get this thing in gear. Conference. Krenshaw, O'Doull, Berry, Bechard. In my office."

O'Doull lagged behind, studying some of Bechard's photographs. Some had been taken with the aid of a Startron night viewer adapted to the cameras. Kerrivan and Nighthawk at Dorval Airport. Kerrivan and Nighthawk getting into a taxi. Kerrivan and Nighthawk in a restaurant talking to two men in black suits. Kerrivan entering a bar. Kerrivan talking to a woman on the street. A blow-up of the woman's face.

Her eyes were on Kerrivan and there was a soft smile on her lips. She was beautiful.

"O'Doull, get your ass in here!"

CHAPTER NINE

Johnny Nighthawk

Testing. Tape Two. I'm sending these tapes air mail, and I just hope they are getting through. Do the cops up there open people's mail? It's against the law, isn't it?

I take you now into the offices of Peddigrew, Lynch, and Westcott, Barristers and Solicitors.

As a result of previous visits to lawyers' offices, I am familiar with the third-storey walkup legal aid lawyer with whiskey on his breath who is supposed to defend me the afternoon of my first appointment – and does not know my name. This scene is different. I will set it for you.

A converted brownstone on Davenport Road. In the waiting room are chintz lamps and stained-glass partitions and wicker chairs. Rubber plants so tall you expect Simba to come swinging down a vine. I would call this motif decadent funk. A receptionist stares at us from between the fronds of a fern. We are asked to wait.

Three men enter. Suits. Briefcases. They too are asked to wait. They are nervous, and sit with the briefcases clutched to their laps.

Facing them, making them nervous, are me and Peter Kerrivan. I am a large Indian with bruises on my face. That will scare anyone. But beside me, glowering at these guys, is something even worse. Pete's flared boots are propped up on a stack of *National Geographics*, and he is slouching back in his worn denim jacket, open over a cannabis leaf T-shirt, his eyes half-lidded behind a pair of spectacles that are hanging cock-eyed, taped at the middle. A black Stetson sits low over Pete's forehead. He is smoking roll-your-owns.

"What kind of trouble are you guys in?" Pete asks.

One of them clears his throat. "We're having a trust agreement drawn up."

"That don't sound too serious," Pete says.

The receptionist glares at him, and he glares back at her. Finally, after half an hour of listening to each other breathe, there is action – the intercom buzzes. The receptionist, who looks relieved, says to the banker-type guys, "Mr. Peddigrew will be able to see you now."

Out he comes, James Peddigrew, beaming and bustling on the surface, but his eyes flicking back and forth, studying the scene.

"Gentlemen, I am sorry," he says. "I was facing a closing date." He does not elaborate. The bankers get up. So does Pete.

"I'm next," Pete says.

Peddigrew chokes on a false chuckle, takes Pete by the arm, and hustles him to the front door, giving me the eye to come, too.

"Hey, man," he says in a low voice, "this office scene is too straight. Why don't you come to the house for dinner tonight?" He gives me an afterthought look. "You, too." He probably wonders if I know how to use a knife and fork.

Peddigrew's is what they call a townhouse. There are old things there that are intended to reflect good taste.

Fragile bric-a-brac. I make a strained effort to relax in this environment, to demonstrate that although a poor boy from Northern Oregon's rain forest, I am a person who can slide easily into any social situation.

Why do I have the feeling that Peddigrew is treating me like somebody's retarded nephew who was brought along because he cannot fend for himself?

Perhaps, you are wondering, why in fact *am* I here. Well, I am here because Pete does not trust his lawyer too well. In this business one does not have written contracts, so it is best to have a witness. I am here as Pete's witness.

I soon pick up that Lara Peddigrew is flirting with Pete. She has bright secret eyes that peek at him, then jump away when her husband looks towards her. She has fine manners and a high-toned WASP quality, but with some wine her good side comes out. She becomes bouncy and bubbly, sort of looser buttoned, and from time to time she teases out a pair of wiggly legs from the slits of her long dress.

Peddigrew, for the evening, has got duded up as your basic farm hand with faded jeans, checked shirt, bandanna, and a big buckle that says "Coors."

We are on our third bottle of fourteen-dollar Beaune when I feel Lara's bare foot beneath the dining table tickle up my ankle. No fool, I know what is happening. Because of my sore knee from the fight, I have trouble bending my leg, and it is stretched across to her side of the table. She is footsying the wrong foot. I know this because as her toes tippy up my shin, she gives Pete a big, secret grin. This is a sly lady. I sense she is dissatisfied with her life, Peddigrew being such a cold fish.

We listen to Peddigrew on smuggling. He talks between mouthfuls of tenderloin.

"I've seen them all. All the scams, all the crackpot schemes, all the dumb deals. I have seen guys get busted in every loony way possible. I am in a business where you see the mistakes people make."

Nobody is listening to him. I have developed a fetish over Lara's foot. I am too awkward to disengage. Pete, beside me, is picking through his salad, trying to avoid the strange things hidden in it.

"It's always some ridiculous mistake," Peddigrew is saying. "Sometimes people get lazy, and talk on the phone."

At this point he looks significantly at Pete, who I have to admit has gotten pretty loose on the phone for a person with his skills. Peddigrew beat the wiretap last time, but it was fortunate the prosecution had a real dumb witness in court, with whom Peddigrew had a field day. He picked him clean like a buzzard.

I am praying that Peddigrew will not suggest we retire to the drawing room for cigars and brandy. I have an erection – Lara's toes are running up and down my ankle. But these stolen moments of furtive sex are ended by Peddigrew dismissing his wife to the living room while he brings out a decanter of cognac from the shelf behind him.

He pours Courvoisier and talks.

"If you just plan ahead, cover all the legal angles before you come back into the country, they can't make it stick even if they do pop you."

Pete is quiet, waiting for him to get to the point. I suspect he does not like amateurs telling him his business.

"There are ways I could tell you that are foolproof," Peddigrew says. "Absolutely hassle free. Let's say you were hired by this company to skipper this old junker from Colombia to North America. Maybe there is a layer of scrap iron on top of whatever else is in the holds. No customs guy is going to hire a crane to pull off the scrap and look underneath. And if he does, so what? *You* don't have to know it was there. You just say to customs, 'Looks like somebody's been playing me for a sucker.' The defence of no *mens rea*. Lack of knowledge. You can't convict a guy if he doesn't know he's carrying contraband. That's the law."

Peddigrew is punctuating his points with a dessert spoon.

"No *mens rea*," says Pete. "That's what I'll tell the boys when they try to take me away. I'll say I got no *mens rea*. James, old cock, tell me about your ship."

"It's not *my* ship."

"Your *company's* ship."

"It's not my company, either. I'm a trustee for the principal shareholder. Titular head."

"Titular head?" says Pete. "Look, who *gives* a shit. We're not going to tell on you. Let's get to the nitty. What's the deal?"

Peddigrew leaves, returns with a file, and produces from it a photograph. We can see that the ship is a rust bucket.

"Five hundred and sixty tons, forty-eight metres," Peddigrew says. "It was built during the war in Norfolk, Virginia. A cable layer, I think, then for years a coastal freighter. Ran through different owners before Juares picked it up."

Peddigrew shows us a photo of a man with big teeth.

"That is Juares. He is an old client of mine. You can trust him. He has a boatyard in Barranquilla."

I look at the photograph and memorize the face. It is the face of a crook, but what should I expect?

"What does this thing run on?" I ask. I am, incidentally, engineer on the various ships that Pete has hired me for. I have a lot of experience on deep sea long-liners and trawlers out on the Pacific.

"It's diesel electric," says Peddigrew.

"That sounds like it will be some trouble," I say. I look at the specs. I will not bore you with the technical end of things, but the ship had a diesel direct-current drive system, same sort of thing as a train locomotive. Tugs, ferries, quick-manoeuvre ships use that kind of system. She had twin Imperial diesel engines, driven off a pair of generators.

Peddigrew carries on. "The official plan – this is what the documents will say – the official plan is to load it with scrap metal and bring it north to be cut up. Juares supplies the scrap."

"Who supplies the weed?" Pete asks.

"Who's got the connection?"

"I'm supposed to have no *mens rea*."

"Nobody's going to make you take a lie-detector test."

"What's your cut?" Pete asks.

"I understand the company would like to go fifty-fifty after expenses."

"Bull*shit*," Pete says. "I run the risk—you get fat. I'll think it over and work out a few numbers. This isn't just a cruise in the Caribbean. I'll need at least six men—Johnny here in the engine room, Kevin as first mate. I'll work on Kevin. He's my buddy. He'll come."

"Juares can find crew."

"Colombians? No, thanks. Also, there is the startup costs. We would need maybe thirty, forty thousand dollars for fuel, maybe double that for high-seas gear and other incidentals. Like food and bribe money. *La mordida*."

Peddigrew rolls his eyes. "My clients aren't exactly in the league of Howard Hughes."

"Aw, come on," says Pete, "what do you earn as a lawyer—two or three hundred thousand a year? James, you got to learn to highroll if you're going to get into the importing business."

At this point Pete pulls out a limp joint that looks like it might have been sitting in the bottom of his shirt pocket for the last year. He hands it to Peddigrew.

"Toke?"

Peddigrew sniffs it like someone's dirty underwear. "What is this?" he says.

Pete shrugs. "Some guy laid it on me."

Peddigrew calls to Lara in the living room. "Twist us some from the good, would you, darling?"

We are sitting around the living room all loaded on the lawyer's sweet Hawaiian buds. Except Peddigrew, who says he is saving himself for later. He does not want to "cloud his palate."

Pete is laying back, thinking things out. Lara is Joni

Mitchell, wrestling with a guitar and singing. I am spaced, staring into the fire. As far as conversation goes, there is silence.

Until Pete, from nowhere, a voice from the far side of the cosmos, starts laying out the commandments.

"You pay a hundred thousand up front for expenses, equipment, and et ceteras."

He is interrupted by Peddigrew. "Lara, darling, would you leave us." He gives her a proprietary hug. She takes her guitar away with her, but I see her give Pete a little tired look as if to say, "Isn't it bullshit?"

"A hundred *thousand*?" says Peddigrew. "Jesus, you owe me that in legal fees, Pete."

Having to repeat himself, Captain Kerrivan sounds annoyed. "A hundred thousand up front. As to the split, half and half is impossible. My supplier – I owe him from the last time. He's going to want half, too. Half to you, half to him – that is a good way for me to stay poor. I'll give you twenty per cent with a minimum guarantee up to a maximum."

"What's the range?" asks Peddigrew.

"A minimum guarantee of five hundred thousand up to twenty per cent of net with a two and a half million top."

I am blown away by these figures. The five per cent crew share that Pete will pay me seems like a poor beggarly sum. I need a union.

"I don't know, Pete," says Peddigrew, "you're not exactly bargaining from strength these days." He thought for a minute. "I'll have to take it up with the directors. I trust you, Pete – don't get me wrong – but how can I be sure my clients will get a fair deal between those figures?"

"What do you mean you trust me? You don't trust me any more than I trust you. If you don't think I'll look after your interests, you'll have to get yourself a sailor suit and join us."

"Oh, sure. I can get disbarred just hanging around you

socially, let alone showing up at your side in Colombia."

"You could be the ship's lawyer. You can make sure we don't make any of those dumb mistakes you talk about." Pete grins. "Or you can send your old lady."

Peddigrew's face hardens. "Don't mention this to her. There is a part of the world she knows nothing about, and I want her to stay that way." He seems to ponder. "I *might* just send an agent along. To look after my clients' interests."

"Long as he don't mind scrubbing decks," Pete says.

Peddigrew is still in thought. "Let me put something to you," he says. "Let's say in addition to the weed, you have a couple of hundred pounds of blow on board. Let's say you didn't have to make the connection. Let's say the company is able to supply itself from its own contacts. Let's say –"

Pete interrupts. "No cocaine."

"Why?"

"I don't trust the *cocaneros*. Too many rats, too many guys working both sides, too much talk, too much heat. The DEA narcs pay up to ten thousand bucks to the snitches for the names of big-time snow removers. That's a lot of *dinero* down there." Pete puts his sock feet on a table; Peddigrew puts coasters under them.

"Also," Pete says, "I don't do any deals I don't set up by myself. It's a rule. In my business, I also see the dumb mistakes that people make."

We are startled by a grating sound. It is the doorbell.

Peddigrew gets up. "Maybe you'll change your mind after you get a little taste of this. It just came up via Air Canada."

We descend briefly now into the Valley of the Bizarre. Coming in the door, graceful and cool, beatific in expression, is Marianne of the Emerald Eyes.

"Gentlemen," says Peddigrew, "I'd like you to meet Marianne Larochelle."

First there is a frown on her face. Then her eyes widen like a scared fawn's. She has caught sight of Pete, who is taking his glasses off, wiping the lenses, putting them back on, not believing.

Without saying anything, she walks to the balcony doorway, pulls it open. She makes a motion, as if throwing something.

Peddigrew is in a state of agitated dismay. "What are you doing?" he yells.

Marianne Larochelle aims a finger at Pete. "This man," she announces, "is a *policeman!*"

Without too much grace, Pete pulls himself to his feet and goes for his inside pocket. "You're under arrest, Peddigrew. We've got it all on tape." He looks at his lawyer with a frown. "You're supposed to say 'Curses.'"

Peddigrew has his hands in his hair. "We'll never find it out there." He is looking out at the thick patches of dirty snow on the lawn.

Marianne says, "James, this man has been following me. He's a narc." Her tone is more confused than urgent.

"This is Peter Kerrivan," says Peddigrew.

"*You* are Kerrivan?" she says.

"Maybe I should have introduced myself." Pete is smiling. He is, of course, proud that he is famous. He has the grace to remember that I am present, and introduces me.

"She just threw half an ounce of mother-of-pearl cocaine in the snow," Peddigrew moans.

Marianne gives Pete her very sweetest mysterious-lady-cocaine-smuggler smile, and extends her hand.

"*Tengo mucho gusto.*"

"*El gusto,*" says Pete, "*es mio.*"

We take this Keystone Cops roadshow outside and pad around in the snow. There is a crust on it from the night freeze, and it has been stomped on from kids playing.

Pete is not much help. He has severe giggles from the Hawaiian pot and finds the situation a source of uproarious merriment. His uncontrollable fits of laughter cause lights to go on in the neighbouring townhouse. Finally, Pete collapses into a snowpile.

"Snow!" he yells. "Uncut snow! It melts in your nose!"

Lara and I, both loaded, are laughing, too. Marianne Larochelle is looking at us as if this is a zoo.

Peddigrew is straight and is the more methodical scavenger, and he comes up with a fat, zip-lock Baggie containing the half-ounce of snob powder. He is waving it triumphantly in the air when a pair of headlights snap on.

Wap. Here is a heavy blow of fate. The bulls have been cruising down the street in the darkness. Two cops jump out of the cruiser and chuff their way across the lawn and I see, from the corner of my eye, Peddigrew flip the bag of coke away. It falls with a soft plump between Pete and me.

One of the cops goes over to retrieve it, saying, "Lady next door was complaining about the noise. She said it sounded as if someone had gone bananas." He peers into the Baggie, sniffs, then smiles at Peddigrew. "You dropped this?"

They had been too far away to see for sure who threw it, I think.

Peddigrew pulls one of his best defences. "No, officer, I just came out here myself to find out what all the noise was about. I'm a lawyer. I live here." He is looking helplessly at Pete.

"Like I said," Pete says in a low voice, "too much heat. What about the terms, then? A fifth, leave it or take it."

Peddigrew mumbles the answer. I catch it. That is my job—I am Pete's witness. "Yes, yes," he says, "it's okay." He has an imploring look. The cops come over, wanting to hear this conversation.

"We got a deal," Pete whispers. "Now get my ass out on bail in time for breakfast." He turns to the bull. "*I* dropped it," he says. "It's mine, I own it, I am in sole possession, and this is a voluntary confession just so you won't have to beat me."

The cop, going by the book, holds the Baggie under Pete's nose and asks the standard question to establish what the lawyer, I guess, calls *mens rea*. "Do you know what is in here, sir?"

"Talcum powder for my bum," says Pete.

Pete gives us a weary wave from the back of the cruiser. Peddigrew sends his wife back into the house, then he, Marianne, and I hustle down to his office, where he draws a large bundle of bills from his safe. "We can use some of this for bail," he says.

We spend an hour trying to raise a justice of the peace to set bail, and following that there is delay and confusion because no one can locate the body.

Finally we check with the lockup. Pete Kerrivan is not there. The cops gave him an appearance notice, told him to show up in court in a month, and let him go. Simple possession of cocaine. I am a little surprised. Half an ounce – fourteen grams – it's usually enough for a possession with intent.

We return to Peddigrew's home, and as we enter the living room, we are confronted by a scene of Bacchanalian abandonment. A blast of heavy metal assaults our ears. "Led Zeppelin II."

I watch Peddigrew. His eyes settle briefly upon an empty bottle of his Beaune, which lies on a red-stained Persian carpet. The eyes roam across a bejewelled stash box sitting open on the table, plundered of its buds. By the fireplace, two more empty bottles of wine.

And, as the final show-stopper, in front of the fireplace we have Pete Kerrivan and Lara Peddigrew grunting and pumping to the screams of Jimmy Page's electric guitar from the big Infinity Reference 4.5 speakers that retail at three thousand a side.

Lara is on her back on the floor, her legs hooked around Pete's thighs, her panties fluttering like a flag from a dainty ankle. Pete is snug between her legs in the throes of a mighty orgasm, woofing and calling to the sweet Lord Jesus. At first I think Peddigrew is just going to stand there with his mouth hanging open. Then he turns off the stereo receiver, and the room fills with a majestic silence, marred only by the decelerating slap-slap of sticky bodies.

Pete rises up on his elbows, fumbles for his glasses, twists the frames around his ears, and obtains a focus, first on Peddigrew – and he knows he can live with that – and then on Marianne Larochelle, right deep into those two green pools.

There is a noisy glutch sound in Pete's throat. The woman with respect to whom Pete alleges he suffers a desperate infatuation is studying him with a soft smile on her face. She slowly shakes her head. Pete, I think, has made some kind of initial impression on Marianne Larochelle.

"You better put something on," she says, and tosses him his Stetson.

Through all this, Lara Peddigrew lies on her back on the floor, covering her eyes with her hands.

"Get him out of here." I realize Peddigrew is talking to me. I think they are the first words he has directed to me.

He snaps open his briefcase and hands to Marianne Larochelle the fat bundle of bills that he had removed from his safe.

"I want you to handle this," he tells her. "I don't want to deal with him. There is a hundred thousand dollars here, exactly. Every dollar is to be accounted for. That includes money he spends on booze and whores."

He turns to Pete. "Marianne will be going with you. As my agent."

Pete's face is a mask of mixed emotion. There is despair. There is joy. He is standing there, covering himself with his hat, assembling himself with a dignity that does not quite come off.

"You're coming down to Colombia with us, Miss Larochelle?"

"I don't think James trusts you," she says. "I can't imagine why."

Pete delivers a large but guilty smile. "You can be cabin boy on the ship," he says.

"Such an honour," she says. "I think I'd prefer to run the galley. It's more my line." She is, by the way, an Air Canada stewardess.

Peddigrew probably hasn't heard all this. He does not look well. His eyes show pain.

"Get up, Lara," he says. "It's time to go to bed."

"Yes, dear."

CHAPTER TEN

Harold Mitchell, damp with the sweat of a difficult night, his muscles clenched in sleep, his body coiled like a spring among bunched sheets, powered himself awake to obey the insistent urgings of his telephone.

It was two A.M.

"I've got good news," said the night duty officer. "I didn't think you'd mind being awakened, sir."

Mitchell cleared his throat. "Yes?"

"It was just a freak shot, but we re-established contact with the target."

"Where? Is he still in Toronto?"

"Out on the front yard of somebody's home. He's been busted."

"What?"

The young officer sounded jubilant. "Yes, sir. Arrested by the Toronto Metro Police."

The cobwebs of sleep evaporated.

"They got him on a possession for the purpose of trafficking. Half an ounce of cocaine. It's solid. Admissions, everything. We got him, inspector."

Mitchell uttered one long syllable which slowly built up and finally exploded from his mouth. "Sh-h-h-it!"

"Sorry, sir?"

"Get him out of jail! And get that charge reduced. Get

hold of Toronto drugs. Aw, Christ, just get off the line and I'll do it myself!"

Operation Potship had almost foundered.

Kerrivan sent Nighthawk on a sales trip through the eastern cities, to Buffalo, Rochester, the Big Apple, Philadelphia, to line up the buyers. This was a task that normally would have been attended to by Kerrivan himself, but, as he explained, with the season under way they had to zip. Kerrivan would stay in central Canada for a few days, contacting buyers there.

"We'll meet Monday in – how about Atlantic City?"

"No, Pete. We'll meet back in St. John's."

"I'll be wanting to see how my luck is running before we go south, Johnny."

"No, Pete."

"Aw, all right, St. John's."

Nighthawk went off to Buffalo suspecting Kerrivan had additional reasons for not coming with him.

Nighthawk was right.

"Here we are," Kerrivan said. He had just been admitted into Larochelle's Toronto hotel room. "Small world, huh?"

"Small world," she said.

"What about the guy who was hanging around with you in Montreal?"

"He was a lover." She smiled. "That's all."

Kerrivan felt his insides stiffen. He twiddled with the leather tassel on his jacket. He had fumbled early on with her and was determined to make up ground. "What about dinner?"

"What *about* dinner?" she said. "Is this an invitation?"

"I am asking you out for dinner." He felt as nervous as a farm boy.

Larochelle was strolling about her room, squinting her eyes to protect them from the smoke of the cigarette that hung from her lips. "A kind of date?" she said. "With you? I don't know. It sounds dangerous. Should I wear my chastity belt?"

"You mean I make *you* nervous?"

"I wasn't prepared to believe the legend until I saw you in action the other night."

"I was an innocent victim. She threatened me with violence. The experience will mark me for life."

"Clients should not fornicate with their lawyers' wives."

"Yeah, I guess it's possible to contract a high-class social disease. How did *you* get to know Peddigrew?"

"Like you, a client. I was nailed on trafficking a few years ago. He did a deal, got the charges stayed. My boyfriend went down for three and a half years."

She was still moving about the room, straightening things, emptying ashtrays.

"That must have been a wallop," Kerrivan said. "What fee did he charge you? I'll bet you had to mortgage the farm."

She blew a cloud of smoke high in the air, tamped her cigarette, then lit a fresh one. "I worked the fee out."

"Oh, yeah, he loves his toots."

"No, he pays for his toots. I went to bed with him."

Kerrivan felt his mouth slide open.

"Lawyers have a way of screwing you every time," she said.

"I'll be going directly to Barranquilla," Larochelle said. "I have a Montreal-Miami flight on Monday, then I'm taking a leave from Air Canada. I'll go directly from Miami. Peddigrew wants me to settle the terms with Juares before you get there. You have the address."

They were in a small Italian restaurant with checkered tablecloths.

Kerrivan would lift his eyes from hers every few minutes and glance around the room.

"What are you looking for?" she said.

"The narco boys. Usually I have company wherever I go. I get lonely without them."

Kerrivan prided himself as a narc-spotter. But the restaurant was crowded, and it was difficult to tell if police were there.

They played spot-the-cop.

"That guy at the door with a three days' growth," Larochelle said.

"No, he's been looking at us," said Kerrivan. "A tail would be pretending he doesn't notice us."

"Maybe it's a woman. What about the one by herself in the corner?"

"Dressed too well. I thought about the longhair in the green jacket, but I think he's a regular here, a lasagne freak. The waiter knows him. Maybe we're alone."

"How romantic," she said.

They sipped Bardolino, and Larochelle chainsmoked. Kerrivan felt mesmerized by her green eyes. But he still felt awkward with her. She was too cool, too assured. She dealt with him in a gently mocking way, and she seemed to have his number. That made him uncomfortable. In his relationships Kerrivan preferred the driver's seat.

He felt particular distaste at the thought that Larochelle was in control of the expenses – she had given him five thousand dollars for spending money. When the bill arrived, he made a show of grabbing for it.

"No," she said. "I'm putting it on the account. A business dinner. That way I don't have to feel I owe you anything."

"You don't," Kerrivan said gruffly. Her hand was on his hand which was on the bill. Her hand felt strangely dry, but soft. Finally, she removed it.

"I'll pay," he said. "This isn't business."

"What exactly is it, Peter?" she asked.

Back at her hotel, still in the taxi, she bussed him lightly on the cheek. "Thank you."

An invitation to come up to her room did not seem to be forthcoming. He was about to suggest one when she said, "I was thinking about a nightcap, but you are probably too exhausted. From last night."

She got out, shut the door, and smiled at the hotel doorman as he ushered her inside.

Kerrivan went to his own hotel in a black funk.

He was at her door at nine A.M. She opened it two inches and her eyes seemed to study him with an expression of curiosity.

"What about breakfast?" he said.

There were beads of sweat on her forehead. Her radio was playing loudly – classical music. "I'll be a few minutes," she said. "I'm rather nude, but if that doesn't offend you, come in."

She opened the door and stood framed in front of him, a slim, damp silhouette in the morning sunlight that streamed through her east-facing windows. Kerrivan's larynx tightened and he was unable to speak.

"If it *does* offend you," she said, closing the door behind him, "I'll give you a pillowcase to put over your head."

Kerrivan stumbled forward, blinded by her body in the brilliant shafts of spring sunshine. He barked his shin on a low coffee table, yelped, and hopped off towards the window, seeking there to reassemble himself, trying to muster an air of nonchalance. "It's a fine, civil day," he said, staring outside at the bleak Toronto rooftops. From the corner of his eye, he saw her swirling about in the centre of the room in time to the music.

"I try to do my exercises every morning," she said. "I do modern dance. Used to perform with a semi-professional group. I was quite athletic when I was a kid. Gold medal in the sprints at the Quebec junior games. I took a black belt in Tae Kwon-Do. Studied for three years at the Yokamura Institute." She talked loudly, over the music. "Sky diving, scuba diving, platform diving. All that stuff. Then I discovered nicotine. Burned out my lungs with cigarette tobacco. I'm wired."

After a while she turned the radio off. Kerrivan turned around to face her. Tricklets of perspiration ran between her breasts. Kerrivan kept his hands in his pockets so she wouldn't see them shaking.

"I'm also a good sailor," she said. "I raced ten-metre yachts, and I don't get seasick. That should make you happy."

She turned and walked to the bathroom, to the shower. At the door, she glanced around at him. "I also like cocaine and sex. Separate or together."

Kerrivan, melting, a failed Mr. Cool, constructed a crooked grin with parched lips.

"Relax, Peter, I'm not going to eat you," she said, disappearing. "Not this morning, anyway."

Kerrivan was able to put some things together with some dealers from Toronto. He found out that the New England Dealers' Association was meeting in convention at Nantucket, and Kerrivan and Larochelle flew there on the weekend.

Kerrivan walked into the resort hotel like a celebrity, and was treated by the dealers as one. He recognized many faces from past business, and there were some newcomers, green and learning. He made tentative contracts with some of the old professionals working out of Boston and Providence, who promised big buys.

Kerrivan suggested to Larochelle that courtesy required they stay the night at the resort and enjoy the party that had been laid on. The best deals, he said, are struck when everyone is relaxing over a smoke or a drink.

"My flight leaves Montreal Sunday noon," she said. "Tomorrow. I've got to be back in plenty of time to pack."

"We'll get up early," Kerrivan said. "I brought an alarm clock."

"Okay," she said, "I'll borrow it and keep it in my room."

Kerrivan raised his eyes over his glasses. "*Your* room? Why waste money on separate rooms? I thought we were partners in this operation."

"*Business* partners," she said.

Kerrivan felt like a limp balloon for the rest of the day.

In the party suite, at night, he sulked in a corner while Larochelle collected admirers, bears hanging around a honey pot. She was wearing a white jumpsuit and shone as brilliantly as a freshly cut diamond in the centre of the room.

Kerrivan engaged in desultory conversation with friends, knocking back straight hits of Johnny Walker Black, growing mopish as he was growing drunk. He was not used to being treated this way. Business partners, she had said. Crap. After a while, he took the bottle and a glass and joined the high-stakes game of lowball stud that was raging at a table in the corner. Kerrivan bet furiously, snarling at the other players, intimidating them. He refused to turn his head to look at Larochelle, but from time to time his eyes shifted and he caught a glimpse of her, grasshopping from group to group.

By one-thirty A.M. he was up three thousand dollars. His bottle of Scotch was down a pint.

By three o'clock he was down two thousand five hundred dollars. The bottle was empty.

By four o'clock, the party burned out. Larochelle had long since left for her room, and the poker game had ended. Kerrivan had lost another thousand dollars.

He got to his feet, clutching at walls for support. His courage was up. It was time to break the ice.

He stood at her door for five minutes, focussing on the number, trying to read it.

She opened it before he could knock.

"I could hear you breathing," she said. "Look, Pete, some time, but not tonight, okay? I've got to get back home tomorrow. Anyway, you're in no condition."

Kerrivan stumbled inside, found his way to a chair, and spent a ten-minute eternity trying to take his boots off.

"I'll show you what condition," he said.

He stumbled towards the bed, collapsed at the foot of it, and passed out.

Kerrivan's last business before going to South America took him back to St. John's, and from there he drove in Johnny Nighthawk's old Ford pickup out the highway to St. Alban's on the Newfoundland south coast. He borrowed a boat and headed out Bay D'Espoir, past the Goblins, to a little cove known to local fishermen as Judas Bight — so named because of its treacherous reefs and rocks.

Kerrivan had spent his boyhood around here, learning the smuggler's trade on an old jackboat schooner on the rum-and-brandy run from the French islands. He had done weekend trips into Fortune Bay and Hermitage Bay with old Captain Pike, motoring in without lights at night, or gliding in with sails when they had a wind. By the age of twelve, Kerrivan had learned the rocks and reefs and sunkers of the south coast, each inlet, island, tickle, and harbour mouth.

It was a cheery day, with the sun burning away the mists, as Kerrivan putted into Judas Bight, up to the dock leading to the old man's rambling boatshed and his square and squat little house. Captain Pike still did a little business there, repairing dories and old wooden seiners.

He was there now, running a paint scraper along the hull of a fishboat, cleaning off the barnacles. As he saw Kerrivan, his lined, bronzed face broke open into a rich smile.

"My son," he said, "y'er a won'erful grand soight."

With the old man, Kerrivan let his speech relax, and he talked with the bouncing brogue he had grown up with.

"Sure and I giss ye know we bate out the charge, uncle," he said.

"I was afear'd you was off an' gone to the penitent'ry for sartin," said the old man. He was nearing eighty.

He grasped Kerrivan by the shoulders with hands that were like steel clamps, and squinted hard at him. "A skinamalink, y'are," he said. "All rames and nary a muscle on ye. Come and I'll bile a bittle and we'll have a drap a tay and somet'in' hot."

"We'll finish this first, Uncle Pike," said Kerrivan, taking up a scraper. "I feels like a little honest work for a change."

They finished cleaning the hull, then sat around Captain Pike's warm kitchen stove for a couple of hours, telling stories and drinking tea and sipping cognac from the bottle Kerrivan had brought as a gift. To the old man, old brandy was an addiction, a legacy of the trade. Finally, they discussed business.

"Ye'll be wantin' to borry the old boatshed," Pike said.

"I'm hopin' to bring in a few ton, uncle," said Kerrivan. "We'll come in at night, as we did afore, and we'll be quiet as mice about it."

"Yiss, y'er welcome to it. The neighbours is off an' moved to Sin Jan's." He sighed. "It's wearyin' here alone, but it'll be a Jasus long day in hell afore I'll go to the city to live. But it's a hard loif alone here, fadgin' for yisself. They gives we old folks a few dollars' pension, an' I gets a bit o' work, as ye see. Now, this here marry-wonna you fellers are sellin', I hear she's goin' about five hunnert dollar a pound."

There would be a hard bargain driven with Captain Pike, Kerrivan knew. Age had little dulled the old man's brain for business.

CHAPTER ELEVEN

The rumble at early twilight stirred the cocks on their roosts in the chicken houses and they wakened and complained. The distant sound of engines, offbeat, ragged, thrummed into the scrubby hills to the north towards the Jackson Company farm, and the plane drifted down to the humpy narrow strip that had been bulldozed there.

Billy Lee Tinker had corrected just east of Pensacola, then had searched for the Conecuh River in southern Alabama. He had corrected twelve degrees to port by the burn-off tower of the new Mobile refinery, adjusted again near the Shell station, then crossed the highway north of Turkey Neck Creek.

Sun's rays now touched the tips of the hills, and Tinker squinted down into the greyness, looking for the row of headlights that should have been lined up along the margin of the landing field. The Jacksons had got his call, and they should have been there, along with some of the other old boys, and their pickups should have been arrayed at right-angles to the strip.

But there was only one pair of headlights. They were at the near end of the strip, where they should not have been.

An uncomfortable shiver tickled up along Billy Lee Tinker's ribs. He had empty gas tanks and twenty-eight forty-pound bags of Santa Marta gold. His options were limited to one, so he came down, nearly skimming the top of the vehicle, a four-by-four that did not belong to anyone he knew. Then his wheels touched, bumped, rose, held, dug in, the B-26 rattling like a Mexican bus. Tinker's teeth gritted as he brought it to a grinding stop. He U-turned, then taxied slowly, almost languidly, back up the strip.

The headlights were moving in his direction. He braked. The four-by-four braked.

Tinker swung the door open and dropped the ladder.

"Douse your cabin lights," a voice said. "No guns."

Tinker recognized the Virginia drawl.

"I see you're still flying missions, Billy Lee."

"Missions of mercy," Tinker said. "Not like Nam."

There was a thin, bright slit of a smile on the pink moonface of Rudy Meyers. Tinker remembered that it was a smile that was there always, a smile that became leaner and sharper when Meyers was about to do something. Usually to someone. He still had a brushcut. There was a camera slung around his neck.

"You still military?" Tinker asked. "Still with intelligence? Or are y'all workin' as a bounty hunter, man?"

"I'm not looking for deserters, Billy Lee. I'm not looking for narcotics, either. As for the army, I gave up my commission. I quit before we pulled out. I didn't want to be a part of it. Rolling over for the Reds."

"Yeah," said Tinker. "Where's my boys?"

Meyers ignored the question. "I was too embarrassed to stay in. After Saigon, it was Iran. Then Nicaragua. We sold it cheap, Billy Lee. Afghanistan. It used to be we kicked ass; now we kiss ass. Some of us are tired of smelling Fidel's excretions, although the president can't get enough of his crap up his nose. Our *conservative* president. I don't know whether to laugh or cry."

"Yeah, well, I never did follow politics, man. What did you do to my friends?"

"I sent them away, Billy Lee. I flashed some tin at them

and they ran. You have cowards for friends. I have their names and licence numbers, and a full roll of film. Those Jackson boys are out on bail, aren't they? They could do a very long shake in the federal prison."

"Are you working for the DEA, man? If you are, you can blow it up your epiglottis."

"I do a little job for them once in a while, Billy Lee. Once in a while. But not today."

That, for some reason, scared Tinker even more. He leaned back against the wing, pulled some papers from his shirt pocket, wet his thumb to pull one loose, then poured a line of Matador tobacco, licked the paper, and twirled it up – almost in one motion. He decided to let Meyers do the talking.

"I have my own business, Billy Lee. Yes, I heard you went hippie overseas. Too much drugs, Billy Lee. Too bad. You had medals coming. You should have stuck around for your last tour."

The crest of the sun sent darts of light across the field. Tinker had *déjà vu*. Billowing balls of fire.

"What do you want?" he asked.

"I'll let you keep the plane, Billy Lee. And your boys can come and get the marijuana. I'll keep a sample, just a sample. I don't wish to turn you in to the police. Or to the military. Unless I have to."

"What's the gig, major? What do you want?"

"Peter Kerrivan. Just an introduction."

•

Johnny Nighthawk

Tape Three. I am not so conceited as to think you are interested in me, but if you will allow a digression, I will tell you how I found myself a continent away from home, upon a different ocean.

110

I was a child of the Pacific, at the age of six a proud fisherboy upon my stepfather's old gillnetter. I graduated early to the great queens of the fishing fleets, the halibut trawlers, and spent many seasons in the Bering Sea. I was a good engineer, if I may be allowed to enjoy a little self-applause. I have never had any kind of ticket, but I have known people with all sorts of paper who cannot keep a thirty-horse outboard running.

I have never had any formal schooling either. But I am not ashamed of that. I am a voracious reader of books – everything: Conrad to Kipling to Arthur Conan Doyle. The result of all this reading and no schooling is that there is a long list of words that I am sure I pronounce wrong. You have already had a laugh about some of them, I am sure. But many fishermen are readers like me. There are no televisions on deep-sea trawlers. When I was in jail, I was made assistant librarian. Kind of proud of that.

We were of the Chinook nation, my family. Before the white man came, ours was a nation of great traders, rich in art, rich in myth and culture, travellers of renown. The tribes of the Plains bought the charms and dentalium shells of my forbears and taught us the joys of tobacco in return.

So it is not surprising that ultimately I bent to the will of my heritage and became a trader, an importer of tobaccos, a traveller between nations and continents.

Colombia became my second home, but it was in Jamaica that I first met Pete Kerrivan. We were down there doing different ends of the same deal. We hung around Montego Bay for several days, had an excellent time. Pete said to look him up in Newfoundland. It was not until two years later that I was able to accept the invitation. I got made by the Bureau of Dangerous Drugs and spent a term in the Florida State Prison. After that, I did look Pete up, which is how I came to be in Newfoundland. An expatriate among the Masterless Men of Kerrivan.

I made my home a while in St. John's, a beautiful city,

especially when you are stoned. (The locals claim it is the oldest city in North America, but I suspect that is a lie.)

So here I am in St. John's, about to travel south again. Because the ever-watchful eye of the law peeps about the airport and peers into every vehicle that boards the ferry at Port-aux-Basques, we decide to leave the island by more secret means. By Bill Stutely's old Cape Islander, a boat he uses for lobstering when he isn't working for Pete.

Bill Stutely is one of Pete's good and faithful boys, one of the original fellows in his band. He is to take us to the Maine coast, then organize the landing party at Captain Pike's in Judas Bight and have a bunch of the boys there ready for our return.

Before we go to Stutely's boat, just as a little diversion, Pete wires a couple of thousand dollars to a bank in San Francisco. He figures it will disperse the heat, send some of it to the wrong ocean.

Also before we go to Stutely's boat, we arrange to meet with Kevin Kelly for a last drink at the Blue Boar Lounge. Pete is coming to pick me up there in a taxi, and he is late, and I am comforting Kelly over a Dominion Ale or two. He is wistful. He is torn. He has not missed a trip with Pete for five years. Kevin is my very good friend, too, but there is hard cement between him and Pete that I cannot share.

Pete has cajoled and begged him to come. He has played slyly and I think unfairly upon Kelly's tortured sense of loyalty. But Kelly remains unbending, immovable. He has paid his back union dues, and this summer he will be working freighters in the St. Lawrence Seaway.

In the bar, he brings me down, predicting calamity. "You'll be going to law with the devil and holding court in hell," he says. He has been visited by sailors' bad omens. "I seen a cat glaring right hard into my eyes the other day," he says. And worse, a lone flying crow passing overhead towards the sea.

Kelly grasps me by the wrist, very tight. "Johnny, don't

go," he says. "Tell Pete – don't go. Ah, God, I woke up with a dream, boy, that you all drownt in the sea. I seen Pete's face in the water." Then he looks long and mournfully into his glass of beer. "Ah, Jesus, Johnny, I sure would like to go." He says this very soft.

Then he is back on the attack. He tells me about his tarot readings, which are full of gloom. He often reads his fortune from these cards. Perhaps he unconsciously manipulates the readings and finds danger where another would find good fortune.

Now occurs an awkward episode with a plainclothes Mountie, whom Kelly spies sitting at a table by himself. His name is O'Doull, I eventually find out. (I had no idea that Kelly and Pete have a friend from the past who has taken such a strange turn in life.) This fellow looks like a refugee from a New Wave band. On O'Doull's surface his twinkle of eye tells me that there is a subtle sense of humour about him.

(I have reason to suspect that this man is your Deep Throat. But I do not pry.)

Anyway, Kelly calls him over, which he should not have done because I fear that this Mountie, who is, after all, a cop, will compromise Pete's and my departure from the island.

"Theo, you old cock," says Kelly. "I hear you got yourself a cushy job in Ottawa, figuring out new ways to defeat the criminal elements." (I am trying to imitate his brogue.) "It's a joy to see a grand b'y loik yerself foindin' the straight path and not laydin' a loose and disarded loif loik some o' yer old buddies went through St. Joseph's High."

O'Doull explains that he is – I find this hard to believe – a sergeant and a scientist in the Ottawa crime lab.

"Only foive years, and a sergeant in the Mounties," says Kelly, sounding delighted.

"I heard you had some minor fling with the law yourself," O'Doull says.

"A case of mistaken identity, to be sure. I was as innocent as a spring lamb."

"The way I heard it," says O'Doull, "you were about as innocent as a ferret in a chicken coop." And he looks very hard at Kelly. "I hope you'll stay out of trouble, Kev. For Merrie's sake, as well as yours."

There is some joshing, a little uncomfortable, and Kelly carries on about his kids. O'Doull seems a little too nervous, and looks at the door from time to time. I wonder if he is part of the operation that is watching us.

You have to know Kelly. As far as he is concerned, cops, deadbeats, nuts, it doesn't matter – they are all friends if Kevin knows them from long ago, part of the old gang. So he asks O'Doull home for dinner. He says, "I got to tell you, though, I thinks me house is bugged. Your boys, the local horsemen, is gunning for me and Pete as if we was a gang of baby snatchers or virgin rapers." Kelly plays the clown with a pantomime face, showing fangs, making claws with his hands. "The Yorkshire Ripper and the Son of Sam, running on the loose with terror on the streets! Ah, there is evil afoot."

Speaking of which, Pete now enters. He doesn't see O'Doull at first, and he yells to me, "Okay, Johnny, we're off!" And he says, "*Embarcamos.*" Which is a Spanish expression meaning we are about to leave on a boat. Not very cool.

Then he sees O'Doull and he starts. He says, "Thewfie O'Doull, for the Lord's sake, boy, and what are you doing off the mainland?"

There is an energetic grabbing of hands and there are expressions of good will, but Pete's eyes are working furtively back and forth among us. I know he has a taxi waiting outside to take him and me to Bill Stutely's boat. Pete sits a while and talks with O'Doull, galloping along nervously, and after a bit he gives me the eye and goes out to his cab. I decide to find my way to the marina by a different taxi and go out the back door on the excuse I have to take a piss. . . .

•

Mitchell was exploding around the Potship offices like a string of firecrackers.

"Somebody find me some goddamn policemen around here," he bellowed.

The wiretap monitors scrunched over their machines, hiding their heads in earphones. A surveillance man, Constable Landesrau, gingerly stepped into the room, and into the line of fire.

"Don't blame me," Landesrau said, taking the initiative. "I was right outside the bar. Kerrivan got into the cab beside the driver, and it took off. I radioed here. That's what I'm supposed to do."

Mitchell turned to Constable McDonald. "I suppose you've got a good one, too. You were supposed to have been watching Nighthawk."

McDonald looked at Landesrau as if to include him in a small neighbourhood of guilt. "Him and me, we never knew there was even a back door to that place. We both checked the alley out before, and didn't see no door." McDonald spotted O'Doull, and pointed a finger at him. "Newf there can tell you more than anybody. He was talking to Kerrivan just before he disappeared on us."

Mitchell followed the direction of McDonald's index finger. Against the far wall, by his work table, was Sergeant Theophile O'Doull, nervously rubbing his fingers together.

Mitchell spoke slowly. "You were *talking* to Kerrivan?"

O'Doull held up a typewritten report sheet, walked up to Mitchell, and gave it to him. "When I heard they had taken off, if they have, and I guess they have, I came down here and typed this up for you to see when you got back."

Mitchell started reading. "The Blue Boar Lounge? That's one of their hangouts. You're not supposed to be seen in there. You know that."

"It's my old bar, inspector," O'Doull said. "They used to let me in when I was under age." Someone laughed, then choked it back. "I kind of dropped in for old times. I wasn't going to stay. Kevin Kelly came in while I was halfway through a beer. Nighthawk was with him. I kind of hunched myself into a corner, but they saw me. Then Pete came in. He didn't see me at first, and he said to Nighthawk, 'Okay, Johnny, we're off.'"

Mitchell repeated, "'Okay, Johnny, we're off.' Kerrivan said that, huh?"

"It didn't seem like anything at the time. He said something in Spanish, too. Then he recognized me—"

Mitchell interrupted, reading from the report. "He says—this is Kerrivan—'I'm off to do my shopping before the stores close.' And Kelly answers: 'I'd like to go with you for company, but I got to help Merrie fix dinner.' Sounds like she pulls him around by a ring in his nose. And Kerrivan says: 'You'll have to have me over for dinner when I get back.'" Mitchell began to mimic Newfoundland speech: "Kelly says: 'Well, oi'll do t'at t'ere same t'ing, me dear, darlin' man. Oi asked Theo but the pore starvin' b'y can't come.'"

"That's pretty good," McDonald said. "That's exactly what they sound like."

Mitchell summarized. "And Kerrivan goes out to the taxi which has been sitting outside the bar running up the meter. And The Hawk excuses himself to go to the back for a piss." He looked up at O'Doull as if seeking to understand the man, to search his mind. "And you sit there for ten more minutes before you and Kelly go your separate ways. Nighthawk never comes back after his piss."

Mitchell let O'Doull's report dangle from two fingers pinched together, as if he were holding a pair of soiled under-

116

shorts. "And you don't come in with this report until some-body phones you at home to tell you that Kerrivan and Nighthawk have virtually disappeared from Canada. Vir-tually? Hell, they're *gone*, Theo. Gone."

O'Doull looked hangdog. He was surrounded by twenty pairs of eyes.

"I'll tell you, O'Doull," said Mitchell, "you make a good scientist. You make a lousy detective."

Mitchell's secretary came into the room. "Corporal Dreidger is on the phone," she said. "Kerrivan's bank man-ager is in his contact group. Kerrivan phoned the bank manager this afternoon to have a two-thousand-dollar draft sent to a correspondent bank in San Francisco. It's to be held for his arrival in the next three days."

Mitchell took a breath. "Okay, let's get moving on that. Do something useful, Theo, connect me with the DEA in San Francisco. Tell them we'll send some men down."

•

Johnny Nighthawk

Pete and I decide to crash on Bill Stutely's boat for the night. Pete says there will be a fog in the morning – he has a sense for such things – and a foggy morning is a good time to say goodbye to Newfoundland.

The next morning at six the wind has backed and fallen, as Pete knew it would, and there is a blind, airy sea, billow-ing clouds from off the Banks. You can see for five feet, then everything is grey. Bill Stutely has been up and started the engine. It is going blurp, blurp, blurp, warming up. Pete and I are fairly tense with the excitement of getting away, get-ting going, getting the trip together.

And then we hear the sound of feet running along the dock towards the boat. I think that these feet sound too fast to be friendly – but Pete knows right away who it is. Before there is even a shout from the dock, he beams a happy smile at me through the fog.

"You wouldn't go without your first mate now, would you?" says Kelly as he throws his duffle bag onto the deck with a clank. The clank, I assume, is at least a couple of horseshoes, because Kevin always likes to nail a couple above the wheelhouse and the door of his cabin.

Also making weight in the bag is a bottle of Newfoundland Screech, which is a brand name for a locally-bottled rum. Kelly pours a few stiff fingers into five mugs and passes them around to me and Pete and Stutely up at the wheel. He knocks one back for himself and tosses the fifth into the sea for Old Man Neptune.

We chug out of St. John's harbour, into the sea, and a wind begins to shred the fog. We hear the caw of a crow, strangely far from land. Raucous, ragged. Kelly catches his breath and looks pale. Then we see it, winging from shore with its mate. One for sorrow, two for mirth . . . Kelly is like a nervous elf, but happier now. Then come two more crows. . . . the third a wedding, and fourth a birth. "Boys," Kelly says, "I think my wife is pregnant again."

It is occasion for another round. And soon there comes an even better excuse for a third. "Potheads!" Stutely shouts. "Off the port bow!"

A pod of these little Atlantic whales. Spouting and dancing upon the waves. Grinning at us.

The potheads lead us southwest towards Maine into a sunny day, a day that shines like a gem.

PART TWO
El Mayor Juan Atrapa

CHAPTER TWELVE

Johnny Nighthawk

You will have to go to the Caribbean coast of Colombia to understand it. Even then, you will not believe it. After you have been robbed once or twice you actually begin to long for an honest cop.

Crime is the way of life here. Personally I do not like it, and it is why I no longer live in Colombia.

A brief travelogue. We will start in the east, at the Guajira peninsula. This is a hard, hot nipple that sticks into the sea near Venezuela, and marijuana flows from it like mother's milk. It is only a thousand miles from Florida. Around this time of year your ears are filled with the roar of planes going heavy, returning light. You can find beaches where the whole village turns out to help man the dugout *canoas* which ferry *bultos* to waiting ships. These *bultos* are sisal sacks full of compressed pot, double-wrapped in water-proof black plastic, and they usually weigh sixty to a hundred pounds. There is deep water just off the Guajira, and in some places a small ship can tie up close.

As I say, there is little in the way of law here. The *contra-bandistas*, even the gringos, carry guns. It is the wild west of American mythology. The Guajira Indians, my people, my brothers, ride the dusty trails in packs, on horseback, rifles slung over their shoulders, warpaint on their faces. The Indians are nomads: virile, cruel, loving, loyal.

I lived with them for a few years. I was accepted, shared their life. What a connection I was for the gringos!

The Guajira is guarded to the west by a great mountain, the Sierra Nevada de Santa Marta. Although it is called a sierra, it is really one massive peak, the highest point in Colombia – from the sea it rises twenty thousand feet into perpetual snow, then descends in a series of cascading plateaus and foothills and waterfalls into the valleys of the Magdalena and César Rivers.

On the lower slopes of the Nevada grow the famous strains of cannabis, the many varieties of sativa and indica: *chiba*, Santa Marta gold, rainbow block, orange *mona*, and last but best, *punta roja*, which grows on the high plateaus where there are cool nights and burning days. It is the pick.

To the west of this is Santa Marta, a shaggy tourist resort and haven for dope traders, squeezed between the mountain and the ocean. This city can rock and roll in season. You wear your wrist watch high up the arm. You carry your wallet in a deep, tight pocket. Women dumb enough to wear pierced earrings have had their earlobes torn away.

Okay, we leave Santa Marta, go west across the red dirt and cactus, the Magdalena marshes, to the horror show which is Barranquilla, then over the humpy-bumpy roads to Cartagena – and here is a city that tastes like fine old champagne. You will picture it as an ancient walled city surrounded by water, containing an old quarter with narrow streets and balconies separated by the reach of a hand. From below, from the cantinas, you hear the plaintive music of romance. The women are beautiful: *mestizos*, blacks, Indians, Castilians. It is a city that goes to my heart.

But back for now to Barranquilla. This is where we arrive on an Avianca flight. It is the centre of the north coast. It is a cesspool. It sits like a lizard along the banks of the Magdalena River – such a lovely name, such an ugly river. There are a million people here in tin shacks. Cattle pick through the garbage which lies smouldering and rotting in the gutters. Vultures hang in the sky. It is the world's ugliest city. It is like the aftermath of war.

Ba-ran-*kee*-ya. That is where our dirty freighter sits, by a dock on the river, beside the offices of Maritimas Manejos del Atlantico, S.A., the offices of Peddigrew's friend Juares. We look at the ship from a distance.

The ship is perfect for Barranquilla. She suits the city.

We crack a few half-hearted jokes. Then we ask the taxi driver to take the three of us to El Golf Hotel, where Marianne Larochelle is quartered. She has been here five days and has been buying supplies.

Pete is nervous about his next encounter with her. But I remember feeling that Pete and Marianne were simply not made for each other. She was urbane, café society. He was rough cut, unpolished. She was Montreal. He was O'Donoghue's Nose, Bay D'Espoir. If Pete met a man who was elegant, he considered him a wimpshit. But he fell for the elegant ladies every time. This one was playing him like a yoyo – which was probably good for his swollen ego. (She would have been good for my undernourished one, but dream on.)

I remember thinking: I will hear about it if he ever succeeds in making out with this woman. Pete enjoyed his own legend as a lover and regularly nourished it with new material from his own mouth. Perhaps I seem to slight him. I should explain: I love this man.

And my heart went out to him in Barranquilla, where Fate dealt him another hard blow. When we arrive at the hotel we find that Marianne has Barranquilla *turista*, a bug of mythical power. She is white, and the carpet in her room has a path worn to the bathroom. Pete will not get close to her this night.

"Juares is a crook," she says, speaking through grey lips. "Don't pay him any money." Juares' end was being taken from Peddigrew's cut – that was our understanding. But people are always on the bite for a little more. *La mordida.* A way of life.

As to the ship, Marianne just rolls her eyes. "Let's not go too far off the coast," she says. "It's just a rusted sieve. It didn't have a single lifejacket. I've been spending money like crazy."

Maritimas Manejos del Atlantico, S.A., is a company in the classic mould for Colombia: grungy, decrepit, crooked. So is Juares. His teeth are rotting and there is five years of grime under his fingernails and in the creases of his neck.

"*Compadres*," he says. We are sorry his mouth opens when he smiles.

He pumps our hands, slaps backs. "Senor James," he tells us, "I meet heem in Toronto." I assume he means Peddigrew. "He speak ver' beneficial to you. We are partner, *no es verdad?*" He winks. "I am like you, Pedro – old client. I am arrest at Canada airport five years ago." With his hands he describes a body pack tied around his belly. "Two kilogram of *coca*. Senor James, he have me out of jail two years, deportation. Is good *abogado*, no? Is best in Nort' America." He was proud of such connections. "He is my partner – *our* partner. And Marianne. How is feeling Senorita Marianne?"

"She still has the shits," Pete says.

"Her is *muy hermosa*." He leers.

"Can we look at the boat?" Pete asks.

She was sitting high in the water by the dock. I hesitate to call her a she. She is no woman. She is a bum.

"We make meellion on thees sheep," says Juares. "Is name *El Mayor Juan Atrapa* after ver' famous mayor of Barranquilla. Is good shape for long voyage, senors. Sound. Ver' sound."

She was a dirty old tub and smelled of dead rats. *It* smelled of dead rats. In the holds, I feel around above the bulwarks and an ounce of rust flakes off and falls at my feet.

"Please not worry," says Juares. "Steel is many repair and welding to do."

There was a guy wandering around with a welding torch; another was sandblasting at the stern, and a third was following him around with a bucket of paint. It had been in drydock, and, from what we could see of the hull, it had been sandblasted, had new zincs, new paint. The colour was a convenient rust red, with brown trim.

Juares shows us some sheets with the thickness readings on the hull, and the disintegration does not appear to be that bad. As long as she will float, that is number one.

Number two is, will she run? Kelly and I spend some time in the engine room. The ship does seem well loaded down with spares, from what is in the storage.

Juares tells us that the *Atrapa* was laid up for a few years before he picked it up, and we could see that the engines seem to have been preserved in heavy oil, which is like a slime over everything. But they are clean.

"A-one condition, the engeens," Juares says. "Like Rolls-Royce."

We tinker around, figure everything out pretty well, then start up the auxiliary generator. No problem that we can see or hear. The auxiliary generator is the key to this kind of diesel-electric system. If it doesn't work, the ship will be dead in the water because it provides excitation power for the engines which in turn run electric motors that go into a reduction gear and power the single propeller. Follow me? You get the idea, anyway. If you lose your auxiliary generator, you lose propulsion.

The engines and generators rumble to life, and I must admit that the sound is not bad to the ears. We will get some horses out of them.

Juares claims that the main propulsion system has been overhauled and tuned up, and we tend to believe him.

We spend the whole day on the ship, checking the electric

motors, the bilge pumps, the water pumps, the switch gear. All the important gauges seem to work. There is a crane on the deck and we check out its motor carefully because it will be used to sling the bales of pot on and off of the ship. We will have to buy some heavy shrimp nets to use as slings.

Pete spends most of his time in the wheelhouse, where there is a Loran A, an old Decca radar, a few local charts, a VHF marine radio, and a single-side band. Not much of an electronics package for deep sea.

Juares takes us to his office, still winking and grinning. We share a few bottles of Bavaria beer.

Juares spreads his hands. "I put my *dinero* in sheep repair beesness." Dope *dinero*, I assume. "What you theenk of sheep? You are please? Her is floating palace for thees beesness."

"She is floating shithole," says Pete, "which is better than a sinking one." He turns to Kelly and me. "What do you think? Can we get this old beater up there?"

"It's worth a try," I say. "It's going to hold a lot of grass." There was enormous cargo space. Bulwarks had been removed to expand the cargo area. Even some of the old crew's quarters had been converted for cargo. With all the bulk that you have when you carry marijuana, we would still be able to squeeze forty tons on this ship.

"It runs," says Kevin. "We better make sure we got spares for everything. And tools."

"Yeah," I say, "and lifeboats. Lots of lifeboats."

"If the Loran packs it in," Pete says, "there's no backup except for the gyro and the sextant." He shrugs. "We don't need anything more." Cruising over three thousand miles of ocean with a sextant is Pete's idea of heroism.

"We have sheep," says Juares. "All we need is *la marimba*." On this coast, that is what they call marijuana. Or often *yerba*, hay.

"We'll get the *marimba*," Pete says.

"You have connection?"

"Yes." Pete is not going to take this guy into his confidence if it can be avoided.

"Now, please," says Juares, "we make plan for loading. Underneath, the *marimba*. We put on top scrap metal." He waves his arm out the window at a pile of scrap: busted-out engines, lines of cable, old rails.

"Yeah, we'll work out the details," says Pete.

Juares shakes his head and takes on an expression of great seriousness, perhaps sorrow.

"Is ver' expenseev to refit sheep and engines," he says. "For diesel gas, twenty t'ousand dollar. I am in need of money, yes? You have money from Senor James?" He pushes a paper with some figures on it towards Pete. "Refit is feefty t'ousand dollar in U.S."

Pete says, "You work that out with Senor James."

"He say you pay me."

"He don't say that, Juares."

I change the subject. "We'll need about five more guys. Assistant engineer, someone for the galley. We can't run this old coaster with four people."

Pete's answer to that is, "Nothing to it." I guess he figures we will all work double shifts or something. Pete knows we can hire on a few local wharf rats for maybe a few thousand dollars a man, but he also knows it will eventually come out of his pocket. I can see myself sweating like a slave in the engine room. Pete can be really cheap, and with the other hand he will throw his money away.

Now we have to locate some weed.

CHAPTER THIRTEEN

Johnny Nighthawk

Bogota. I lived here for a year. It is a deranged city. Dishonest. Vibrant. Dirty. It seems to simmer for weeks, then
explodes. Then settles back into a hum. A couple of decades
ago there were a few thousand people here but there are
now – who knows? – six, seven million. Some of them are
very rich, but not many.

The people are a torrent on the streets, and you will see
them in their *ruanas*: peasants and pushcart vendors, shop-
pers and businessmen.

The best time is as the evening comes, as the sun rolls into
the dirty haze. Then a frenzy ignites the city. The voices of
the *vendedores* grow rich with songs of praise for their offer-
ings, and meaty smells of *chicharron* and *chorizos* fill the
streets. Women with a special beauty glide mournfully
through the shops, and in the squares near the *Centro*, the
kids come out, the *gamines*, abandoned children who beg
and steal and work the crowds.

You step carefully along the broken concrete sidewalks
and are assailed by gusts of diesel billowing from the trucks
and the *busettas* and the ancient Dodge buses. These vehicles are dressed like floats in a carnival parade. They are
driven bravely at night, without headlights. They prowl the

128

streets like wolf packs, howling their horns.

As the sky turns blacker, the rows of little shops near the *Centro* begin to close. At nine o'clock, their corrugated metal doors roll clanging shut, and the whores come out and watch the men strut by.

Calle 26 divides the city north and south. The north is the better side, so-called – at least by the better people. But Pete and Kelly and I, we have always liked the south side, the easy side, where there are few gringos. Near Calle 26 are the luxury hotels, the Tequendama and the Hilton. The Hilton is where we stay, incidentally. Not because we like it, but because it is necessary to impress the Colombians, or you get nowhere.

As the night lengthens, you will see the rats begin to dance openly in the litter of the park behind the Hilton, and the street dealers, the *marachaferos*, scurry about with them, looking for Americans. They are armed with samples and testers, pipes and coke inhalers.

There are cops all around. Soldiers. Narcs. They do not give a shit unless it earns a dollar.

Gold was once the colour of wealth here, but now it is green, and they push green on the streets: dart-eyed little men with quick tongues. In their palms they hold out emeralds wrapped in tissue. They hold out paper bags with green buds of pot and let you smell them. They worship the other green, U.S. green. Twenty times a day, people will come up to you: "Hey, boddy, change you dollars for pesos?"

But the real deals are done in the air-conditioned boardrooms of the skyscrapers, the *rascacielos*. The gringo *marijuaneros* and *cocaros* sit for long hours with the captains of the families and their representatives and lawyers. Never is grass mentioned. One speaks only of *la merchandisia* or *el producto*. There is an air of legitimacy. Pete will wear a sports jacket. I bring along a white shirt for such an occasion. And of course I have to cut off my braids.

Now I bring you right into such a boardroom – into the offices of Articulos Exportados de Colombia, S.A., on the thirty-third floor of the Bogota District Bank Building. Kelly is doing I Ching hexagrams at the hotel, so there are only Pete and I – and Senor Felix Ugarte and his simple cousin Jorge, plus an *abogado* for the family, plus two sinister gentlemen standing by the door, men I am sure have killed for the Ugartes.

Pete is hungover and mean. We had arrived in Bogota the previous day, and that night we kicked back, smoked some *basa*, hung around the Club Ocho-Nueva, a fancy hook shop, although as far as women were concerned, Pete had kept back, suffering, as he alleged, for the love of Ms. Larochelle. She was still sticking it out in Barranquilla, trying to keep her eye on Juares, buying supplies from a list we gave her, and recovering from *turista*.

The session starts off with coffee in the American style and with the usual politenesses – token inquiries as to health, happiness, and general state of contentment, the whole Latin American two-step that one dances on such occasions. Even if they are planning to slit your throat, they will first greet you and ask after your health.

Pete knows from previous deals that Ugarte has a penchant for cigars, although local ones are of dubious quality. So Pete has arrived with several two-dollar Cubans, Escepcions, and offers one to Ugarte. When he turns it away with a flick of his hand we know there is going to be trouble. Ugarte appears unwilling to owe Pete anything, however small. So the old man lights up a smelly Colombian and Pete lights up a powerful Escepcion, and the atmosphere quickly becomes heavy.

Pete's main error in how he handles people is he is too blunt, and also he is unwilling to play the games. Throughout, Pete is overconfident. He had believed that when it came time to visit Ugarte he would be able to temper the hard feelings over the Mounties' eight-ton bonfire of the previous year.

There is a complex legal point here – the weed *was* fronted to Pete, although with a small downpayment, and theoretically the ownership passed to him, and therefore he was in debt to Ugarte for the full value of the cargo. Not being a lawyer, I do not know the implications.

But on the other hand, Pete had on four previous occasions bought Ugarte's cannabis and had become a favoured customer, and had always, within six months of delivery, made full payment when they met on one or the other of the Caribbean islands.

The preliminaries over, Ugarte's cheeriness slips. He says – now you will not enjoy the pure flavour in English translation but I will reconstruct as best I can – "Senors, my associates and I were at the Intercontinental Hotel in Aruba at the appointed time. We waited for three days, as was agreed, plus two more. Then I made telephone calls to Canada. I found you were in *la cana*." He says it as if it is Pete's fault.

Pete expresses sorrow about this, explaining that the police had burned the product and thus there was no money for Ugarte in Aruba, and Pete, in jail, was unable to make the appointment.

"If what you say is true," Ugarte tells us, "I find it difficult to understand why you are now sitting in this boardroom. If what you say is true, why are you not still in a Canadian prison?"

Pete explains he was found not guilty.

"But how can that be? You have been arrested. The merchandise was seized by the police. Is there not a long sentence to be served?" Ugarte, with this, folds his fat hands and leans towards Pete. "It seems you have perhaps friends in the Canadian police."

Pete shoots a look at me and I return it. It is dawning on

us Ugarte believes we have pulled off a scam with the pot. He thinks we have paid off the police and sold the eight tons without cutting him in. Ugarte, of course, believes all the world is like Colombia.

His *abogado* hands him a paper with figures on it, and Ugarte starts reading out his costs from it: two DC-6 flights for the drops to the beach, the trucks, the compacters, the peasants who had to be paid, the *mordidas* that were taken by the *federales*. It turns out to be a staggering sum, much exaggerated – twenty-five million pesos, or six hundred thousand dollars U.S.

Plus – and this is the grabber – eighty million pesos on top of that. I do not know how they figure this. Ugarte knew we had a fast sale lined up at two hundred a pound on site, or two-fifty delivered in Boston. Ugarte was to have gotten half.

Anyway, Ugarte folds the paper and presents it to Pete. It is a bill. It comes to one hundred and five million pesos.

Pete looks at it and starts talking fast. He explains that he has a big ship and can make Ugarte a fair profit on a makeup deal, plus pay back his out-of-pocket costs on the previous one.

But Ugarte keeps on talking, and as he talks his smile dribbles away from his face. The account, he says, will be paid. *Totalmente*. In one week. And he gestures towards the two big gazoonies standing by the door. They nod to Ugarte. We look at them, too. They smile at us. "Totally," Ugarte repeats. "There will not be more business with *los fraudes*."

This is a very hard expression. One must now either suck ass or show valour.

There is a flash of colour on Pete's face. His eyes glint like ice. These are danger signs. He slides his chair back from the table, and he pats his crotch.

"*Mama mia verga*," he says.

What this means is: "suck my cock."

There is no sound – just a slight hiss of air escaping from between someone's teeth.

Then Ugarte slams his fist down. *"Hijo de puta!"* he yells. "Son of a whore!" There is a torrent of spit as he sounds the hard consonants. This insult, in Colombia, is a prelude to battle.

Pete – I think he is crazy, by the way – says, *"Doble hijo de puta."* Most of us dealers have learned our Spanish in the hook shops and on the street.

Ugarte ups the ante. *"Doble hijo de puta remalparido!"* Literally, this means: "Double son of a whore with birth defects." You have to hear it in Spanish to get the full effect, with the R's rolling like a drum tattoo.

Pete crumples the bill in his fist, makes a motion as if using it for toilet paper, then throws it on the table. *"Coma mierde,"* he says to Ugarte. Very calm. He beckons me to leave with him.

"One week," Ugarte hisses. He nods to the two goons, who you can tell from the unnatural bulges in their suits are packing pieces. Ugarte requests that they "teach us manners."

We urge our asses out the door to the elevators, followed by Ugarte's bodyguards. I look at Pete to let him know I think he is crazy. "You can't let the jerks walk all over you," he says.

The hoods get on the elevator with us. There is a young lady already on board, a secretary I guess. "They'll wait until we get out on the street. It would be bad manners to spill blood in front of this pretty *muchacha*." Pete tips his cap to her. *"Buenas, señorita."* She smiles. "You take the fat one behind you," he says to me. "I'll take the ugly fart with the big teeth." He turns to the man and leers. "You are an ugly fart, aren't you?"

The man smiles and nods.

We hit the twentieth floor, from where the elevator will go nonstop to the ground. Pete gives me a nod and at the same time unleashes an elbow to his man's midriff. The other guy is looking away as I hit him on the jaw with my fist. It was a pretty hard hit, I guess, because I can hear a crack as if a bone is splitting, and there is blood coming between his teeth. Pete's guy is slumped over, retching. The girl is screaming.

At the ground floor, we tear ass.

CHAPTER FOURTEEN

Alfredo J., sitting beside Flaherty on their customary park bench, was wearing a grey linen suit with a scarlet kerchief around his neck. Flashy dresser, Flaherty thought. She felt like a frump in her baggy jeans and tennis shoes. She was a little upset about Alfredo's lack of progress.

"I thought you were close," she said. "If the target doesn't trust you, who in God's name does he trust?"

Alfredo J. spoke calmly, trying to reassure her. "There is very little trust in this business, Miss Flaherty. Not to mention this entire world. You and I, we are still learning to trust each other, are we not?"

True. Flaherty hoped she was not being set up. The CIA would have a real laugh on her. Their man had been warning her away from this operation. "Washington wants us to keep our hands off for the time being," he had said.

Flaherty had exploded at the CIA officer. "This isn't some candy-ass hippie operation with packsacks and duffle bags," she had yelled. "We're talking about the biggest damn thing *anybody* has *ever* had out of Colombia. I need something damn hard for Washington to pull me off this one. Hard, man. Not limp. Hard!" The Agency could play all the wink-wink, nudge-nudge games they wanted with the April Seventeen Movement, but she wasn't going to buy their bullshit.

"Do you think your government will try to block you in this?" Alfredo asked. It was as if he had guessed her thoughts. "This is what I mean by politics," he said. "We should discuss politics, you and I."

He cupped his hands over her cigarette and lit it for her. "You have a good spirit," he said. "You are a fighter. I like such women."

He had a way with her. She could feel her heart flutter.

"They are talking about coming in through Canada," he said. "North to the island of Newfoundland, then south. It is a straight run, deep into the Atlantic, away from the shipping lanes."

"I have heard about the plan," Flaherty said.

Alfredo's eyebrows arched with surprise. "You have?"

"I get other information, Alfredo. I also meet with Meyers."

"Of course. I forget."

"I just hope Operation Crackpot doesn't bugger it up for me."

"Operation Crackpot?"

"Never mind."

"Perhaps I should meet with the Canadians," Alfredo said.

"No, don't do that. I'm working with them. I'm just trying to make sure they don't blow it."

At Operation Potship, everything was in slow motion. The men and women from the surveillance team were sullen and bitchy, and particularly so was Harold Mitchell.

"What is that bastard doing, anyway?" Mitchell railed. "Why can't we raise him?"

No one tried to answer.

Theophile O'Doull, meanwhile, had put together his tracking device and teed everything up with the El Paso Intelligence Centre. The equipment was ready to be delivered to Meyers for installation on the ship. If there indeed was a ship. And if indeed they could get access to it.

But they had no information. No idea where Meyers was. No news from Colombia. Kerrivan could be in Outer Mongolia, as far as they knew.

Ottawa was starting to grumble about wasted manpower, wasted hours.

•

Johnny Nighthawk

Tape Four.

Aguardiente – too much drives you crazy. You are left with licorice headaches.

We drank too much of it after the session with Ugarte. You would not believe how close Bogota can become. The local families run it like a cartel. After Ugarte put the word out about us, Bogota zipped up like a fly after a fast piss beside the road. We got the Bogota blacklist, and were turned down by the Perrarra family, by the Lorcas, Hernandez, and by a couple of smaller groups.

We got deep dirty depressed. The thought of Ugarte's *asesinos* is a thought that brings one right down, along with the fact of being in Colombia with an empty freighter and no prospects. Have you ever gotten *into* a depression? Have you sucked gloom enough inside your system so you feel depraved and damned? That is what this business does to you.

I have a history of such depressions. The worst one was back during the counter-culture revolution. War in the streets. Beads and bare chests. Native peoples' power. Riding shotgun on the reservation. Dope. Right in the middle of it I got convicted of smuggling weed into Canada, doing a dirt-road border-run into British Columbia. Seven years for a rucksack full of pot. So it goes.

Anyway, at the end of another day in our fruitless quest

for a connection, we were sitting around El Ingles bar in the
Hilton with some fellow *contrabandistas* from Miami and
New York. El Ingles was buzzing, as it does at this time of
year. Everyone else at our table was already connected, and
we were pretending to be happy with them. Pete kept getting drunker and drunker, and started to dominate the
table, ranting about Colombia, about the garbage and the
poverty and the corruption.

He stopped in mid-harangue as Billy Lee Tinker wandered through the hotel lobby door.

Pete shouts, "Hey, Billy Lee, you southern-fried
chickenshit, haven't they busted you yet?"

Billy Lee has trouble adjusting his eyes to the light.
Basically that is because he is wearing sunglasses. But he is
standing there with a shit-eating smile on his face – Billy Lee
Tinker is always stoned – and he knows the voice of Pete
Kerrivan.

"I hear they reamed a hot poker up your ass, man," he
says.

"Billy Lee Tinker," says Pete. "It's worth a round."

Billy Lee Tinker. He's worth a few rounds. He is standing
there in a patched military tunic with a big cannabis leaf
sewed on where the medals would normally go. He is the
ace of the Marijuana Air Force. He has never been shot
down.

Billy Lee was already hot when I first met him in Nogales
in the early seventies. We were both waiting for a big diesel
camion from Oaxaca, with some for me, some for him, some
for a lot of other guys doing the border run to Arizona. I
had a jeep and he had a Piper Seneca, and we were five miles
from the U.S. border. The semi was three days late, so we
kicked back and got to know each other. Then we helped
each other with our runs.

He was a daredevil flier – he had been a wing commander
in Viet Nam. He liked to get down real low, just above the

top knobs of the cactus trees, when he made his drops onto the desert.

For a while, later, he was contracting out to a guy who owned a Lear jet, and what he used to do was follow the big jetliners north from Colombia, piggybacking behind them so they shared the same blip on the ADIZ radar screens. Airliners don't have rear-view mirrors.

Like I say, he was an ace, but later he came to be in the shadow of Pete Kerrivan, who had become number one. I am not just talking about volume. And I am definitely not talking about the fat cats in the Miami offices who make the big deals and pay off the cops and run their operations by phone and telex. I am talking about the guys who *do* the trip. The guys who sail or fly in with their loads. I have often wondered whether Billy Lee liked being number two. Maybe he was jealous.

Pete and Billy were different, but in ways they were the same. One was a flier, the other a sailor. Billy Lee was from the Deep South, and Pete from cold, cold Canada. They both came from small towns, and were easy going, and neither of them actually cared a shit, and both of them were in it for the game, mostly, not the money, which they lavished on others and on good times. They were both highballers, both gamblers.

As to what Billy Lee looks like, he is like Pete: tall, fluid, loose. You could see him as the short guy on the local NBA team, only white. He sees the world through dark glasses behind drooping eyelids.

In the bar, Billy Lee cheers us up. He has tall tales to tell about pirating the flight plans of registered cargo planes, getting radio clearance that way. He informs us he bought a war surplus B-26 bomber, got it flying, and has been going like crazy at a hundred thousand dollars a trip. But one of his engines just blew out on him, so the plane is sitting up in Alabama and he is grounded.

The night ultimately simmers down to just Billy Lee and Kevin and Pete and me. Billy Lee drunkenly puts his arms around Pete's shoulders, and he says in a soft, confiding voice, "I hear you old boys ain't got yisselves any weed this year."

"They've painted our balls black here," Pete says.

"Wal, I got a contact with some real Juan Valdez, man. *Punta roja*. A hundred acres of *punta roja*. I got the hardest connection since my dog Skeeter got his cock stuck up a spaniel's cunt. You interested?"

"Is the bear Catholic?" Pete says. "Does the Pope shit in the woods?"

CHAPTER FIFTEEN

Johnny Nighthawk

We will look at the crop and meet the connection. The
family is that of Victor Publio Paez, and this is a connection
muy grande. He is big on the north coast, bigger than Ugarte
in Bogota. The Paez group has *palanca*, which is what power
is all about in Colombia. *Palanca* is a useful word – it means
"lever."

His agents want to look us over, all of us. So we arrange
to meet Marianne at the Barranquilla airport. Paez will send
someone to pick us up there and take us to the plantation.

Plantation. That is what Billy Lee tells us. Paez has a plantation on the southern slopes of the Sierra Nevada. Large-
scale cannabis farming is something new in this country.
Usually marijuana is grown by the poor farmers on small
acreages, *ensembrillas*. The farmers are beholden to the
Mafia families, who are the liege lords over the feudal serfs,
and who come by each season to collect the crop.

"These folks is sharpies, man," Billy Lee tells us. "They
got more money than Bunkey Hunt before the fall of silver.
And they're putting it all into *sinsemilla*. They got theirselves greenhouses, man, they got trained aggies, and
they've come up with some kind of rainbow *punta roja*, all

flower, no seed. I ain't seen it yet, but it's pure female, man."

We are sitting in the bar at Barranquilla airport. Marianne enters. She waves.

"Speaking of pure female," says Billy Lee.

His shades have dropped down over his nose and he is staring at her. Marianne still looks as if her insides are churning a bit, but she has her far-away mysterious smile. She should patent it.

"Look but don't handle," Pete says. He narrows his eyes at Billy Lee. "Maybe you better not look too much, either."

"Purebred, man," says Billy Lee. "Purebred." He glances slyly at Pete. "You sure you got papers say you own her?" He stands up, takes off his old tractor cap, swings it down in front of him, and bows in what is supposed to pass for a gallant Southern gesture.

"Since Pete here ain't likely to," he says, "may I have the pleasure of introducing myself. Billy Lee Tinker from Turkey Neck Creek, Alabama, ma'am. Tales of your grace and charm have superseded your arrival."

When Billy Lee goes to sit back again, he falls straight to the floor. Pete has pulled his chair away.

Pete offers the chair to her, and she sits on it, cool and dainty.

Billy Lee talks from the floor. "Hey, Pete, man, seein' I'm savin' you guys from going on the rocks, maybe you could offer me a job on the boat, man. I navigate, I'm handy with engines, and I know some funny card tricks. I also reckon I'd like to learn how to speak French."

Pete gives him an arm-lift up to his feet. "I want to have some weed left on board when we finally get this ship north. If you come, there's no guarantee."

"Yeah, well, fifty tons, man. I might just not be able to smoke it all."

Marianne widens her eyes. "Fifty *tons*?"

"Yeah," says Billy Lee, "this is gonna be the trip of the

142

century. This century or any other, man."

"They told me we should go to the Satena counter and wait," Billy Lee says.

So we are at the Satena counter. It is one of those little airlines that fly to little places. Owned by the Colombian army, I believe.

We have all had a couple of beers, except Marianne, who is not drinking, and Kelly, who is our taster. With all the new hybrids coming out these days, a good taster can't afford to dull his palate. Anyway, we are joking and carrying on, being the typically ugly American tourists, when this fat guy arrives, wearing a uniform.

"Senor Billy Lee and party of four," he calls out in Spanish. He gives us all boarding passes. There are other people here, and they are harrying the fat man, wanting to know about their flight.

"*Lo siento*," he says, "sorry, the flight is full."

We follow him outside the building. Billy Lee is looking nervously at the row of tired airplanes on the field. "These planes are falling apart," he mumbles. The word is that Billy Lee is a very poor flier when he is not at the controls.

The fat man staggers a bit on the tarmac. It would appear that this fellow enjoys strong drink.

Our plane is a DC-4 scarred by oil and grease and scorch marks. Our pilot, as we feared, is the fat man. As we enter, the plane creaks and Billy Lee makes a strained face.

"Where are we going?" he asks in Spanish.

"Don' worry, meesters," says the pilot, strapping himself in. He hands a bottle to Billy Lee, who is standing at the cockpit door. "*Quieres ron y cola?*"

Billy Lee asks, "Is anyone helping you fly this?"

The pilot answers with a happy smile. "God is my co-pilot, senor," he says in Spanish. Billy Lee turns white and slumps into the seat nearest the cockpit entrance.

Three of the engines grunt into action, but the other one

coughs and gags. Billy Lee is white-knuckling his chair arm. The fourth engine finally bursts into a cloud of smoke and catches, and as the plane begins to stumble towards the runway, Billy Lee lurches to his feet, goes forward, buckles in beside the pilot, and starts checking out the controls. He takes a hit from the rum bottle.

We circle around over the ocean, north of Santa Marta, then cross the Guajira. There are some heavy winds coming around the Sierra Nevada that have me concentrating on my anus.

This is our introduction to the Paez dope plantation:

We follow a river into a high pass, slip between the walls of a wide canyon. The river disappears. I turn back to look, and I see a waterfall that drops six hundred feet into a valley so lush it shines. I see buildings, and hundreds of neat rows of plants. There is a landing strip, and two small aircraft at its edge.

The plane hits an enormous blast of wind that comes rushing up the valley. The aircraft seems almost to explode open, my seatbelt snaps, and I am somersaulting out of my seat. We are banking a hundred feet from the stone face of a granite cliff, and we come swooping down like a falcon in the tightest U-turn a plane like that can do. And all of a sudden we are levelling off at the right end of a dirt runway – with a sweet, gentle, gut-settling two-point landing, like an L-1011 coming in on Runway 3 at JFK.

"That," says Pete, "was a rush."

The pilot turns around and waves the bottle of rum at me. I knock one back.

"Thanks for the flight," I say.

"Don' worry, meester," he says.

"I nearly had a heart attack, man," Billy Lee says. "I kept tellin' him to give over the controls, and he kept sayin' 'Don' worry, meester.' What a fuckin' flier, man!"

The valley is walled to the north and south. The north cliffs reach a thousand feet. The hills on the south side are low, and do not hide the sun. A jewel-blue river rolls down the valley from the foot of the falls, where a mist balloons into the sky. Behind us is high-altitude jungle. You can hear monkeys screaming high in the canopy, and see parrots flashing by.

And the cannabis plants march up the valley in rows like an army, about three feet apart, with gaps where the male plants had been. They are mature, but they are short – maybe five or six feet. And dense. Thick with bud, weeping resin. The odour is powerful, a sweet, rich stench, and the plants seem to droop with the effort of supporting their weight. The air seems yellow, and when a breeze brushes the plants, we see why. The wind carries the resin into the air in billowy clouds.

The pilot hands us gauze masks. We see that the men and women working in the fields are wearing them, too.

I am assuming you know something about the horti-culture of pot. Perhaps you do not. Cannabis is dioecious – as with people, there are two sexes. If the male dies after it pollinates the female, the female gives seed. But if the male dies just before it can deliver its pollen, the female secretes only juice, no seeds, and the resin in the juice is what con-tains the bulk of the THC, the active ingredient, the stuff that gets you off, the stuff they make hashish from.

Sinsemilla: it is a Spanish word meaning "seedless." Co-lombian pot is normally characterized by the fact you are always cleaning it, picking out the seeds before rolling it up.

There is an administration building. As we walk towards it, we can hear the thrumming of a generator that is work-ing the pumps and the sprinklers. The harvest is under way. A group of farm workers is going down the first few rows, hacking them down with machetes. A tractor and baler are following behind. By the administration building, heaps of flowertops are drying. A couple of men are running a com-pacter, others bagging blocks of pot into sisal sacking.

I am awed. I am also stoned – just from breathing the air. I am brought down very fast, though, by the sight of a couple of guys wandering around with automatic rifles slung over their shoulders. "Parrots," they are called in Colombia. There is a saying here – when reason fails, the parrots do the talking.

"What's the elevation?" Kelly asks Billy Lee.

"Sixteen hundred metres." He looks about. "Must get full sun all winter."

Kelly gets down on his haunches and sifts the soil. It looks dark, feels moist, seems full of nutrient, probably manure.

The pilot, correctly guessing that Kelly is our taster, points to a heap of dry stuff. "*Lo proba,*" he says. "Try it."

But Kelly goes first to one of the growing plants, breaks off a bit of flower, sniffs at it, rubs it between his hands, licks them, rolls his eyes.

He takes a jeweller's eyepiece from his kit and does a hair count.

"Nearly forty to the millimetre," he says. Then he goes to the dried material and weighs out a gram with his scale and rolls up a little J with it, using very thin test paper. He gets a nice burn, then really puts his lungs on it, and sucks it about halfway. Then he pinches it out and holds his breath. I can see he gets a good one, a full-size toke.

We are all standing around like interns watching a great surgeon.

Kelly is staring off into space. He has a little leprechaun grin.

After a couple of minutes he says, "Blast-off."

Another minute or so passes. Then he says, "Orbital velocity now."

A few minutes later, "It's star wars, boys."

He lets loose a long, low whistle and shakes his head. Then he lights the roach, the *cucaracha*, and smokes it right down. "It's a point three-five, maybe a point four." After a few seconds with a quiet voice. "Maybe five."

We have some *punta roja* mindfuck here. Your average hemp comes in anywhere from point zero-eight to point one-five on a THC scale. Top-shelf pot might average about two-five.

"Real light," Kelly says. "I'm seein' Sergeant Pepper stuff out there." There is a soft calm to the face of Friar Toke, and he is smiling, and he is looking up into the valley towards the waterfall. "It's an elegant fine smoke, b'ys," he says, turning to us.

"What did I say?" Billy Lee is grinning. *"Supremissimo."*

The morning sun is slinging spears at us. Birds are gossiping in the jungle. I feel the power of the waterfall. I hear the river whispering nearby. I feel calmed. I realize I should have been wearing the gauze mask.

There is a voice behind us. And suddenly I feel a chill.

"Good morning, gentlemen. Welcome to the farm." An American.

The sun is behind him and at first I do not make out his features. But I see he has broad shoulders and a round face with a stiff military moustache and a brushcut.

His face seems to glow pink. We used to call such white men bum faces when we were kids. The man shows us a compressed, thin smile, a smile without teeth. He stands erect like a king and stretches out a hand.

"I am Rudy Meyers." He has an arm-wrestler's grip.

CHAPTER SIXTEEN

Johnny Nighthawk

Behind Meyers, someone else emerges through the door of the administration building. This guy *does* have teeth. He poses for Pepsodent. He is Ricardo Montalban in a monogrammed polo shirt and a dashing red bandanna. A brier pipe, to boot. He is about fifty, but in very good shape.

"May I introduce my aide, Colonel Augustin Escarlata," Meyers says.

The dark eyes of Colonel Escarlata flit from face to face, then settle on Marianne. As we introduce ourselves, he shakes hands. But Marianne's hand, he kisses. This guy is smooth as chewed sealskin.

Meyers turns to Billy Lee. "Thank you for the connection," he says.

Billy Lee shrugs. "It's nothin', man. You wanted a ship. You got a ship."

"I'm sure Captain Kerrivan will be happy to give you a finder's fee," Meyers says.

"How 'bout that, Pete?" Billy Lee says. "Throw in a regular crew share, and we're laughin'." He sneaks a look at Marianne. Pete sees this and *he* looks at Marianne. She is not looking at either of them. She is looking at the colonel. Oh, boy, I think. It is like the look she first gave Pete in that

bar in Montreal. And Escarlata is looking at her as if he is
taking her picture. I am liking none of this.

"You with the army?" Billy Lee asks, trying to distract
Escarlata.

Escarlata turns to look at him, takes the pipe from his
mouth. "I suspect that by now I have been stripped of my
rank," he says, with good English. "Let us say I am in retirement from the Cuban army."

"Castro sent us some very good people," Meyers says. "I
recruited Colonel Escarlata from the last boatlift."

"How about that?" says Billy Lee. "I'm a deserter, too.
Bunch of shit, the military, ain't it?"

The colonel merely says, "I had reasons for leaving."

"So did I," says Billy Lee. "Hated fuckin' killin' people.
Didn't bother you, though, huh, Rudy?" Billy Lee turns to
us. "Rudy liked it, man. Rudy and me, we're old Nam buddies. Real good buddies."

"*I* had an honourable discharge," Meyers says.

"They can take their honourable discharge, man, and
shove it up their joint staffs," Billy Lee says.

Meyers smiles at us. "Billy Lee was never what you could
call one of your great American patriots. A little too much
Southern rebel inside the hillbilly. That's what we used to
call him – Hillbilly Lee Tinker. Maybe it comes from smoking too much marijuana, Billy Lee."

Pete is studying Meyers through all of this. Then he says
to him, "We've met."

"Do you think so?" says Meyers.

"Six years ago, West Indian Club on Grand Cayman."

Meyers' smile seems to contract by just a hair. He says,
"You have a good memory, Captain Kerrivan, a very good
memory. May I call you Peter?" Pete nods. "I work for
Senator Paez, Peter. I provide various business services to
the family, services that require some expertise. For instance, Peter, one such service involves the movement of
this," he sweeps an arm out, pointing to the field, "to

149

America. I have friends in New York. I have asked them to guarantee fifteen hundred dollars a pound."

Pete does not bat an eye.

"The money will be going to a good cause," says Escarlata. Meyers flashes a hard look at him and Escarlata winks at us. "The cause of our patron, Senator Paez, who no doubt will put his profits towards the benefit of mankind," he says. I suspect this guy has studied at an American university, so good is his English.

"Yeah," says Billy Lee, "Senator Paez – he's just a bigger crook than most of them, ain't he? Well, we're all here to make him even richer, I reckon, so let's do a deal. Don't let these boys squeeze you, Pete. They're fat, man. Squeeze *them*."

"You got the senator's go-ahead?" Pete asks Meyers.

"I have his full power of attorney." Again Meyers waves at the flowering pot field. "Do you know how much marijuana is out there?"

"Enough to fill our holds," Pete says. "You got about a hundred acres out here, and you're running about half a ton an acre." A ton an acre is about average, but these plants have lots of growing space. "We can take it all. For the right price."

"I don't think you'll complain about the money," Meyers says. "It is risk-free this side. Our people will handle the loading. All we ask of you is to guarantee delivery, through whatever are your usual routes in Canada, to a designated warehouse in New York."

"Tell me about the money that I'm not going to complain about."

"Ten million dollars."

I can feel my eyes popping. Ten million dollars. Crew share is five per cent. I am on a coral beach in the South Pacific and Polynesian girls with no clothes on are dropping little purple grapes into my mouth.

Pete is saying something, and suddenly I am sucking air.

"No way. I don't work for chickenshit like that."

Meyers' pretty pink lips hold their smile.

"You're not going to sell this for fifteen hundred dollars a pound," Pete goes on. "This will go better than Thai stick rates – two, two and a half. Most of the Guajira crop has gone seedy with the rain, and that's going to drive up prices like crazy, especially for *sinsemilla*. They could gram-bag this stuff in New York, or at worst deal it off at a hundred a quarter. Even ounces, you're talking three hundred dollars, and at that price it'll go like Cheezies. Wholesale, you've got a three-hundred-million-dollar crop." Pete flashes Meyers his three-hundred-million-dollar smile. "We'll take a tenth," Pete says. "Thirty million dollars."

Says Meyers, "We can buy twenty ships for thirty million dollars."

"You don't have time to buy ships," Pete says. "You don't have the people to run a ship. Let's face it, you're not going to take a chance on a Colombian crew, not with this stuff. They'd be lucky to get the ship out of the harbour, and if they did, they'd stash the dope somewhere in the Bahamas, and you'd never see them again – or the grass. You got to get this stuff north and into an air-conditioned warehouse before the THC starts to bleach out. You got to start moving it in a week." Pete has a bland expression. "There's only one reason you came to us. We're professionals."

I am trying to be like Pete, nonchalant. I hum, look at the scenery.

"And don't give me that risk-free bee'swax. I've heard that from other suppliers. We take the risk – Senator Paez and you guys, you splash around in your swimming pool while we're breaking our eyeballs watching out for the Coast Guard. They don't give a damn if you're out on international waters. They grab you, anyway." He looks at us as if we should get ready to go. "Meyers, I can get thirty million on a consignment deal with any family in the country."

Meyers and Escarlata look at each other. Then Meyers

laughs. It is a high-pitched laugh. "Come, Peter, have a cup of tea with us. We will talk, is that all right? We will talk."

They take Pete to the administration building.

The rest of us find some shade and sit.

"What the fuck does he think he's doin', man?" says Billy Lee. "Bargainin' for bananas in the local fruit market?"

Kelly, stoned right out, lies back on the grass. "Don' worry, meesters," he says, and rolls up a few joints for later.

Pete comes back.

"We're getting screwed," he says. "We're up against the wall. Meyers knows about Ugarte's blacklist."

"How much?" Billy Lee asks.

"Twenty million. Fifteen on delivery, the rest a month later when it hits the streets."

That is why Pete is number one.

The fat man and his scary DC-4 stay on the runway. We leave this pot-plant paradise by Cessna Citation executive jet.

"One of El Patron's little toys," Meyers says. "We borrowed it for the day. The senator has actually never been out to this farm. It is not considered – how do you put it, Billy Lee? – cool? It is not considered cool for so public and important a figure to be seen standing up to his neck in marijuana plants."

Escarlata gets behind the controls. Billy Lee starts to get up front with him. "Hey, man, I used to fly something like this, a Lear."

Escarlata gives him a freezing look. "Maybe the young lady would care to sit up front. Mademoiselle Larochelle?"

She smiles sweetly at Billy Lee and moves up past him.

"Good luck, Pete," Billy Lee says in a loud whisper. "Did you see the way that guy kissed her hand?"

Kelly gets in on it. "Yeah, he's a real Latin charmer, boy. Must be the Aqua-Velva. He sure smells good."

We leave Captain Jackpot to simmer while I study this

character Meyers. Billy Lee had already told us about how he met him in Viet Nam. Meyers was with military intelligence. Billy Lee had caught some flak and gone down over no man's land. When a chopper picked him up, he had two Viet Cong prisoners.

"Shouldn't have turned them over to Meyers, man," he told us. "That's when I started thinking war is shit city."

On the plane, Kelly offers Meyers a joint. Jokingly, of course, as if the man might be right out of stash.

Very icy, Meyers says, "Put that away, Mr. Kelly. I don't touch it."

Okay, I am thinking, it's a free world. But Meyers does not stop at that. We are sitting around a table in the cabin of the plane, and he is telling us how drugs have destroyed America, how pot has "created a generation of useless, apathetic, and spineless slugs." He keeps repeating, "Spineless slugs, Mr. Kelly. As far as I am concerned they can rot in it. America can decompose in its own fetid compost heap."

This is a guy who is putting together a third-of-a-billion-dollar deal in *sinsemilla*. I think possibly he has a very subtle sense of humour. I do not know if I should be laughing to prove I share his sardonic wit.

"Let it rot," he goes on. "And then the hard and the tough and the clean will take over. Then we might shoot the pushers."

He is smiling but that is not very reassuring, because he is always smiling. You would have to *call* it a smile, but there is no warmth in it. We are exchanging looks back and forth, Pete, Billy Lee, Kelly, and me. Do we laugh? Will he shoot us if we laugh?

After a while someone asks where we are going.

"Cartagena," Meyers says. "El Patron has set aside several rooms in one of his new hotels. An entire floor, in fact."

We have left our bags in Bogota. We complain about this.

Meyers waves the complaints away with a flick of his hand. "Please, gentlemen," he says, "your Bogota hotel is being taken care of. Your luggage will be brought to Cartagena."

We are in a station wagon driving in to Bocagrande Beach outside the old city. Escarlata is driving. Marianne is beside him. It is getting obvious that she likes his style, which is somewhat more subtle than Pete's.

Meyers is briefing us. "I will come and get you in a week. The senator will want to meet you, probably at his villa. The goods will be ready by then. We will air-freight to a drop near the Magdalena River and barge it down to Barranquilla and onto your ship. Oh, yes, I know your ship, the *Juan Atrapa*. It is being supplied to you by one Juares. A sleazy fellow. My men were watching while you inspected the ship. I hope you don't mind. You must watch your wallets with Juares. He is a dishonest fellow."

Meyers has this imperious air about him. King of the big connections.

"There will not be a problem moving the goods out of the country. We will look after all the bribes that are necessary. I have arranged for short-range air cover up to the north Florida coast."

"*Air* cover?" This is me.

"Yes, right through the Windward Passage, up the Bahamas Channel and the Strait of Florida."

"We'd be crazy to go that way," Pete says. "I always take the Mona Pass and head straight into the gut of the Atlantic." When you are carrying a shipload, you want to be as far off the coast and the main shipping channels as possible. That's always been Pete's *modus operandi*. Deep-sea trucking, he calls it. Set a course a hundred miles east of Bermuda, and you're on a straight line to Newfoundland.

"There are eight Coast Guard cutters working the Mona Pass," Meyers says. "Eight cutters, all anxious to stick one more cannabis-leaf decal on their bows. It's a choke point. There is an operation going on there, Peter, out of Puerto Rico. The *Steadfast* is there, the *Dauntless*, the *Hamilton*, and they are operated by some of the best shallow-water sailors in the Coast Guard. Each of those vessels has bagged at least ten drug ships in the last year."

I am wondering how he knows so much. He tells us.

"I have a large information gathering service, gentlemen. And I have connections – far-reaching connections. Take the Windward Passage, Peter, and go between Cuba and the Bahamas, and up the Strait of Florida."

The Florida Strait – we cannot believe this. We would be just off the U.S. limits, in the main shipping channel.

On the other hand, we have never before had the luxury of air cover. Meyers says he will give us a frequency and a single-engine aircraft will alert us by radio to the dangers of any lurking cutters. Meyers himself will be in the plane. Fortunately, the Coast Guard boats are easy to recognize – white, with fat diagonal red racing stripes near the bow.

Pete is not happy with this route. "You're putting your dope on the line. We're putting our nuts on it."

"I have *connections*, Peter." Meyers says this slowly, as if he is telling us he wants us to get the hint and not ask dumb questions.

The hotel caters to middle-class tourists from the United States. We are not allowed to dawdle, but are taken right up to the eighteenth floor – which is ours.

"You are to stay put here until one week from today," Meyers says. "When I say stay put, I mean right here on this floor. You are to keep away from the bar, away from the pool, away from the beach. And away from the city."

What he is trying to tell us is he thinks we are heat collectors.

"There are only two types of gringos in Cartagena," he says. "Crooks and tourists. You don't look like tourists."

"Yeah," says Billy Lee, "the tourists are the fat people with red bodies, who smell like coconut oil and ride around in them little buses."

"To *la policia*, you will stand out like billboards," Meyers says.

Escarlata has a scotch in his hand and is lounging in a chair. "I think Mademoiselle Larochelle is an exception," he says. "She does *not* look like any crook, Rudy. I think she may be permitted to leave the hotel. Escorted, of course. This is not a city where a woman cares to walk alone."

"Depends on the escort, I guess," says Pete.

Marianne is pretending she does not realize how much attention she is getting.

Meyers takes Pete and me through the rooms like an eager bellhop. "There is scotch and rye whiskey and bourbon. There is beer. There is marijuana. If you need anything else, call room service. For meals. Magazines. Girls, if you desire." He counts out twenty thousand dollars and gives the bills to Pete. "I'm on an expense account. Enjoy."

At the elevator, as he and the colonel are about to go, Meyers says, "By the way, I'll see what I can do about getting Senor Ugarte off your back. He's an old friend, of course."

He gives us this little bum-face smile, and he is gone. Bang, bang, zip, zip. The fix-it man. American efficiency. No drug rot in this guy's brain.

"He's a narc," Kelly says.

"He's a crook," says Billy Lee. "Just like you and me. A *tramitor*. A fixer."

Kelly is looking at the business card he left us. Private investigator, it says. Out of Miami.

"He's a narc," Kelly says.

"This country is full of these guys," says Billy Lee. "Ex-U.S. military, ex-CIA, ex-mercenary. They run dope while they wait for the next war."

Friar Toke, a paranoid, is insistent. "If a guy talks like a

156

narc, looks like a narc, thinks like a narc, nine to one he's a narc. I don't trust him. Boys, I had a five of swords reversed yesterday on the tarot spread. 'Disaster, malice, treachery. Beware of false friends.'"

"Come off it, Kevin," Pete says. "Meyers worked for Ugarte. I know that for a fact. He works for the Paez family now. And you heard him rapping about dope. A narc would *lie*. Besides, his hair's too short for a narc."

CHAPTER SEVENTEEN

Kerrivan was strung out, although he had taken neither drug nor drink during the evening. Exhausted, he had gone to his room at ten o'clock, undressed, lain down, tried to sleep.

And the hours passed, and the night trickled slowly away, and he lay on his bed, his eyes staring at the darkness, something in his stomach gnawing at him like a rat.

It was three o'clock.

Kerrivan felt used. He had a sense of dancing to the pull of a puppeteer's strings. Trucking drugs for other men: it was not his way. Until now, he had bought his own and sold his own and taken nobody's orders. He was the Masterless Man of Newfoundland, the heir to the great Peter Kerrivan of the Butter Pot barrens, beholden to no person.

Kerrivan remembered Mitchell's words from the trial: The syndicates come in; they hire people like Kerrivan to do the hauling. Kerrivan, so proud of having been his own man, was now something he had always scorned – a mule. Carrying a load for El Patron. Taking orders from Meyers, a strange piece of warped humanity.

For all his career, Kerrivan had been working up to the big one, the multi-million-dollar trip. It was here, it was set, it was organized. If he got out of it with his skin intact, he would be many times a millionaire. And he was feeling shitty.

He was *not free*. Then add to that the nagging, constant doomsaying of Kevin Kelly, who had been getting to him. Over dinner, Kevin had not stopped bitching.

And on top of it all, this goddamned crippling infatuation with a woman he so little understood. Was it just a physical thing, straight-out goat lust? Or had he somehow fallen for her mystery? What was it about her? Something, perhaps, off centre. A slight lateral drift a few degrees off course. Something, whatever it was, that held him fascinated. But, shit, he wasn't going to follow her about forever like some mooning fool. He decided to work at blotting her from his mind.

And as he reached that resolution, she came to his door, tapping gently on it.

He let her in, and they sat on his bed, and she touched him. They did not speak. For several minutes her fingers moved gently along his neck and arms, and she began to work his muscles with her hands, loosening them. He felt them release, one by one. Laying him on his stomach, she worked her fingers along his upper back.

"Cocaine," she said. "The more I do, the more I want. The more I want, the more I do. The more I do, the less I sleep. I think I'm wired. Bitten by the white mosquito."

Her hands went down his spine, working at him, working at him. Her fingers were strong and seemed to emit energy, to concentrate fields of force and send them deep into his body.

"Juares gave me a half-ounce rock of crystal yesterday," she said. "Just laid it on me. I've been shaving crumbs from it all night. I can't stop. Like some?" She took the coke from the pocket of her robe, and a razor and a ballpoint-pen tube, and put them on the bed table.

"No," Kerrivan said. "Not now."

She moved down the bed and began massaging his feet,

and her hands moved slowly up his legs.

"I've never felt anyone quite so tense," she said. "Relax. Roll over."

He was naked, his cock up and hard.

He felt a whisper of air on the head of his penis.

He heard her voice, soft and a little teasing.

"Are you certain I can't offer you a little blow, Peter?"

He felt the sharp tip of her tongue touch, touch, darting, withdrawing. Then her hands closed around his cock and her mouth came down wet over it.

Larochelle paused each half hour to cut more powder from her glittering white stone, and by the time the sun was in the sky she had taken Kerrivan through the book of sex, paragraph by paragraph, chapter by chapter. Her hands played music upon his body. Her mouth whispered over it. Her cunt seemed to suck him inside her, and held him like a clamp.

"You're going to remember this night," she said. "You're going to remember me."

At noon, Escarlata arrived, exuding charm and gentility.

Kerrivan followed Larochelle into her room and watched her packing her bag.

"I don't believe it," he said. "He's old enough to be your father."

"That's how I like them, Peter, my *cheri*. Fairly used."

Which is how Kerrivan felt after she had left with the Cuban. Fairly used.

O'Doull's solid-state creation was a little device called a Sat-Track transmitter. Approval had been given by the National Aeronautics and Space Administration to beam UHF signals from the transmitter to its Nimbus-6 satellite which, as O'Doull explained to Mitchell, was "in a sun-synch orbit over the poles," circling the earth every hundred and seven minutes.

160

Mitchell was surprised at how small the device was: eight by six inches, and three inches high.

"How does it work, Theo?"

"How does it work?" This was not going to be easy. "Okay, it's a digitally encoded beacon."

"Digitally encoded, yeah."

"Every sixty seconds it gives off a one-second burst of information which is binarily encoded in the digit screen. It gives up three hundred and forty milliseconds of plain carries and sixty-four bits of encoded information, including its own ID code."

Mitchell wore a bland look. "Carry on."

"The data is transmitted to the satellite and time-tagged. Each time the Nimbus-6 passes over Alaska, the data is dumped by ground command to a station at Fairbanks, and the tape made from the down-links is transmitted by way of landline and microwave to the Goddard Space Flight Centre at Greenbelt, Maryland. There, the information is computer-formated and processed."

Mitchell was nodding his head, so O'Doull decided to carry on.

"The computing uses a mathematical out-rhythm which involves taking data from four up-links from the Sat-Track on a particular satellite path. When the satellite time-tags, it measures the frequency at which it received the signal, then measures three more frequencies on successive link-ups."

"Successive link-ups, uh-huh."

"Using those four frequencies and measuring the Doppler effect, we calculate the change in distance from link-up to link-up."

"I see."

"In other words, how far the Sat-Track—and the ship carrying it—have travelled within those frames of time."

Mitchell nodded.

"At Goddard, they take a read-out from the system: times, locations, the confidence value—that's a statistical measure of accuracy of the data-fit to the algorithm. All right?"

"Sure, yeah."

"The print-out at Goddard gives the platform location – that means the transmitter location – at Zulu time."

"Zulu time?"

"Greenwich-Meridian time. It'll read something like this: 'Day one-two-nine of year one-nine-eight-two at zero five-three-zero Zulu.' Then it gives numerals which translate to co-ordinates of latitude and longitude."

"Uh-huh. That's pretty good, Theo."

"From Goddard, they will relay to us at Potship telephonically at timed intervals."

"And what do we do?"

"What we do is we stick pins in a map of the Atlantic Ocean." O'Doull smiled. "That's the dangerous part. We might prick our fingers." He looked at the blank face of Inspector Mitchell. "You understood all that?"

"About three words, Theo." Mitchell shook his head. "I got lost somewhere between the Zulus and the algorithms. Jesus, Theo, sometimes I worry that the days of old-fashioned cops like me are passing. I can't understand half the stuff that's happening. The age of computer electronics. The bad guys don't have a chance any more. It's not going to be any fun, Theo."

"All we need is a ship, inspector," O'Doull said. "Heard from Meyers?"

"No. I called Flaherty, and he hasn't been in touch with her, either. He hasn't been in touch with his own goddamn office. Maybe somebody iced him. Or maybe he's not the great hotshot that Flaherty claimed."

"The Sat-Track has to be installed in the battery-charging compartment on the ship," O'Doull said. "I'd like to do the wiring myself, if you'll send me to Colombia."

"We'll cross that bridge later. Tell me, Theo, can we also

hook into a ship's radio? Can we bounce their radio transmissions off the satellite?"

"Not the Nimbus-6," O'Doull said.

"Why not?"

"Wrong type of satellite. We'd have to buy some time on
a communications satellite." O'Doull was in thought, staring down at the floor as if he were fascinated by something
at his feet. Some men stare into space, Mitchell thought;
O'Doull stares at his feet.

"We *could* intercept their radio. I *could* put something
together, inspector. Can we get NASA clearance through
EPIC?"

"Why not? That's what we pay EPIC for."

The RCMP was one of a group of North American policing agencies subscribing to the El Paso Intelligence Centre,
which co-ordinates all major continental operations, including smuggling investigations. The DEA, FBI, CIA, internal
revenue, customs, and Coast Guard were all on a feed from
EPIC by way of teletype messages that unscrambled upon
receipt.

"Call EPIC, Theo, and see what you can do."

On Day Sixteen of Operation Potship, Rudy Meyers finally
materialized. Telephonically, as O'Doull would put it.

"Twenty-Nine G-K in Miami," he said.

Mitchell was in a controlled fury. "You're not a one-piece
band, Twenty-Nine G-K. I've got sixty other full-time people on this case. Everyone's sitting on their butt and chew-
ing their nails waiting to find out what you've got for us.
Why the hell haven't you been in contact?"

"Inspector, I could spend half my working time talking to
you on the phone. But I wouldn't be getting much done that
way."

If only Meyers were a member of the force. Mitchell
would ream him out hard.

"Things got a little more intricate than I had expected," Meyers said. "The targets lost their connection. I had to arrange an introduction with some other people. I have expended a great deal of energy on behalf of this operation, Harold, a great deal of energy. This is going to cost me dearly in the long run, because when this is over, I will have lost a very important connection on the Caribbean coast. They will not trust me after this."

Mitchell had no tears to shed over it. "Just tell me what's happening. Where are you?"

"Colombia. Don't be impatient, Harold. You see, I have news that will please you. There is a ship. There are goods to be put into the holds of the ship. The load will start moving in one week exactly if we are not thrown off schedule by accidents of fate."

O'Doull rapped on Mitchell's door and poked his head inside. Mitchell waved him in, pointing to a chair.

"How much goods?" Mitchell asked.

"I have a nice fat one for you, Harold."

"How much?"

"Oh, maybe a hundred thousand."

Mitchell sagged. "A hundred grand, is that all they could afford? They can't buy spinach with that."

"A hundred thousand *pounds*, Harold. P-O-U-N-D-S. If I have to make myself that clear, I hope your line is absolutely safe."

Mitchell put his hand over the phone. "A hundred thousand pounds of pot, Theo! We've hit pay dirt!"

"What about the Sat-Track transmitter?" O'Doull asked.

Mitchell relayed the question to Meyers, explaining the satellite-tracking concept.

"It may be impossible at this stage to get something like that on board," Meyers said. "The vessel is under guard twenty-four hours. If I send some of my technicians on board, there are going to be too many questions asked."

"We've *got* to track them," Mitchell said. "There's a million square miles of ocean out there."

"I may have something just as good," Meyers said. "First, air observation. They will think it's air cover for *them*. We'll have eyes on them as far up as northern Florida. Second, Harold, I may just be able to put someone on board."

"Good. Who?"

"I'm not telling, Harold. Not on the phone."

O'Doull spoke to Mitchell in urgent tones. "What does he say about the Sat-Track? Can he get access?"

Mitchell looked up at him. "No. Sorry, Theo."

O'Doull struck his forehead. "You mean after all that *work?*"

"The transmitter," Mitchell said into the phone. "It's important, Rudy. I trust machines more than people. Let's try for double protection, like they say in the deodorant commercials."

"Send it to me in Miami, Harold. I'll give it some thought."

CHAPTER EIGHTEEN

Johnny Nighthawk

Pete's ego has been punctured. Marianne has run off for a few days with the flashy Latin romeo.

"That bastard, he has kidnapped her," says Pete. He mopes around all day like some depressive psychotic, staring at a blank wall, a bottle of scotch at his elbow, his eyes like hot coals. "I am in love, Johnny. I am in love."

He is in lust. He plays well the role of wounded martyr. I don't know about Marianne. I wonder about her heart. She has played Pete as Pete Townshend plays an electric guitar.

But after two days in this gilded cage, we are *all* going crazy.

We play a lot of poker – dealer's choice. Billy Lee is down three hundred bucks to Pete. I am down fifteen hundred.

On the third night, we hear distant melodies of fiesta. We see happy people, brightly dressed, walking towards the source of music that tinkles up the street, to our aerie.

We crack.

That night we spend a thousand dollars in the city. We do the fiesta. Nighthawk, like his namesake, beats around the city after dark and makes a lot of noise. (Incidentally, I gave the name Nighthawk to myself. Johnny Little was the name that was forced upon me at birth, presumably by some agency. What kind of Indian name is Johnny Little?)

At midnight, we are lost, loaded, loafing in the maze of thin streets. People swim by. Tinny music comes at us from a hundred portable radios. It is a raunchy, muggy ass end of an April night, with a moon slipping furtively behind clouds that roll in from the sea.

We are arm in arm, singing shanties, trading easy taunts with the pimps and the hustlers and the dealers.

"Hey, man, you want some grass?" A street dealer approaches us.

Billy Lee says, "No grass. No feelty pictures. No cheeks."

The little dealer bustles up to him. "Hey, man, where you from? You from the States? Hey, man, I been to America. I got a cousin in New York. Hey, I got some really far-out grass, really outrageous shit, man. Hey, you want to come up to my place, do some coke?"

We tell him we are tired.

"Aw, hey, man, buy some grass. I got a cousin in New York. I live in the States for five years, man. Come on, I'm really low on bread. I got a sick kid. In hospital."

Billy Lee slips him a five-thousand-peso note. The guy hands him a bag of weed. Billy Lee does not want to take it, so the guy stuffs it into his jacket pocket.

And then he yells to someone behind him in Spanish, "He bought the marijuana. Can I go now? Will you let me go now?"

This is one of those set-ups – fairly common – where the local cops force street dealers to set up tourists, then blackmail them for some *mordida*.

The cop comes running up to Billy Lee. "Departimento Administrativo de Seguridad," he says. "You have papers, senor?"

Billy Lee is really pissed off, just keeps walking down the street, the cop waddling after him. "Why don't you go off

and pound your beat? Pound your meat, while you're at it."
He says this in English, which the bull does not understand.

"*Pasaporte*?" The cop is bristling. "*Pasaporte*!" He gets in
front of Billy Lee, stopping progress. Pete, Kevin, and I
stand around and watch this spectacle.

Billy Lee starts screaming at him in Spanish. "Passport?"
he says. "Passport? I don't need no fucking passport. I am
here at the personal invitation of the Minister of Tourism! I
am a correspondent with *Time* Magazine!" He grabs a
bunch of papers from his wallet and flashes them. They are
the usual dope dealers' bullshit papers. Colombians really
love paper.

The cop obviously cannot read, but he makes a gallant
show of pretending. Billy Lee has him worried and presses
his advantage.

"I am a secret agent with the FBI. See this?" He shows
him a business card from an aircraft spare parts company,
which the DAS cop holds upside down. "*Cristo*! I am a
special guest of the mayor of Cartagena. Read that – you will
see." He swears at him. "*Cerdo! Guevon! Bacilo de gonor-
rhea!*" Then he shoulders past the bull, stabs a finger at the
crooked little street dealer who had tried to set him up.
"Arrest this *trafficante*." He hands the cop the bag of dope,
grabs back his five-thousand-peso note and gives it to the
lawman. "You keep the evidence, of course, officer." Billy
Lee takes back his papers and stalks off to where we are
standing around.

Afterwards, we are walking down the street, laughing,
making obscene noises, and another guy steps out of the
gloom.

"It is good you paid off the *cerdo*, senor. I do not want to
have to shoot a police. It causes much problems." He is a
heavy with scars, as in the movies.

"Senor Meyers wishes you to stay in the hotel," he says.
"Senor Meyers says if you do not stay in the hotel, we must

step on toes, maybe break them."

This man is very professional. We had no idea he had been tailing us. We tell him *"Gracias"* and return to the hotel.

There is a pretty *puta* outside looking for customers.

"Deseas un buen rato?" she says to Billy Lee.

"No hablo espagnol," he says.

"You wan' good time, meester?"

"No hablo ingles," he says.

On the seventh day in this luxury prison Meyers arrives.

"The merchandise is on the river," he says. "It will arrive tomorrow in Barranquilla. Perhaps you might authorize Mr. Juares to allow my men on board. We will load it during the night. You gentlemen, of course, need not run the risk of being present."

Pete shakes his head. "No, it's my ship. I'm the captain. I'll supervise."

"I'm afraid that will simply not be possible. Senor Paez wishes to entertain you tomorrow night, at his villa. A going-away dinner. It would be *quite* indelicate to refuse this invitation."

"Why does he want to dirty his hands?" Pete asks.

"I am sure you do not hold yourself in such low regard, Peter. El Patron has heard of the famous Captain Kerrivan. He would feel honoured." Meyers has found the direct pathway to my friend's vain heart.

"Okay, I'll go. My boys will oversee the loading. Johnny, you're in charge."

"But everyone is invited, Peter," Meyers insists.

"Naw," says Pete, "these boys wouldn't know how to handle themselves in such fancy company. They don't know the difference between a gravy boat and a finger bowl."

"Our people can handle the loading," Meyers says.

"Uh-uh. Johnny, Billy Lee, and Kevin will look after it."
"Do you have a suit?" Meyers asks.
"No."
"Buy one."
"Where's Marianne?"
"She'll be there."

CHAPTER NINETEEN

Costumed in a stiff, white polyester suit, Kerrivan sat slumped in Meyers' station wagon as it pulled up at the gates of the Paez villa, south of Cartagena.

A uniformed guard nodded to Meyers, raised the barrier, and waved them through. The walls were of brick, three feet thick, topped with a layer of cement and broken glass and four lines of barbed wire. Dobermans strained at their leashes near the guard hut.

The road weaved grandly through a jungle thicket which opened near the sea. Gardeners were mowing grass and pruning ornamental shrubs on a flat, five-acre oval, part of which served as a putting green, part as a polo field. Behind the oval was a manse in the Victorian style, of red brick and tinted marble.

And sitting on the terrace, her green eyes dazed, was Marianne Larochelle, her lips puckered around a plastic straw which dangled in a frosted glass of pina colada. She was wearing riding breeches. The fingers of her right hand were resting on the upturned palm of the left hand of Colonel Augustin Escarlata.

Kerrivan thought the man's smile was proprietorial, as if he had purchased her. He was wearing a bright ascot. This guy was once a Cuban revolutionary? He didn't seem to fit the appropriate image of beard, khaki fatigues, and fat cigars.

Escarlata began to tamp out some white powder onto a small silver spoon. A cocaine-snorting ex-Cuban revolutionary? Or had he discovered that the quickest route to Marianne's heart was through her nose?

Kerrivan, steeling himself, walked up the stairs to them.

"Hi," she said.

"Obviously," he said.

"Care for a blort of stardust?"

"No. It makes me too happy."

Senator Publio Victor Paez was stout, ruddy, affable. About mid-sixties. He was as genial in touring Kerrivan about the estate as Kerrivan was glum in looking it over.

The senator walked with a limp—a wound, Kerrivan assumed, from his early days. He had heard that Paez had gained his power base during La Violencia, the Colombian civil war which had spent two hundred thousand lives three decades earlier. The Colombian family gangs were spawned during that turbulent time, and had grown affluent on the corruption and wealth of the country.

Smuggling was the foundation stone of the power of these families: guns, coffee, radios. Cocaine, quaaludes, cannabis. The only South American country with ports on both oceans, Colombia sits on the equator at the axis of the new world. It had become, under the reign of the smuggler barons, an international pivot with spokes connecting it to all the nations of the Americas.

Kerrivan wondered: Why, with his people, his money, his power, had Senator Paez chosen a cold-seas sailor from Newfoundland?

"The main thing is trust," Paez said, switching at clusters of white flowers with his cane. "One loses millions of dollars of merchandise each year because of misfeasance, Captain Kerrivan. Sadly, we have created a nation where theft and disloyalty are the rule, trustworthiness the exception."

He turned and faced Kerrivan, squinting his eyes at him. "I want a man I can trust. They say you are reckless. I am not happy with that. They say you are also lucky. That pleases me. But they say you are an honest man. You drive a hard bargain, but you will not steal. This shipment is very important to us. It is the single most valuable shipment of merchandise that has ever left the shores of Colombia. There are thousands of *marijuaneros* to choose from. We have chosen you. If you succeed, you will be able to work for us for many years."

"Senator," Kerrivan said, "I don't normally work for others. I have my own business."

"A small business, Captain Kerrivan, and a business that is doomed, as all the small people are doomed. You grow or you die. That is the rule of all business. I want you to think about this. I want you to think of joining us when this endeavour is done."

"No. I'm sorry."

"You must face some facts, my friend. The day of the small entrepreneur is over. The market has grown too large. The competition has become too strong. But for the aggressive young man who knows how to make profitable alliances, there will be a future. Soon these products will be legalized. It is a matter of time. I am preparing our family for the day when it is legal, in this country and in America. Remember the lessons of history — some of the great distillers of your country were once men who were lowly bootleggers, smugglers of alcohol. They prepared themselves, waited for the laws to change. Now they own empires. Perhaps one day you could share in such an empire, Captain Kerrivan."

They had stopped walking, but Paez began picking his way again along the path.

"In any event, Captain Kerrivan, whether you work *for* me or whether you freelance on contract, as you prefer, I will say this once, and then we will get on to more amiable topics of conversation. What I must tell you is that if you try to steal this merchandise, or if you attempt to swindle me in any way, I will have you killed." It was stated calmly, matter-of-factly.

"Perhaps it is unnecessary for me to say that," Paez continued, taking Kerrivan by the elbow as they came to the waterside. "As a professional, no doubt you understand the rules. But please know there is that unwritten term to our unwritten agreement. As my lawyers would put it, it is an implied term of contract—because in this unhappy country, where larceny is such a way of life, deterrents must be effective."

He seemed to contemplate the vastness of the sea.

"I have read a statistic," he said. "Across these waters, in America, there are fifty million who enjoy an occasional—what is the word?—toke. There was a time during the last decade when it appeared that my country would become quite wealthy in supplying this great market. Five years ago, we were the world's greatest supplier of marijuana to America and to Canada. But we have not progressed. And the market no longer grows as fast."

"So you are doing something about it," Kerrivan said.

"My family has put millions of pesos into the technology of agriculture, Captain Kerrivan. We are determined to make a major move on the American market. Ours is the first Colombian experiment in *sinsemilla*. It has been done successfully near Oaxaca. It is done in Hawaii. *Sinsemilla* is now being grown in great quantity in California. The North American strains are becoming very popular. If we do not compete, we perish. This entire country will collapse."

Kerrivan almost expected Paez to say the country's future was now in Kerrivan's hands. But all he said was, "You had better take some guns, Captain Kerrivan. There are pirates in the Caribbean."

"I can manage without guns, senator."

"Meyers will provide you with hand arms, anyway." Paez doodled in the sand with the point of his cane. "Do you think he is an honest man—Meyers?"

"I don't know," Kerrivan said.

"Yes." He seemed to muse. "Yes, he is an enigma. But I pay him well for the information he obtains and for the people he brings me. I told him to bring me someone I could trust. I trust you, Captain Kerrivan. You have an open face. You look me in the eye. I am told you have had ten years' experience, and have never lost a shipment."

"Then Meyers gave you bad information. I have lost two loads. One of them belonged to Mr. Ugarte. I was arrested once."

Paez slapped him hard on the shoulder. "Yes, these things I know." He sounded hearty. "This is just a little test of your honesty, Captain Kerrivan. Yes, Meyers has indeed investigated your background. He is very well connected with the authorities in North America." He looked sideways at Kerrivan. "You do not find this strange? Perhaps not in my country, but in America?"

Kerrivan shrugged. "Some people play both ends, senator."

"But you play just one, eh? *My* end, Captain Kerrivan. You would not be reckless when it comes to my property. Because you understand that if you are careful, you will be a millionaire, is that not so? Twenty million dollars, less your expenses and your crew shares. That will leave you enough? You will not starve?" He chuckled and slapped Kerrivan on the shoulder again. "And you will be paid when you deliver to our people in New York City, yes? That is the arrangement."

"Fifteen down, the rest in a month."

"Yes, it will tax my reserves of capital. And you have a hidden inlet, a secret cove somewhere in Canada? How will you bring it back down into the United States?"

"I'd prefer not to tell you."

Again, Paez slapped him on the shoulder. "Excellent. It is better not to speak of these things. There are ears everywhere, yes?"

A flock of sandpipers came running up the beach, following the surf, pecking at its leavings. Paez picked up a stone and skimmed it. They rose with a clatter, swirled through the air, then settled farther down the beach.

"Will it not be very expensive to pay off the customs at your border with the United States?"

"It won't be necessary. There are no fences at the border. It's five thousand miles long."

"Tell me nothing more, Captain Kerrivan. I am reassured. You have safe harbours on the Atlantic, and you have a border that has no guards. And few people expect shipments of *la merchandisia* to come from the north, from Canada. But tell me nothing more. I understand. It is not that you don't trust me."

"No."

"You do trust me."

"I don't have to trust you, senator."

Paez smiled. "And why is that?"

"Because if I am not paid the fifteen million, your people will not have the merchandise."

"Of course," Paez said. "Of course. Now, perhaps you would enjoy a dip in the pool before dinner."

At the table, servants swarmed about them. Kerrivan sat beside Paez's brother, who was in the full-dress uniform of a general of the Colombian army. Kerrivan conducted a desultory, tentative conversation with him, while ignoring the existence, across the table, of Marianne Larochelle, whose breasts were barely hidden in a gown that seemed to be buttoned two stops above the navel. Escarlata was in a dinner jacket and punctuated his conversation with a gold cigarette holder which he moved like a baton.

Escarlata was telling heroic tales of the days of the Castro insurgency. The revolution, he was complaining, had failed. All revolutions fail, he said, because men who fight so hard for power fight harder to retain it. He looked at Kerrivan, and followed his eyes to Larochelle.

"She is stunning, don't you think?" he said. "Exquisite taste. I'm afraid she literally dragged me through the boutiques of Caracas. Many of these places import from Paris."

"Did you have a good time?" Kerrivan asked. He tried to control the edge in his voice.

"Yes." The pupils of her eyes were pinned. Two dark stars in a green softness.

"I have a little surprise for you, Mr. Kerrivan," Escarlata said. "I understand you might need an extra crew member. It has been suggested that I join your ship."

"Oh, yes, I forgot to mention that," said Senator Paez, from the end of the table. "Colonel Escarlata has kindly offered to join you. As I said, the Caribbean is a sea of pirates. Colonel Escarlata is experienced with small arms, an outstanding shot. I know, because we were out on the firing range this morning. He made me look like an amateur."

Kerrivan felt sick.

"I guess you've been on boats before," he said to Escarlata.

"Unfortunately, my background is as a soldier and an airman, not a sailor. Perhaps my most useful function will be in keeping out of everybody's way."

Kerrivan didn't smile. "You understand this is *my* ship, Colonel. There's only one captain on a ship."

"Of course. By the way, Mr. Kerrivan, when you know me a little better, you might get to like me. There seems to be an obstacle in the way of our friendship. But I am going to apply myself diligently to the task of liking you, and I wonder if *you* would try as well. I plan to enjoy this journey. I am a lover of adventure."

Kerrivan offered a stiff smile. His eyes remained glacial. "I like you better already, Colonel."

"Excellent," said Paez. "A happy ship is a healthy ship." He stood up with a glass of champagne. "A toast, ladies and gentlemen. To health, to happiness, to riches. To a successful journey. *Salud!*"

Kerrivan poured a little champagne into the crystal goblet that was in front of him, and pulled himself to his feet.

"Health," he repeated. "Happiness. You bet." The rims of the glasses touched and rang like bells.

Kerrivan looked at Larochelle, who smiled her seraphic smile at him. He looked at Paez, the patron, who seemed contained in an aura of power. He looked at Escarlata, whose white teeth seemed to reflect the gleam of candles from the chandelier.

He looked at Meyers, whose glass contained only water. Meyers was smiling. He was always smiling.

CHAPTER TWENTY

Johnny Nighthawk

We are drifting down the Magdalena River under a fat moon. Lights blink and fade along the shore.

The river spills into the long swell of the sea.

We have laid a course due north to the Windward Passage. We putter along at thirteen knots, a good speed that we have urged from the old engines.

Kevin Kelly, awaiting his turn at the engine watch, is wobbily standing on his head on the deck. The *vitaripakarini*, the hatha yoga headstand. He explains, "You fix the moon in the navel and a radiating sun in the palate."

Marianne Larochelle has been dancing Tai-Chi. She alternates this with a flurry of Kung Fu movements, whirling, spinning, kicking. This is done incongruously to the sound of Santana from the speakers. The driving, urgent rhythms of Latin rock.

Later, Kelly is seated under a lamp at the galley table, facing east, incense swirling around his neck. He is laying out the Tarot spreads, predicting morose futures. The atmosphere in the galley is heavy with fish stew.

After a five-hour shift in the engine room, I escape and go

atop the pilot house to help Pete with the aerials. The VHF is non-functional. Likewise the Loran A. Juares has installed a used Loran C, but we are south of its range. The gyrocompass is suspect. The single-side band, we have discovered, has the wrong crystals. There is a sextant of great age, doubtless a relic from the days of the Spanish armada. We have trusted the word of Juares as to the condition of all these things, and of course we were fools.

Eventually, Pete and I discover that the aerials are not the problem. We will have to look *inside* the Loran and the VHF. It will be a complex task.

But Pete doesn't really seem to give a shit. He has the sextant and a magnetic compass, and he is Captain Kerrivan of Newfoundland. Horatio Hornblower at the helm of his ship of the line.

Augustin Escarlata is useless. He wears a yachting cap, looks like he is out for a day's sail in a twelve-metre sloop. Pete has him tying things down. He cannot tell a bowline from a half hitch.

I have sized Escarlata up as an aging romantic, a revolutionary whose dream was doomed to fail, a fifty-year-old Cuban warrior unable to admit to himself he lacks the stuff and mettle of a Castro or a Guevara, and who blames his country for his own deficiencies. So he has run away from it. But this is cynical. I envy him for his *savoir-faire*, his flashing teeth. In this, Pete is my brother, although he suffers more, of course.

By unspoken agreement, Marianne shares a cabin with Augustin. Billy Lee, Kelly, and I are in another. Pete has the captain's night room. The captain's day room is filled with marijuana. Everywhere we are crawling over these sacks. After we filled the holds, there were a hundred *bultos* still left on the barge. So we stowed them in the cabins, in the storage rooms, in the passages, on the deck under tarps. As for the scrap metal, I told Juares to forget it. We left it behind.

The *bultos* are double-wrapped in heavy-gauge black plastic inside sisal sacking. Despite that, the aroma of the flowers often drifts through the air. You become acclimatized to being ever-so-softly stoned. . . .

Marianne is now at the wheel. She and Billy Lee have been given this watch, and we have instructed them as to the control console. Pete or Kevin will take the wheel if we see a ship near our course. Marianne is sultry in cloth that wraps around her hips like a sarong, braless under a denim shirt.

Billy Lee is picking a course off the charts with a pair of dividers. He glances at Marianne from time to time. As I do. As Pete does. Where her shirt is open, one sees a perfect curve of breast and a brown nipple. She has been doing nose candy all day.

Standing near Pete, I feel the power of his tension, I feel vibrations exploding from him, I see the silver sparks of bitterness that flash from his eyes when he looks at her. Pete should be sleeping, taking a break.

But none of us sleep much, day or night.

We keep the speakers out on the deck during the day. They are KLH's from the Barranquilla black market, five feet tall, driven by three hundred amps each side. We have about fifty cassettes. There is a reggae tape on now. Bob Marley. It seems to suit the climate and the space. We will soon be coming into the Jamaica channel.

Every hour on the hour, Meyers' plane, a Cherokee 6, gives us a little flypast. We have an aircraft radio tuned to his frequency.

"All clear to the north," he tells us. "All clear east of Jamaica."

"I do not trust the man," says Kelly. "There is an evil presence among the influences guiding us. I see him in the cards."

The sun rises over a trembling sea. A thick bank of nimbostratus climbs the western sky to windward. A high cirrus curls above us, showing red. Red sky in the morning, sailors take warning. And the barometer has started to pump hard to average. Jamaica marine radio predicts a blow, a snotter.

But Pete is unconcerned. "It will keep the Coasties off our tail and snug inside the cocktail bars," he says.

There is a smell of bacon and eggs from the galley. Pete has decided to put Escarlata in charge there, where he can do limited damage. How did he fight a war without losing an arm or a foot? Or his life? His tales of heroism in the Sierra Maestre – perhaps they cannot be believed.

By ten A.M. it is baking hot. The sun has room to travel, but the clouds are packing in even thicker to windward.

Marianne is lying atop an inflated dinghy, on her back. She has stripped her clothes off. This makes us suffer. She breathes in, breathes out. Her breasts are dark and show no tan line. Billy Lee can't stand it any longer. He goes to his cabin to try to sleep.

Soon the air has grown muggy and soft. An unsettling calm augurs a storm. Jamaica says the blow will be coming in later today at around nine or ten on the Beaufort scale, with forty-knot winds and up. The needle has started to jerk, and is falling very fast.

I go to the engine room. The engines are groaning like sick dogs. There are ominous clanks, but the gauges are deadpan, revealing nothing. Somehow, between Kelly and me, we have to nurse these machines, urge them on.

It is early afternoon, and the clouds eat the sun. The wind hits us a hard slap, and from the west, the sea is building up, sending curling smokers at us, hurling foam. We are chugging into the belly of a Force 10 gale.

I am praying the engines will hold. If we go dead in the water, crosswise to the swell, we are in danger of broaching to, of capsizing. I have been in rougher water, but in better ships.

Kelly relieves me for a while in the engine room. I poke my head into the pilot house. Pete has a maniac look on his face, a grotesque smile that is out of place. His arm muscles, like whipcords, are straining to hold us steady on.

I hustle around, battening things down. In the galley I find Augustin Escarlata, and now I know why Pete was smiling. The ex-revolutionary is on his knees before a basin, his face as green as the ocean, and he is heaving his breakfast.

An hour later, we are whooshing wildly up and down a roller-coaster sea, pitching and yawing, slewing heavily from side to side. The rain comes hard and sudden, a great, grey curtain. In the wheelhouse, Pete's screams can barely be heard above the roar of the wind. "You cocksucker!" he calls out. "You dirty cocksucker!" But there is a great smile crinkling across his face, and his screams are screams of joy.

As evening comes, the sea continues to heap up, and there are bomb bursts of green water as the gale spits foam from the crests of the waves. We are sliding down wave fronts, surfing into the troughs, the bow splitting the stomachs of the waves with the sound of thunder.

The generators are now acting up: the voltage fluctuating, the breaker kicking out intermittently, causing the gyro to tumble, making it useless.

None of this seems to dim Pete's joy. "I'm going to stick this sucker right up the gut of the Windward Passage!" he boasts.

Marianne and Billy Lee are sick now, too, and mostly useless. Pete and Kelly and I are alone with the *Juan Atrapa* and the sea.

I am in the engine room again, offering love and prayer to these awful machines, coaxing them, sweet-talking them. I have no idea where on the expanse of the Caribbean our lit-

183

tle ship might be found, and I have visions of cleaving open the hull on a Cuban rock. I am becoming a fearful believer in Kelly's black portents.

The winds back around and carry us north fast, faster than we wish, although we have slowed to release the strain on the engines.

But Peter brings us through the passage. I do not know how he does this. He has the instincts of a migrating salmon.

At five A.M. the sky suddenly splits open, and Pete takes a star shot with the sextant as we cruise the crest of a long rolling wave. We are through the pass, he says, north of Cuba, southwest of the Bahama Islands. The sea is hissing and swirling, but it is now settling as the gale shows us its ass and runs away to the northeast. Soon, in the glow of early twilight, we see the storm clouds shredding into long rips. And quickly the sun comes over a crisp, clear horizon.

"Nothing to it," says Pete. And in his triumph, he looks around for Marianne.

I do not tell him that she is below with Escarlata, spooning split pea soup into him. Perhaps she has no room for heroes in her life.

In the evening, we are picked up by the Gulf Stream, and we nestle into it, gaining a couple of knots, hoping to soar right up the Florida Strait before the sun comes up.

Meyers' spy plane has been a frequent visitor. We have told him our navigational aids aren't working. (Predictably, the Loran C is also haywire, although we are now in its range.) Meyers promises to drop a packet in the morning with a new Loran C, or an Omega. "We really don't need that fucking stuff," says Captain Jackpot.

Pete has now given Escarlata some dirty clothes, and the colonel is helping us change fuel filters. We have sixty thousand gallons of dirty Colombian diesel aboard, and we are constantly changing filters. Pete has decided it is a good job for the Cuban to learn.

By now Escarlata must not like Pete very much.

Later, about midnight, the number-two generator starts heating up, cooking itself. It takes us two hours to get the plant back on the line – and then the other one starts to freeze up. What do we have – gremlins?

We are up all night with flashlights and lamps. We have shut everything down and are getting back to basics. It has something to do with shorting problems, and we are going over the wiring millimetre by millimetre, cursing Juares with language that is majestic.

In the meantime, we are dead in the water, the current sucking us up the Florida Strait.

"Aw, God," says Kelly, "this is the shits for sure. We should be a thousand miles out in the middle of the Atlantic. What in the good Lord's name are we doing here, drifting who knows how far off the shores of Florida? This is Coast Guard country, Pete. And us with fifty tons of flower-top all over the goddamn ship. I warned you, Pete. 'Don't go,' I said. No, the great Peter Kerrivan has to do one more trip."

Pete grunts, searching for a little bolt and washer he has dropped. "I'm doing this for you, Kevin, my boy. All I want to do is make you rich and happy. I have no other dream."

Kelly goes on. His mouth is a motor that grumbles incessantly, and when he is depressed, he speaks in a toneless mutter that can drive you crazy. "I'm telling you, Pete, this trip is going to go down. When I say going to go down, I mean *down*. I warned you, Pete. I told you so."

"A hundred thousand times," Pete says sharply. "Lay off, for Christ's sake!"

Everything is really bitchy in here. I am angry with Pete, too, because I regard him as the major fault of all the sexual tension that exists aboard the *Juan Atrapa*.

"Dead in the water," mumbles Kelly. "With generators half burned out. No spare parts, because that's another thing Juares lied to us about. Ah, sure, the engine storage is full of stuff, but none of it was meant to fit on *this* floating piece of garbage. We got no radio that works a good damn, no radar, nothing to steer the ship by. Even the magnetic compass is off twenty degrees. You are going to take a hundred-and-fifty-foot ship all the way to Newfoundland with an antique sextant? Shooting the northern star and the rising sun? You're crazy, Pete, that's what I think."

"I'll get it up there," Pete says.

"*You'll* get it up there?" This is me.

I can see Pete's crazy grin in the lamplight. "*We'll* get it up there, boys. You and me and Billy Lee. With a little help from our friends."

That sets off Kelly again. "Who—Meyers? He's setting us up, boys. He's in cahoots with somebody that's out to get us, to be sure. Juares is part of it, I am starting to think. Your lawyer's business partner. Do you think they've bought your lawyer to set us up for a fine bust?"

"Kevin," Pete says, "paranoia will rot your dirty soul. Sure, and the Mounties have bought a third of a billion dollars' worth of pot so they can put Pete Kerrivan in the slam for good."

"*Just* Pete Kerrivan?" This is me, again.

"Let's try those terminals now," Pete says. He is sounding testy.

"Meyers will go where the money is in this operation," Kelly says. "If he's working both ends, let's hope Paez is paying him more than the cops are offering."

"You're not happy unless you got some disaster just over the horizon," Pete says. "Sure, Meyers is in it for the money. That's why he's babysitting us all the way. How much do you think he's getting paid for this little operation? I'll tell you, it's not under five million, I'll bet you that."

186

My hopes are that Pete is right. Meyers has a big stake in this. He checked out the names in the world of sea smuggling and of course came up with Pete Kerrivan. He made contact with Billy Lee Tinker, and twisted his arm hard for an introduction to Kerrivan. That, I tell myself, is what happened.

"One more thing goes wrong," says Kelly, "I'm jumping ship. One more thing, and it's goodbye, boys, I'm going home to Merrie." There is a pause. All this talk mingles with curses as we work away. "I don't know if this ship has got zombies in it, or the ghost of old Mayor Atrapa, or maybe we're being sucked right into the Bermuda Triangle, but I'm telling you, boys, there's some kind of weird force going on, and it's doing a shockin' heavy number on all of us."

"Shut up, Kevin!" Pete orders sharply. "Let's start getting this thing connected up again."

There is a period of silence and then Kelly starts going again.

"We are on our way to get ourselves busted out here, boys. If we don't get this tub out of here before the sun comes up, we'll be like a wounded duck in a shooting gallery." Kelly raises up, and says in a loud voice, "Boys, I'm going to suggest that before we get ourselves boarded, which like as not is going to happen in a short time now, I say we hook up that crane to the auxiliary generator, I say we open the holds and sling the weed out into the sea and take the lifeboats into shore. Because if you don't come with me, boys, I'm looking to take some extra gas on the longboat and I'm going in by myself!"

Pete snaps. He shouts at Kelly, "For the sake of the sweet Lord, Kevin, *take* the Jesus longboat and take the Jesus Johnson 2000 and take yourself and your gloomy Jesus attitude to the Jesus Florida coast!"

Kelly might very well have done that, but I have now combined the right wires and there is a sputter and sparkle of lights.

Yet Kelly has more to say. "While I'm on the topic of this ship, Pete, another thing, and I'll say it – the vibrations alone are going to do us in. I mean, Mary Mother of God, the sexual energy is so tight I feel the boat is going to explode sometimes. So she likes to screw around. You should be prepared for that, Pete. You're no different."

I say amen to that.

With the plants once again on line, the creaky old ship chugs back to life. Pete takes a shot when the sun touches the lip of the horizon, and we learn we are somewhere midway, hopefully, if Pete is accurate, between Florida and the Biminis. To the west is a pall of smoke. Meyers' plane will be along soon, now that it is light, so we can get an accurate fix of how close we are to that smoke and mist – which is a distant landfall, marking the city of Miami.

Already, fishing boats are putting out to sea in the distance. A few small planes buzz, going east. In a couple of hours, this will be a beehive.

And then it happens.

We hear Meyers' voice crackling over the radio. "Take a heading northeast!" he yells. "Get out of there!"

We see his plane.

And then we see what Meyers has seen – coming at us like an ugly giant hornet.

The dawn is shattered by the chattering of helicopter blades. We are staring up at the fat belly of a Sikorsky HH3F Pelican, with a diagonal red racing stripe.

CHAPTER TWENTY-ONE

Johnny Nighthawk

Understand this: with my record of one long stretch behind me, plus a collection of bits and pieces, this will be the long count, the last count, the big out, *finito*. There will be no comeback for The Hawk. They will squeeze his juices out, wring his spirit dry, bend him, break him, crush him, and when twenty years pass by, if he survives in body, they will open the steel doors of Raiford Federal Prison and the shell of Johnny Nighthawk will stumble through them, his tired old-man bones covered by a Salvation Army suit. He will go to the gutter. The others will be fairly young when they get out. They may get off with five to ten. That is because they will take no criminal records into jail with them. I will be used, of course. The judge will give me the book – the heavy book, the one they save for three- and four-time losers. A lesson to those who would dare follow the path of greed and crime. Deterrence: it is the favourite word of judges, sanctified, enshrined, hallowed.

"You guys are fucking crazy to be coming in right off Miami."

Those are the only words I can remember from the first hour or so. Everything is recalled with blurred edges. A kind of amnesia sets in, protecting one from the shock.

I stood on the deck, frozen to the rail as if welded, while the chopper danced in the air above us, waiting for the Coast Guard cutter to come alongside. She was a big mother, the cutter, over two hundred feet, one of their long-range ships. I remember it being armed with cannon, and I remember semi-automatics being trained on us.

I also remember a guy slashing open one of the sacks as if he were gutting a pig. I remember a cloud of resin exploding into the air from the *bulto*, and the guy's eyes enlarging. "Mother lode!" he yelled. Everyone could smell the sweetness of it.

I remember thinking there will be promotions for these guys.

I recall one of the Coasties saying something about thirty million dollars' worth of pot. I guess they had no idea. They had probably never seized a shipment of pure flower.

I remember thinking, kind of laughing to myself hysterically, that the custody crew they put on board the *Juan Atrapa* was going to have a good time trying to run that tired, complicated old boat.

We are all herded to the stern of the cutter, and they zip through the routine – numbers pinned to us, photographs taken, identification examined, names, addresses, some woman giving us the Miranda speech in a fast monotone, probably hoping we will not be paying attention, although what difference does it make – knowing we have a right to remain silent, knowing we have a right to a lawyer – when we have got so much cannabis aboard this ship that we are stumbling over sacks of it in the corridors.

I am thinking: why did I not listen to Peddigrew, hide the weed under the scrap metal? I was too greedy, of course.

I am thinking: why did we not listen to Kevin Kelly, who seemed to divine this calamity?

I can't look Kelly in the eye. None of us can. Greed had blinded us to his truth.

What else do I remember? Rows of boxlike cheap hotels

in Miami Beach. Sailboats beating into the wind in Biscayne Bay. A white cruise ship. The buzz of speeding cars on the MacArthur Causeway. The mouth of the Miami River. The U.S. Customs Building, where we disembark.

We are cuffed, of course. Marianne is taken away by the hard-talking female narc. The rest of us in a van. A jail. I am not sure if this is the Dade County jail, or some place else, a Coast Guard lockup, a drug squad lockup. Fingerprints, mug shots. We are taken out separately for interviews. In my case, as I recall, my interview consists of all questions, no answers. I am the cigar-store Indian. I am down, depressed, haunted, two guys working me over verbally, scorn in their eyes.

How is it that the Coast Guard has so suddenly zeroed in on us? It is no blind luck case of stumbling upon a marijuana ship. I feel a dull ache in my head, like the throbbing pain that comes when the novocaine wears off, the pain that comes with the knowledge that we have been betrayed. By someone.

Meyers. I see his clean, pink face smiling in my mind.

The clang of metal doors. A cold cot and a blanket. Darkness. Distant cries. I hear the tick of time, slow seconds dropping away. Tiny rivers of cold sweat creep down my body.

In the morning we are taken to court to be arraigned. The sign on the old stone building says U.S. Post Office and Court House. The marshals, big, easy-going men, lock us in a large room on the second floor.

Kelly is crouched like a ball in the corner. Pete and Billy Lee stand by themselves, quiet, closed in. Escarlata is ashen. Marianne is shaking.

Someone barks, "U.S. Magistrate's Court of the Southern District of Florida in session." We rise numbly, sit again.

Names are called, words briskly spoken.

"Estreat the bond."

191

"Waive reading of the indictment."

"Case number 801173."

"Is your man here, Fred? Call the case."

"Let's get on with the list, we'll be all day."

The magistrate is moving people in, moving people out, setting bail, chatting with the lawyers. They still do not call our names.

A door in the back opens.

It is Meyers. He is smiling, nodding at us, greeting people. They will kill me if I move at him, but I want to.

Behind him comes a man in a grey suit. He confers with Meyers.

Now our names are called, and we are motioned to stay in our chairs. The grey suit moves to the centre of the courtroom, in front of the magistrate.

"This your case, Ben?" the magistrate says, informal, nonchalant.

"Benjamin Ardell, for the record. I represent the five men and the woman, Your Honour." Benjamin Ardell has lank hair, liver spots, and a red, bulbous nose that speaks of a taste for strong drink.

Where has Benjamin Ardell come from? And why has he come in here with Meyers? Who is this man, this attorney, who seems to be speaking for us?

And what do these words mean: *habeas corpus*? He speaks them in triumph, waves a document at the magistrate. The U.S. attorney sits with his back to the bench, glum, tapping a pencil against a clipboard. A woman – the narc that I remember from the bust – whispers in his ear. She is bouncy; and cute. Flaherty, I find out later, is her name.

"I am directed by Judge Evans of the District Court to request their immediate release," Ardell is saying.

"That's fast work, Ben," says the magistrate, grinning.

Ardell drawls, "Well, sir, the judge wasn't too happy about getting out of bed before seven o'clock this morning, but we wanted to get in front of you before more damage was done. The government realized the error of its ways when we looked at the Coast Guard reports last night. Even the Government of the United States isn't entitled to commit acts of piracy."

The magistrate says to the U.S. attorney, "What's the government's position?"

The attorney doesn't get up from his chair. "Yeah, he's right," he says. "No real damage done. They can go."

The magistrate looks at us. "All defendants in the case of the United States versus Kerrivan *et al* are free to go. Charges are dismissed."

Billy Lee scratches the stubble on his face, and says to the magistrate, "Sure like to know why. Just as a matter of passing interest, Your Honour."

"Well," says the magistrate, slow and relaxed, "seems the Coast Guard boys did a bit of a botch-up on you fellows. When they rechecked your position, they found out you were sitting about a thousand yards outside the twelve-mile limit. That entitles everyone to a get-out-of-jail-free card."

"What it comes down to," says Ardell, our lawyer, "is you were kidnapped by the Government of these great United States."

I am thinking I have fallen down the white rabbit's hole. I am in Wonderland.

CHAPTER TWENTY-TWO

Johnny Nighthawk

We are gathered, completely zenned out, in a large government office at the courthouse. The six of us from the ship are there, and a grinning Rudy Meyers, and our lawyer, an assistant U.S. attorney, and Special Agent Jessica Flaherty.

There is steam hissing out of this woman. She is looking at Meyers with undisguised hatred. To me, Meyers is an object of affection. A sort of uncle.

"Don't sit down," Flaherty tells Meyers. "We don't want your stink settling into the upholstery."

Meyers ignores her. His eyes, usually as hard as pebbles, are shining. His mouth has puckered into a muscular little smile under the bristles of his moustache. He seems almost merry. He and the lawyer are passing us sheets of typewritten paper.

"Sign these, please," Meyers says.

They are in legalese. I am trying to read the document, but my hands are shaking, and the words are flowing into each other. Something about forgiving the Government of the United States and its agents and attorneys and et cetera, et cetera, from all manner and means of claims et cetera, et cetera.

"These are releases," Ardell the lawyer says. "You are

agreeing not to press charges or suit against the government." I can smell a whisper of morning alcohol on the man's breath.

Of course I am expecting Pete to pipe up with something to the effect, hell, no, we're going to sue the pants off the government. But he is spaced out, like me, and he is blinking his astigmatic eyes at the paper.

"You will, of course, be allowed to take your ship and its cargo back into international waters once you sign the releases," the lawyer says.

Pete says softly, "They can't seize the cargo?"

"International law forbids seizure without the consent of country of registry of your ship, the *Atrapa*," says the lawyer. "The Government of Colombia did not give its consent."

"Somebody's been bought off," Flaherty said, giving Meyers another freezing look. "They seem to be able to buy anything down there. And anyone."

"Looks like the Coast Guard and the DEA were a little trigger-happy, Jessica," Meyers says. "Jumped the gun."

"We'll be watching them," she says. "We know the ship, now. We'll tail them every fucking foot of the way. They drift just one inch back into U.S. waters, and we'll scoop them so fast their socks will fall off." She gives the fix-it man a crooked smile. "Maybe we'll put a tail on you, too, Meyers."

"Oh, I don't think there's much of a chance they'll be back here," Meyers says. "No, I don't think this ship will be back in this jurisdiction, Jessica."

"The Mounties," she says, "always get their man."

"Yes, but Jessica, do they always get their ship?" He chuckles at his poor joke.

"Just sign the releases and move everybody the hell out of here," the U.S. attorney says. I think he just wants the episode to close. It is embarrassing to watch Flaherty and

Meyers squabble. Between them, love is not lost.

The releases are signed, collected.

Flaherty smiles sweetly at us. "We *are* in touch with the Canadian police, you know. What do you plan to do – come in at night?"

"You don't have to say anything to that," our lawyer tells us. "Please, Miss Flaherty, you know better."

She shrugs. "Enjoy the hospitality of Miami. The Canadians have one day before immigration warrants are issued. In the meantime, folks, don't get caught doing anything I wouldn't do." She turns to Meyers for one last shot. "I hope you sleep at night."

"I sleep quite well, thank you. As well as you."

"I don't have to wash the scum out of my sheets every morning," she says.

Scummy though he may be, this man has saved our dirty skins. I am prepared to kiss his round, pink head.

Outside, I drink deeply of the free air of Miami, U.S.A. I am feeling reborn.

"Send me your bill," Meyers tells the attorney.

"Don't think I won't. I'm charging by results, not by the hour. Don't collapse when you open the envelope." He starts walking to his car, then turns to us. "I'll give you guys credit for guts and luck. Not brains."

Escarlata smiles a wan smile. "Can someone tell me where I can find the next boat back to Havana?" he says. "I think I would have a better chance at home with President Castro than on the high seas with Captain Kerrivan."

Meyers scowls at him. "You are not carrying on?"

"A team of elephants will not drag me back to the *Juan Atrapa*, *amigos*. I am deserting Captain Kerrivan's little navy. The sea and I, we do not love each other." He turns to us. "I have a hotel suite in Coconut Grove, a penthouse. You are all welcome to shower, bathe, shave, soothe your souls and bodies in the sauna, the Jacuzzi, or the swimming pool, as you prefer."

The six of us smell like gorillas' armpits. It is an offer one cannot refuse.

Meyers suggests we stop at the ship to get some of our things. "I have a few surprises for you."

"I think maybe I have had enough surprises, Rudy," says Escarlata. "I will skip the ship. You can join me later."

With that, this Latin lover of adventure hails a taxi, blows Marianne a kiss, bows low, and bows out.

The ocean liners and the container ships tie up along an enormous manmade island in Biscayne Bay. But the hustle-bustle boat traffic – and I mean everything from runabouts to hundred-foot trawlers, yachts, tramps, and old merchantmen like the *Juan Atrapa* – hide out in the Miami River or the deep canals that spiderweb away from it.

There seem to be hundreds of little boat and ship repair businesses along these waterways. And there are some which are big, with boat sheds like Boeing 747 hangars.

If you can tear yourself away from the beach scene, take a stroll along the Miami River. It is a dark artery that pumps through the heart of the city and it is ribbed with drawbridges. You will see rust buckets and junkers, shrimpers and long-liners, houseboats, tall sloops and ketches, and speedy little Cigarets and Magnums. (Many of these little things are dopers' boats – they can outrun any cutter when they come in from their mother ships.)

You look around at this floating carnival, and you wonder how many of these thousands of boats and ships earn a legitimate living for their masters. It is a smugglers' haven, this river, this city. The Miami River has a mouth that sucks up hundreds of tons of Colombian marijuana every month. It is trucked by night into warehouses, and importers' headquarters here are often as busy as your local stock exchange, with new crops being posted on the walls almost every hour during the season. It is called, of course, the high season.

Two or three miles up the river, into the Miami Canal, is
where we find *El Mayor Juan Atrapa*, bedraggled and sad
beneath the tin roof of one of these huge ship-hangars. We
cannot see her from the outside. We see just tarps and
canopies, part of the pilot house, and the radio masts.

"When the Coast Guard released it, we had it moved
inside this hangar," Meyers says. "These fellows here," he
points to a couple of narcs lounging outside the marina office, "are hanging around to make sure no one tries to rob
us. Aren't you, gentlemen?"

Neither of the DEA guys shows us any expression as we
brush by.

"If anyone walks out of here carrying a large package,
make sure you search him," Meyers calls back to them. *"Los
stupidos,"* he mumbles to us under his breath.

He explains to us that the marina business is in
bankruptcy. His security service is guarding the premises.
Inside the door a couple of his staff, mean-looking guys,
nod to Meyers, who takes us through, out into the shipyard
and the hangars. There are a couple of leaky old trawlers
sitting low in the water near the *Atrapa*. Our ship is a wasp
nest of action. There are guys crawling all over, working
with paint brushes.

The *Atrapa* had been a nice rust-red colour. More rust
than paint. Now it has become dark blue. This is the first of
Meyers' surprises.

"I thought we might try to confuse things a little," he
says. "Blue gives better camouflage from the air."

I go up to where a guy is stencilling a new name on the
bow. *Alta Mar*. "High Seas," it means.

"Bad luck to change a boat's name," Kelly says softly.

"Bad luck not to," says Meyers. "You will have to move
out at night, of course." He has not asked us whether we
want to move out at *all*. We have not had a chance to discuss this strange business.

"They will be looking for a vessel of this configuration,

but with a different name and colour. I have provided Portuguese and Panamanian flags, and you can fly one or the other at the stern. Lots of Portuguese ships near Newfoundland, I hear. Just to be safe, try to move out of aircraft range. Perhaps if you take a heading almost due east to about sixty or sixty-five longitude, you can then do a left and go straight up to Newfoundland. That *is* where you're going, isn't it?"

Pete says nothing, just looks at him.

Meyers says, "The tanks are topped up. Another forty barrels for emergency are lashed onto the deck."

"We've got to talk about this, Rudy," Pete says.

Meyers gives him one of his not so reassuring smiles. "I'm sorry about what happened," he says. "When I saw the helicopter coming, it was too late. No damage has been done."

"They knew we were out there," Pete says.

"Then there is a leak," says Meyers. "I will find it and plug it."

He takes us by the elbows, hustling us up the gangplank, one by one. He carries on as if there is no problem. Our arrest has been a minor irritant, an unimportant aberration in the grand scheme of things.

There does not seem to be much free deck space left, with all the barrels of diesel and all the *bultos* of weed piled up under the tarps. The sack that the Coast Guard guy slashed open is still lying there, its contents scattered and tracked all over. There is three hundred thousand dollars' worth of female flower spilling out of this sack. It is ignored as if it is a pile of tree leaves.

In the wheelhouse we are stunned. It is like the dashboard of a space module. Our old electronic gear has been stripped, and we are looking at an array of radios and navigation devices. They are being wired in by three guys chattering in Spanish.

"The Russians trained them very well," Meyers says.

"They are skilled technicians. I pay them top dollar."

"Let's talk about this," Pete says again.

Billy Lee and I are exchanging a lot of looks. Kelly is shaking his head. Marianne is very jittery. This pretty snowbird is pretty wired. I worry about her.

"We junked your old Lorans," Meyers goes on. "Put in a new Loran C. Also, over here, an Omega 1127 DC and a radio direction finder. I'm sure you know how to use all this equipment. Nothing radical about it. The Loran and Omega charts are under the chart table."

He is talking very fast. "Now what do we have. Radar – a new Decca 101 to get you through the fog. Echo sounder. Radios: ship-to-shore, Regency Polaris VHF Transceiver. Try not to use the VHF, they can beam into it from shore stations, although you'll be out of range most of the time. Larange Receiver. Titan Marine Radio UHF. Yaesu CB transmitter-receiver with linear amplifiers. I've given you a call number. If there's an emergency, just try to patch through to me somehow. You're running a cattle drive north, I'm the owner of the ranch. Just develop some code around that, so the ham operators won't get nervous. Let's see – a Zenith Transoceanic portable over here, a Sidebander II single-side band, twenty-three channels, and a Simpson 85 to complement it. Arkas Autopilot. Recording fathometer."

Meyers is beaming like a used car salesman. "Okay, here's something you may have to use. It's an electronic counter-measures pod. That's what the U.S. Air Force calls them. For jamming enemy radar. You won't believe what this cost. It is *not* available on civvy street, gentlemen. Billy Lee will know how to operate it."

"These things are illegal, man," Billy Lee says. "We can get busted if we're caught with this."

"If they try to follow you out of here at night, jam up their radar. That will give you a good edge. There's a lot of ocean out there."

200

He looks around to see if there is anything he has missed.

"Oh, yes, I'm not sure if you are familiar with this handy item. Bearcat 250 Police Scanner. We've pre-programmed it so it locks onto any police or Coast Guard channel that happens to be broadcasting. They don't scramble as much as most people think, and code confuses their simple minds."

He glances around, admiring the artistry. "A new gyro, and we've reset the magnetic compass as well, although you'll have to adjust it again when you get out to sea."

Out to sea. I am thinking – why is somebody not telling this jerk that we have no intention of going back out *anywhere* on this ship? But all we do is make nervous jokes.

"Where's the automatic shoe polisher?" Billy Lee asks.

"You don't suppose you could lay on a couple of destroyer escorts," Pete says. "How about a nuclear sub?"

"We've done what we can about the generators," Meyers says. "I've had a couple of men working on the number-two generator all day. That's the bad one. We'll load you up with spares."

Billy Lee says, "And I take it you've attended to the wine cellar. I prefer a dry Bordeaux, although a 1976 Beaujolais would tempt me."

"There is booze in the storage, hard and soft. I don't drink myself, so I don't know anything about people's brands. Lots of frozen meat in the locker. I threw out all that Colombian tinned stuff and substituted American. Better quality, fresher. I hope you won't have to use them, but there's a .30-.30 rifle and some handguns in the locker below the wheel. You may encounter sharks. Or pirates." A pause. "As you can tell, I am very anxious to get this cargo moved."

We look at him. There is a silence. The silence seems to expand, to fill the cabin.

"I am suggesting a midnight departure," Meyers says to Pete. "You're the captain, of course. But at dawn you will want to be eighty miles at sea."

"I'd like to talk about this, Rudy," Pete says. "You got to admit things are sort of crazy."

"There is nothing to talk about, Peter. Nothing at all." Meyers' voice is barely above a whisper. He is from an old Peter Lorre movie. "You have a contract, Peter. A contract with me and with Senator Paez. I want you to understand that your end of that contract is going to be fulfilled."

I am watching Pete's face. The face says nothing. He says nothing.

"If you do not bring these goods in, Peter, Senator Paez is going to be unhappy. Unhappy to the tune of over a quarter of a billion dollars. That will make him a *very* unhappy man."

Their eyes are locked together.

"We'll talk it over," Pete says finally. "The five of us. We'll be down in my cabin. We'll let you know in half an hour."

Meyers gives Pete a punch on the shoulder, playful but hard. "Good man, Peter. I'll be in the office making some calls."

We are all in Pete's cabin but Kelly. No one is talking. Pete is staring into space, glassy-eyed.

Kevin comes into the cabin, swings his packed duffle bag in after him.

"I'll meet you boys in Newfoundland," he says. "If you're lucky. I've been on some amazin' trips, but this one makes the *Guinness Book of Records*. Miami is where *this* dumb Newfoundlander gets off. It's women, children, then every sane man for himself."

"Well, Pete?" I say. I am expecting to hear some sense from this man. We have false passports, lots of different IDs. We can try to find some work in the Caribbean.

"I'll take the load up by myself if I have to," says Pete.

I should have known better. Peter Kerrivan, the brave outlaw of the Butter Pot. Captain Ahab alone at the helm, with the odds favouring the whale. Randolph Scott strapping on his guns once more, going alone into the O.K. Corral.

"I made a contract," he says. "Billy Lee?"

"Wal, if this here weed don't get moved, man, Senator Paez ain't gonna be suin' us in no court of law. I'm a gamblin' man, like Pete. I say we go."

Pete looks at me with his penetrating grey eyes. "Johnny," he says, "I won't feel let down."

"Aw, fuck," I say.

I know I will go with him. He knows that, too.

"You boys are stark *mad!*" Kelly yells. "Mad as gomerils. Pete, Lord livin' Jesus, boy, even the rats know when to abandon ship!"

Exasperated, Pete slams his hand flat on the table, shouting, "For God's sake, Kevin, fuck off! Take the next fucking plane back and take all your fucking doom and gloom with you!"

Then he sighs and shakes his head, cools a bit. I know he feels he has lost control of this trip. "Sorry, Kev. Look, I was thinking of sending you back early, anyway. You're going to have to help Bill Stutely get the landing crew together at Uncle Pike's." He starts to take charge of himself. "Have everybody there in ten days and wait for us. We'll come in at night or first good fog."

"Pete, I'll be sitting around that boathouse with a gang of the boys ten days from now and this ocean-going shithouse will have wrapped it up somewhere, upside down and sending up bubbles. Or you'll come in on a tow from the Canadian Coast Guard, with The Bullet holding a shotgun to your belly and smilin' in your face." His tone is urgent and pleading. "Pete, do you know how weird this is? They release this ship to this guy Meyers, who's been playing both ends so long he don't know which end is which. I mean, pick your brains off the floor. This trip is going *down.*"

"Johnny and Billy Lee and I can take it in by ourselves,"
Pete says. "With all this gear on board, the three of us can
sleep all the way to Canada."

"The *three* of us," says Marianne, who has been sitting on
the edge of the table, watching, listening. "I keep hearing
the three of us. Did somebody forget I'm here?"

Then Pete says, "You're not going. You don't have a vote
about whether you go."

"How damn democratic."

"He's right," says Billy Lee. "No point in takin' a chance
of gettin' your pretty ass busted. Too dangerous,
Marianne."

"You can *kiss* my pretty ass, Billy Lee!"

"You'll get half a crew share, plus what Peddigrew pays
you," Pete says, becoming businesslike. "Kevin gets one
crew share. I'm doubling Johnny's and Billy Lee's. Hang out
with the old Cuban for a few days, Marianne. Kick back and
wait for us."

She glares at Billy Lee and Pete. "Why don't the both of
you take a flying jump at a hole in the ceiling? The old
Cuban, hey? He's got more finesse in his little toe than both
of you put together can supply working at it for the next
hundred years." This is the first time I have seen this lady
angry. "Who do you macho twits think you are? You wave
your cocks around like flags and think every woman twenty
miles around is going to drip for you. The only goddamn
one among you who's got his male trip together is Johnny.
What do you think, Johnny, do you think I'm a poor,
weepy, helpless, inferior female? Or what *do* you think?
You never talk."

This is where The Hawk steps right into it. "First of all," I
say, "it's dangerous. Inspector Mitchell and the RCMP
aren't concerned about the letter of the law, like the Americans. Second — how do I say this? — second, there's just the
simple fact of you and three guys on board a ship for a long
time together. With you on board, Pete is liable as not to run

us onto the Sable Island lighthouse. Too much electricity, Marianne, with three guys and a lady."

She is staring at me, her mouth wide open.

"Johnny," she says, "you're the worst of the lot."

She looks us over as if we are pigs squatting in the muck. "How wimpy can you get? Three guys and a lady. What a load!" Her cheeks are lit with fire and her eyes are sparking. "I'm just damn happy to get *rid* of you, if you want to know the truth. I won't have to be ducking out of the way of all the colliding male egos!"

There is a long, strained silence as she goes to her cabin to pack her things. When she comes back she throws Pete a roll of bills. "The rest of the expense money from James," she says. "Christ, I'm going to score some coke and get happy."

Pete sighs. "Let's try Escarlata's whirlpool, folks."

"I'll stay behind," I say. "I'll check out the engines, get everything warmed up for midnight."

Kelly scoops a bag of flowertops from the open *bulto* on the deck as they head for the gangplank. Then he turns to me. His eyes are damp as he gives me a bear hug. I return it hard. I am happy for him. "Give my love to Merrie and everybody else," I say.

"*Le vaya bien,*" he says.

I watch them disappear into the office building.

I am still standing at the railing. I have not slept for three days and two nights. Eventually, I glimpse from between the tarps a taxi going over the swing bridge. It carries Marianne and the guys. The stoic Indian stands there for another half-hour, staring at nothing.

It is near rush hour. Cars are buzzing over the bridge by the marina. In my exhaustion, I am given to hallucination. I think I see Inspector Mitchell pass by in a station wagon. Every time I see someone's shining head, it is The Bullet. I think, God, I have to get out of this business.

I will check out the engines. I will have a shower. I will try to sleep for a few hours. This is my plan.

CHAPTER TWENTY-THREE

Rudy Meyers gripped Kerrivan hard by the hand. "I knew you would continue the trip," he said, "because you've got guts and you're a man of honour." He shook Billy Lee Tinker's hand, too, and ignored Kelly, the defector.

Meyers saw them to the door. "Incidentally, those two DEA agents outside – I think they'll be looking the other way when the *Alta Mar* pulls out tonight. Money tends to distract one's attention. I won't be here when you get back, but my guards know you."

"I'll call you when we get to New York," Kerrivan said. "We can meet there. You bring the dollars. I will have the merchandise."

"Absolutely," Meyers said. "No question. Piece of cake. *Hasta la vista*, Pete, *hasta la vista*."

Meyers watched from the window as Kerrivan, Tinker, Kelly, and Larochelle, in their taxi, disappeared up the street and over the bridge. Then he went into the inner office, closing and locking the door behind him.

"I think it was a cheap shot sting," Flaherty said. The others were standing, but she was leaning back on a swivel chair, her boots on the desk.

"You didn't *have* to be a part of it," Meyers said.

"I did. Direct orders from Washington – as conveyed to them, I suppose, by Inspector Mitchell, who just happens to

206

be in charge of combined U.S.-Canada operations." She shot a dark glance at Mitchell. "If it had been up to me, I would have been a thousand miles away. Far enough that I wouldn't have to hold my nose."

She punched a cigarette from her pack, struck a wooden match, and lit it. "But I'm a good soldier," she said. "I obey orders." She blew a smoke ring over Meyers' head. "Just like the Nazis." She turned to Mitchell. "Is this how you Canadians usually run your operations? Entrapment? You *should* call it Operation Crackpot."

"It seems to me you've had some experience in the area of entrapment, Miss Flaherty," Mitchell said. "Didn't we hire you a couple of years ago as a – how shall I put it? – an undercover seductress?"

"That involved a corrupt cop," she said. She blew five more perfect rings in Meyers' direction. "I'll go the extra mile when I'm putting together a case against a corrupt cop."

"Jessica," Meyers said, "it *was* you who instructed the U.S. attorney to co-operate. The holier-than-thou doesn't wash."

Ardell, the lawyer whom Meyers had hired for the courtroom scene, tilted a small flask of bourbon to his lips and wiped them with his hand. "She may be right," he said. "A judge would call it entrapment. I can't see how you'll get a conviction, inspector."

Ardell spoke with a slur. Mitchell was repelled by him. He felt Meyers should have been able to put the courtroom business together without having to bring in an outsider, but Meyers had claimed Ardell could be trusted. With a big alcohol monkey on his back, he needed the money.

"Mr. Ardell," Mitchell said, "you may be interested to know that in Canada there *is* no doctrine of entrapment. It is one of your strange American legal conceits."

"No, sir, I didn't know that," Ardell drawled.

"We have advice from our staff lawyers," Mitchell said.

"There's a precedent: an operation on the West Coast a few years ago. Some smugglers bound for Canada ran out of fuel and we arranged for DEA undercover people to pull their boat into San Diego Bay, refuel it, and send it on its way north. It was a controlled delivery, like this. The courts okayed it."

"Controlled delivery." Ardell spoke with the smiling cynicism of an old alcoholic. "That's what you call it, huh? Don't worry, inspector, I'm a lawyer. I'll keep my mouth shut."

Among the four others in the room was Theophile O'Doull, who looked as if he were trying to hide in a corner, his eyes shifting nervously from speaker to speaker.

"Well, Theo," Mitchell said, "the whole point of this interesting little diversion to Miami is the Sat-Track transmitter. I want to know if it's functioning. If it's not, we've wasted a lot of my time, your brains, Meyers' undercover ingenuity, and we've lost the services of Colonel Escarlata."

"He is a coward," Meyers said. "He seems also to suffer a tendency to lose himself in the pleasures of the flesh. I intend to get rid of him."

"I want to know if the Sat-Track is functioning," Mitchell repeated.

"I'll call Goddard," O'Doull said. "They'll have word by now." He dialled direct to the number in Maryland.

"Kerrivan won't find it?" Mitchell said.

"Not behind the jungle of hardware that's in there now," said Meyers. He turned to Flaherty. "That was an impressive performance, today, Jessica. It shows your stage experience."

"If you mean the part where I asked if you wash the scum from your sheets in the morning, yeah, I liked that role. I do a better job if I believe in my role."

O'Doull waved them quiet and spoke into the phone. "Repeat, please. Latitude north twenty-five degrees, forty-six minutes, thirty-seven seconds. Longitude west eighty degrees, eleven, and thirty-two." He hung up. "I think those are Miami's co-ordinates."

Meyers nodded, and everyone – except Flaherty – seemed to relax.

Operation Potship was no longer running the risk of human frailty, Mitchell thought. It was equipped with the perfect informer – a space-age informer that couldn't be bought off, a faithful electronic fink which would keep in touch with Operation Potship every one hundred and seven minutes.

"Congratulations, Sergeant O'Doull," Meyers said.

O'Doull smiled a faint and nervous smile.

Later, taking Mitchell and O'Doull back to their motel, Meyers said, "I don't want Agent Flaherty involved in this any more if it can be avoided. She can be very annoying. A very mouthy dame."

O'Doull found it curious how the man's lips did not seem to move when he talked.

●

Johnny Nighthawk

A late start. A golden moon hangs over the city and paints the ripples in the wash.

Another swing bridge opens, and we move through, and the jaws of the bridge shut behind us.

To starboard is the U.S. Customs Building. A lone sentinel light glows in the yard. My heart pounds as we pass by. But there is no one.

A last bridge. We slow. We wait. Finally it opens. Its arms rise in an invocation to the moon.

The river casts the *Alta Mar* upon the sea.

PART THREE
The Gypsy's Witch

CHAPTER TWENTY-FOUR

Theophile O'Doull lay under a single sheet in a Biscayne Bay motel room, bathed by the wash of the air conditioner. The moon's white eye glared through the window and painted a silver rectangle on the wall beside him.

In O'Doull's hand was a tumbler of Barbados rum, half-full. He searched for patterns in the darkness then closed his eyes to dream . . .

His flight had been late, and he had slipped past the brass that had gathered to meet him. O'Doull had always preferred to work alone, without orders. A Citroen taxi shouldered rudely past the others in the line and the rear door opened for him. He got in.

"I am Maria von Koenig," the woman said. Her hair was blonde, her eyes green. "I am your contact here. We will go first to my hotel room."

O'Doull knew she was from the other side. But she was beautiful, and he would play along. . . .

Jessica Flaherty, chainsmoking, stood at the window, cursing the moon, listening to the sounds of rut that ascended with a shriek. "*Dios!*" Then voices moaned in release.

That bastard, Flaherty thought. Alfredo J. who was to have come tonight had come indeed, but not to her. She

looked at her watch. She would wait. This was critical.
This was the night.

The electric glitter of the flashy, glassy bars of Mayfair Centre brought Kevin Kelly no joy, and he became frightened of the lonely people in them, plastic and brittle. He hungered for the warmth and love of his woman and his babies.

Escarlata had offered him a couch until the morning when Kelly's plane was due to leave. The night would be long.

He rolled up a fat dooby of Senator Paez's flowertops, shared it with some freaks sitting in a park under the moon, and strolled back to the Mangrove Arms Hotel.

J.R. Peabody, the night clerk at that hotel, was trying to hustle Cherrie, a natural blonde who believed that gentlemen preferred redheads. Peabody expected free rides from the quality whores who used the hotel. He figured his job got him more free ass than a movie star.

Cherrie would come across if her john failed to show. He knew that.

The phone rang. A woman spoke urgently: "Please send someone to the penthouse! Quick! Please!" She rang off.

Peabody wondered if it was the full moon that made people strange. He went to the elevator.

Detective Braithwaite took the call from the Mangrove Arms Hotel. He wished he hadn't. "Shit," he said to himself. It would be another long night. He desperately wanted to transfer out of the Miami police force, and move to somewhere sane. He strapped on his gun harness and went outside.

The air in the room was cool and dank with the sweat of death.

214

Feet shuffled softly and voices murmured. An air conditioner puttered. A bulb flashed, and, in the harsh white light of its split-second of time, there appeared a frozen tableau, etched sharply in the eyes of Detective Braithwaite. The tableau showed a dead man wedged behind the door clutching the empty air with curling fingers. It showed the homicide team moving through the room like dark spectres – dusting for prints, rummaging in drawers, scraping blood into vials. Complaining.

J.R. Peabody stood by the door, biting at a fingernail. Men from the morgue waited nearby.

Braithwaite, a black man, a senior investigator with the Criminal Investigation Section, homicide detail, was speaking in a sonorous monotone. "No other signs of disorder. Nothing broken, nothing overturned. From the condition of the face, I would say blunt instrument. No weapon so far. Initial ID from Jessica Flaherty, drug enforcement." He pushed the stop button of his cassette recorder. "Give me that again," he said.

"Escarlata, Augustin." She spelled it out.

He repeated it into his machine. "Apparently Cuban national, came over on the Ariel boatlift. No next of kin here. Lives here, at place of death."

He turned again to Flaherty. "This is pretty expensive digs, Miss Flaherty. What did he do for a living?"

"Worked for Rudy Meyers."

"That explains it. Part of Rudy's goddamn army, I suppose."

"Meyers had him playing double agent. Working for the RCMP."

"That why he got offed?"

"I don't know."

Braithwaite leaned down over the body, and continued dictating: "Can't see any injuries other than to face, but the face is a job for a good mortician. Appears to be caved in towards the middle."

Flaherty couldn't look. Even Braithwaite turned his head away with a sour expression.

"Looks like he got hit on the nose with a swinging nine-pound hammer," he said.

Flaherty wasn't used to this. She was feeling sick, holding her stomach down.

"Okay, the other man," he dictated. "There is no pulse here either, but it ain't cold yet. They'll have to do anal temps. Can't figure this one out at all. No exterior injury. Something internal, maybe. We wait for the medical examiner on this one. Okay, who's he, Miss Flaherty?"

She was staring out the sliding glass doors, to the roof, to the moving lights on the water, watching the moon over Key Biscayne.

"Miss Flaherty?"

"Detective, I think we should have a talk in private."

"You've got some operation going with Meyers and the RCMP. You don't want it compromised."

"You've got it," she said, then paused for a breath or two. "And there's more."

"Well, I got a murder here, Miss Flaherty. It's priority over drugs."

"Let's have a coffee when you're through here."

"Okay. Let's get this guy's vital statistics."

"Kevin Kelly," she said. "Citizen of Canada. Newfoundland some place. Smuggler by occupation. . . ."

CHAPTER TWENTY-FIVE

A daydreamer, a worshipper of heroes, a shy seeker of glory, Theophile O'Doull was acting out a fantasy when he became a cop. He joined the force at twenty-five – over-ripe for a rookie Mountie. But he had been in school, taking a Ph.D. in electronic engineering.

The fantasy that most possessed him had to do with being a police detective, a solver of crimes. It was this fantasy that held him infatuated six years ago when two puzzled recruiting officers sat him down for his interview. They knew industry would offer him four times what he could get being a cop.

The RCMP were happy to grab him. They stuck him in the central crime laboratory, and made him chief electronic technician. He suffered there, sought transfers to the field, and was continually rejected.

Denied his dream, he began to see in his disillusionment that there had lurked behind the dream a real and personal reason for becoming a Mountie: the need to make reparation for the sins of a loved father. The father had made corporal, a rank that allowed him to command one-man detachments here and there in Newfoundland. Corporal O'Doull and his wife raised three daughters eager only to marry, and the son, a brainy dreamer. His father invested heavily in his education in distant and costly schools.

At the age of fifty-five, on the eve of his retirement, a scandal destroyed Corporal O'Doull. There had been allegations of bribe-taking; small payments in cash and in kind from the rum and brandy smugglers who did a hectic trade from the French island of St. Pierre.

Innuendo and rumour were followed by a quiet internal inquiry, a hearing at which O'Doull's father had no lawyer. Soon after came a recommendation of retirement six months before his due date.

Then, unexpectedly, a rehash loud and undignified before a public commission of inquiry. Another sudden burst of headlines when the commission released its report. The report assumed the guilt of the policeman and excoriated his seniors for covering up his misdeeds.

Theophile O'Doull remembered the time: the family gathered in a tight, wretched knot in their waterfront home, his mother despairing, his father seeking oblivion in whiskey. O'Doull, sunk in gloom, began to wonder if the charges of graft were true. His education *had* been expensive. Shortly after, O'Doull joined the RCMP. As if this would give his father back his pride, redeem his name.

It wasn't medicine enough. O'Doull watched his father die slowly of the scandal and the pain – and the alcohol that calmed the pain. Cancer had got into his liver, had spread, and he had refused to fight it.

A year ago, O'Doull had flown back to Newfoundland for the funeral, then returned to Ottawa: moody, contemplative, immersed deeper in his dreams. Again he asked for a transfer to the Criminal Investigation Division and again was refused.

His workmates considered him a character. Eccentric. Vague. Forgetful. Lately, there was a new quality. With his father's death had come a toughness, a cynicism, a dry bite to his quiet humour.

They called him "Newf." He hated that. His given name

was worse. There had been an uncle Theophile, and in remembering Uncle Theophile in the name of their only son, his parents had been the cause of later suffering. The name led to an apparently comical appellation: Thewf the Newf. Or often, worse: Thewfie the Newfie. One of the seemingly endless drawbacks to being a Newfoundlander was that one's origins were the source of an unceasing flow of humour. The image advertised was that of a seacoast hillbilly, a hick from the land of fog.

O'Doull worked at the fringes of criminal investigation and learned the processes, but came no nearer to a real criminal than in the courtroom, where often he would be sent to testify – trying to assemble in words easily understood the answer to a lawyer's fumbling question while peering at the nervous prisoner in the box. But the real stuff of CID work was denied him: the assembling of a case, the questioning of suspects, the joining together of the jigsaw.

His daydreams, however, counted hundreds of successful cases, brilliantly resolved. Often, at the end, a woman who had earlier been wrongfully accused would throw herself into his arms. She was dark, alluring, her eyes filled with mystery. If he were alone, at night, his mind would conjure bed and passion.

But the call to action had finally come, late one afternoon as O'Doull was lost in the routines of the laboratory.

"Good news," said the lab superintendent. "You're finally going to the front lines. Kerrivan and Kelly – those dope dealers you went to school with. Inspector Mitchell wants you on the case. Voice identification."

O'Doull thought for a few seconds. Then he said, "No."

But he wasn't given a choice. He was flown the same day to St. John's, and was introduced to the strange world of Operation Potship, where surveillance teams brought back more rumours than fact, where the inspector in charge seemed to operate from a messianic sense of mission.

To O'Doull's disgust, he found himself prying into the private lives of old friends – like Kevin Kelly and his wife Merrie, whom O'Doull had dated in their high-school days. Ultimately O'Doull reached a truce with himself. Kelly's conversations, after all, were the kind that all the world could hear: breezy, easy, and direct, as if he were shouting to a friend across a crowded room. Merrie was the same as ever – unaffected, without malice. O'Doull began to feel like a silent hidden member of the family. He worried when one of the babies was ill; he triumphed quietly when Kelly announced he had gotten work on the inland freighters.

Hidden in a hotel on the edge of the city, O'Doull had been ordered not to see old friends, and not to be seen by the targets. He staved off boredom by working late and poking through the files. Meyers' photographs from Colombia were professional: clean and sharp, and some of them showed Marianne Larochelle's sea-green eyes. In one picture, which O'Doull filched (he had it with him now, in his Miami motel room), she seemed to stare at the lens, as if aware it was there. She seemed to be smiling at him. . . .

The terrorist, armed with a stolen Colt AR15, came at him, firing wildly in all directions. O'Doull, squinting, snapped a shot that sent the man spinning off the wall. There was the sound of semi-automatics burping fire in the embassy drawing room. O'Doull gambled – he flung the door open and dived low, catching the ambassador's daughter around the legs and carrying her, with the momentum, behind a settee. Her skirt had risen, and his hand had slid up her thigh to her hips. His immediate sense was of a gentle, teasing perfume. But there was no time. He lobbed two gas canisters in the direction of the Arab commandos. . . .

O'Doull was battling an unbidden morning erection through all of this. He was disgusted with himself. He turned off the movie in his mind, and got himself to the shower. He felt dragged-out. He realized that last night he had drunk half a bottle of rum.

Thirty minutes later, he was downstairs in the restaurant, looking for Mitchell and Meyers. He saw the inspector at a corner table, by himself. When their eyes met, O'Doull suddenly felt enshrouded in a pall of gloom.

"Did the ship get out?" he asked.

"It's about eighty miles at sea," Mitchell said. "Kelly isn't on it."

Good, O'Doull thought.

"He's in the county morgue."

O'Doull blinked. His mouth went dry.

Mitchell sketched the details Flaherty had given him. "They think Kelly killed the Cuban, but they're not sure what killed Kelly. Heart attack, probably. They're opening his body up now."

O'Doull felt lightheaded. He took a coffee, then waved the waiter away. "My God," he whispered, "we have to call his wife."

"We'll let the Miami police do that," Mitchell said. "It can't come from us. I know you had been friends, but I'm sorry, Theo. We still have an operation."

O'Doull fumbled with the creamer, and squeezed half its contents onto the tablecloth. "The police have made a mistake," he said softly. "Kevin didn't kill anyone. Somebody has dressed some bullshit up on a plate, and we're being asked to eat it." He felt his anger rising.

"You know, Theo, it's time you said goodbye to dreamland and woke up to the real world." O'Doull had an image of the battle-scarred veteran lecturing the green recruit. "We're dealing with hundreds of millions of dollars' worth of narcotic in this operation. The obvious scenario is that Kelly found out Escarlata had been spying for us. He killed him, died himself in the process. That's the way the system works, Theo—if an informer's cover is blown, *he* gets blown. Blown right away. Rats are marked men in the narcotic industry. Targets. I just hope Kerrivan doesn't know. He might abort the trip."

O'Doull's face had turned from white to red. He leaned towards Mitchell and spoke hoarsely. "That scenario reeks, inspector. Kelly committing murder? A heart attack? Come *on*, inspector!"

"Theo, you can't be a cop with tearstains on your face. Let's let Miami homicide do the figuring. They're paid to do it."

O'Doull felt himself teetering at the edge of control, and he was hanging on tight. He looked up to see Meyers peering down at him.

"Massive heart attack," Meyers said. "That's the word from the county medical examiner's office. Still no sign of the murder weapon. That part of it is a little hard to figure out. Good morning, Theo. Hell of a thing, hey?"

Beneath Meyers' bristle military moustache, his mouth was set. The smile was missing.

"*Goddamn it*, Meyers," O'Doull said, almost shouting, "what's going on?" Several other customers turned around to look.

"That freak turned out to be a vicious little fellow, didn't he?" Meyers said. "You never know about people."

O'Doull thought for a second he was going to slug Meyers. He half-rose from his chair. Mitchell put a calming hand on his arm.

"All right, Theo," Mitchell said, "you look into it. Stick around here for another day, and bring me back a report."

"The local boys aren't going to be happy about some outsider butting in," Meyers said.

"You're not going to play Sherlock Holmes, Theo," Mitchell warned. "Just keep from under people's feet, and don't fall over your own. Talk to the pathologist, talk to the detectives. Meyers will show you around. Let's get together a nice clean report on this, without any blurred edges. I don't want Ottawa asking questions we can't answer."

The point is, thought O'Doull, Kelly could not take another's life. Such an act lay beyond the domain of the conceivable. In Newfoundland, Kelly had been a member of a small brave band who stood against the killing of fur seal pups. To him life was a sacred flame. He was awed by all things that grew, or hopped, or creeped, or flew, or swam. He was awed by the magic of life, and had talked about it seemingly forever during those long sessions after lights-out, when adolescent boys debated life and the cosmos, God and eternity.

Kelly had not been much of a fighter. Unless backed to the wall, or defending Kerrivan's name against a slander. A school friend whose imagery was crude once complained that Kelly "thinks the sun shines out of Kerrivan's asshole." He had always been the odd kid in the crowd – following along behind Kerrivan with a sniffly nose, or going off by himself to moon over some private adolescent grief.

O'Doull remembered that Kelly had gotten into mysticism in his teens. He had studied birth charts, Buddhism, Taoism, the *Book of Change*.

Kelly had disappeared suddenly in the summer of 1966. Letters arrived from New York, where he had discovered the East Village scene. O'Doull now realized Kelly had probably been selling pot to support himself that summer. He had come back to Newfoundland in the autumn: a long-haired pilgrim from the land of Leary. He turned people on. O'Doull toked up a few times, but didn't get off. Perhaps he had been too scared to let go. But Kerrivan, of course, flew wide-eyed and feet first into the world of drugs, and he let Kelly lead him through pot, acid, peyote, and the whole roller coaster.

It was soon after that that O'Doull's path diverged from theirs. He refused to reject his parents' values. Corporal O'Doull had been old-line, old-fashioned, stern, disapproving. But he had also been loving, generous, weak. O'Doull had loved him too much to hurt him.

Kerrivan and Kelly sailed the Atlantic a few times, working the hash run from Tangier, then began to operate from Colombia.

Kelly became a full-time smuggler. But he was not a killer.

CHAPTER TWENTY-SIX

From his motel room, while Meyers drove Mitchell to the airport, O'Doull called Operation Potship, raising Constable Hughes in the wiretap room.

"Anything from the ship?"

"I'll check."

After a minute. "Jeez, there's about five minutes on here."

"What time?"

"I don't know. It's a six-hour tape. We put it on at nine o'clock last night."

O'Doull remembered: the transmissions were voice-activated. Unless a monitor happened to be listening, there was no way to pin down the time of a conversation. O'Doull asked the constable to plug the tape machine into the phone.

The first voice on the tape was that of the Miami marine operator. *"This is the marine operator, WOM, calling the* Alta Mar. *Whiskey Bravo, six six three three."* O'Doull presumed the call sign was pirated.

After a few repeats of that, Kerrivan's voice came on. He was angry. *"Jesus! Yeah, this is the* Alta Mar."

The caller was Kelly. His voice was wavering, distant, rising, falling, subject to the blur of static.

"Pete. Pete. Can you hear . . . can you . . ."

"Jesus, boy, all the world can hear!" Kerrivan's voice said. *"What the hell are you doing?"*

There was some sound from Kelly's end, but O'Doull could not make out the words. Kerrivan continued to shout: *"I can't read you. Repeat, I can't read you! Over."*

Then Kelly's voice, suddenly coming in clear: *"Just a minute. Stay with me. Hang on. I'll be back to you."*

The static was gone. There were sounds, muffled or distant. About eight seconds passed. Then Kerrivan's voice: *"Kev? You there?"*

Then Kelly's voice, strong and urgent: *"Deep-six it, boy. Deep-six the cargo."*

Kerrivan: *"Get off your paranoia, Kevin, and get off the fucking phone!"*

The static came back, and Kelly's voice faded into it. Something about "alpha, alpha." A code? "Meyers," "the gypsy's witch," something. The gypsy's witch?

"I can't read!" Kerrivan shouting.

Kelly's voice warbled and died, sputtered back. O'Doull thought he heard the words "jettison the cargo." Then his words were coming clearer: *"Scuttle the ship, Pete!"*

And that was it. A sound like a grunt. A harsh clunk and a clatter.

The operator: *"Sorry, sir . . . noise . . ."*

Kerrivan shouting to her to keep off the air.

Something else, distant. A cry? Or a shriek of static from the ionosphere? The sound triggered a shudder that shot up O'Doull's spine.

A click.

Kerrivan: *"Operator, operator, goddamnit! Come in. Over."*

The operator, distant, wavering: *". . . party . . . hung up."*

A loud *"Shit!"* from Kerrivan. Then his voice calling WOM Miami, requesting the phone number of Escarlata's hotel. Then asking the desk for the penthouse.

"The party does not answer."

"Keep ringing!"

"I am sorry. Your party does not answer."

O'Doull had the constable play it again for him. Then he asked him to send the tape, air dispatch, to his hotel. "Send the original. Keep a slave copy."

"Yeah. Hang on. Maybe you want to listen to this, sergeant. It's a call coming over on Kelly's phone. The missus, talking to her sister."

Hughes plugged him into the Uher tape machine. It was Merrie Kelly's voice: *"He phoned yesterday. He's coming home, sis! He's coming home! God, if I'm preggers, like I think I am, he'll die!"*

"It helps to have friends in the police," Meyers said. "The chief investigating officer, Braithwaite, he's pretty smart, for a spade. He'll give you all the information you need. Mind you, they're busy, busy, busy. We got a couple of murders a day in Dade County. Good name for it: *Dade* County. Get a lot of dade people out here."

O'Doull stared out the window of Meyers' car at a city bleaching in the sun. He had only been in Miami one day, but already the skin of his face felt burned.

"Mostly drug murders," Meyers continued, "although the police have a pact with the tourist bureau to try to tone down the statistics. Scares off the money, you know. The rich Jews from New York, that's what keeps Miami Beach going, and Miami lives off the Beach. Lives off dope, too, if you want to know the truth. Well, we all do, don't we? Me, you, drug cops, the lawyers, the judges – where would we be without drugs?"

A high, dry chuckle.

There was a beep from the pager strapped to Meyers' belt.

"That's my office. I'll have to let you find your way around town on your own after this. I'm too busy, Theo – can I call you Theo? – much too busy. I have a big agency with too much work. Thirty men full time. God knows how many on contract. Spying and protection, that's my business. Security service, uniformed guards, the whole razzle-dazzle. I use Cubans, they're the best. A lot of sickos and dipsticks came over on the boatlift, but some good people, too. We screen the nuts out. Escarlata: I thought he was top-grade material, but he turned out to be a patsy. Soft. Cotton candy. Fell for Marianne's wet vagina and she left him behind. She's a stewardess. You know what they're like. Short on brain, big on pussy. She's been stuffing nose powder up her hole, walking right through customs. The ship whore. That's why Kerrivan brought her along. Nice-*looking*, though, Theo. I'd pay a month's taxes for a little go or two."

O'Doull thought the man was an obscenity.

"Bad luck for Kelly that the little freak left the ship after the caper we pulled. He'd be alive if he hadn't been a coward. By the way, I like your Inspector Mitchell. He went along with it all the way. A lot of cops wouldn't. They like to tie you up with routines. Safe, unimaginative, no room for initiative. I spend half my time fighting my way out of the red tape the snivel servants use to tie up private policing agencies."

Meyers dropped O'Doull at the modern, rambling fortress which was Miami's police building. "Homicide detail, fifth floor. Get a pass at the desk. We'll have a drink before you go back to Canada. You shouldn't be long here."

"As long as it takes."

"Like I said—not long. Dope must give hippies weak hearts."

Braithwaite did not seem anxious to spend any time with O'Doull. "I've got exactly five minutes, then I've got to get out of here. I'm on overtime. We got a murder in Liberty City, and that's the sixth body this week, including the two you're interested in. And the week's only half over. I'm going to quit. We're two hundred men under staff, and I'm

228

working on nerves and chocolate-bar energy."

He went to a drawer and pulled out a thin file. "Look, if it was a politician or a tourist got themselves offed, we'd spend some time at this, but these dirtbag dopers are a dime a dozen. Informers, rip-offs, double crosses – there's a thousand ways and reasons for drug murders. Strictly speaking, you got no business looking at these reports, but the DEA has asked us to co-operate, and we'll do it."

"What time were the bodies found?" O'Doull asked.

"Two o'clock this morning. About there. It's in the report. I've got to go. Look, hell, take a Xerox. It's not as if you're a private citizen."

O'Doull read the sheets as Braithwaite fed them through the duplicating machine. "Who called in the report?"

"Anonymous. A woman. Called the hotel desk downstairs. It's all in there. Maybe there was a hooker in the room. The place is full of them. She does the decent thing at least, by calling the desk. We'll never find her." Braithwaite was edging his way to the door.

"You dust for fingerprints?"

"Yeah, of course." Braithwaite sounded offended.

O'Doull was about to tell him about the taped ship-to-shore call, but he hesitated, then decided to hold onto the information.

"You lift any prints from the phone?" he asked.

"You better check with ident on that. The prints aren't back. Look, I got bodies out there."

O'Doull walked with him. "Did you take a brief from Rudy Meyers about our operation?" he asked. "Do you know what's been going on?"

"Enough to know it's none of our business. I talked to him. I talked to Flaherty. Some big drug deal on its way up to Canada. The Cuban was working for you guys. He loses his cover. He gets killed."

"Any suspects?"

They were at Braithwaite's car now, and the policeman

paused. "What do you mean, suspects? The suspect died already of a heart attack. Talk to the county medical examiner, Jackson Hospital." He opened the door, swung into the car, and started the engine.

"What about the other people from the ship? Could any of them have stayed behind with Kelly?"

"How the hell would I know? Ain't Meyers supposed to be on top of all that?" He slammed the door, tramped the gas pedal, and laid rubber.

O'Doull went back inside and got directions to the identification section. One of the officers checked the file for him.

O'Doull looked over the photographs. "This is the phone? It was on the hook when you arrived, like this?"

"Yeah."

"Prints?"

"Jeez." The man riffled through the cards. "I don't know how we forgot to take lifts from the phone. Jeez, it was right near the body, too."

O'Doull borrowed some fingerprinting equipment.

The assistant examiner at the morgue, Dr. Benitez, was young and eager.

"I state cause of death, that's all I do. I don't say murder, I don't say suicide, I don't say foul play. I say, like here, massive cardiac arrest. Or I say, about the other guy, contusions and lacerations to the brain. That's all I do. Or I can tell you if there's anything in the bloodstream or stomach or urine. High THC content in the cardiac fellow, by the way. That's the narcotic ingredient in cannabis. Marijuana."

"Anything else?"

"Very light alcohol intake. Point zero four at time of death. We took bum temperatures at half-hour intervals. Cooling rate gives us two A.M. time of death, give or take a quarter-hour. That's the cardiac case. Now, with the older guy, we got massive brain injury. The bone and cartilage of the nose are twisted right up into the mid-brain, ripping it to shreds. Both frontal lobes lacerated. Heavy haemorrhaging in the subdural space. Instant death. Near instant, anyway. Zap. Eternity."

"How . . ."

"How does a man get such an injury, you ask? I say foul play. I am not supposed to say it, but I say it. You do not drive your face into your brain by falling on your nose or against the corner of a table. We have a driving blow, enormous force, up and in."

"The guy you call the cardiac fellow. Kelly. Did you check for bruises, cuts?"

"None. No, you couldn't do this with a fist. Everything twisted in." He paused. "Personally, I think there is something strange here. A murder and a heart failure. Coincidental in time. I tell Detective Braithwaite there is something strange here, and he tells me the police have a great many other fish to fry. I talk to the state attorney, and he tells me the police, as he puts it, 'don't have the time to investigate variables other than the scenario that commends itself to obvious reason.' He's a lawyer; that's the way he talks."

"A heart attack could happen during a fight," O'Doull said.

"What fight? I saw photographs. Not a lamp knocked over. The cardiac fellow: no bruising on the chest. The heart just fails. An explosive coronary. No evidence of thrombosis, no arterial blockages. But one of the lungs collapses. Why? It just collapses. I don't have a theory. A couple of bruises on the arm, but they could be old. Well-nourished, well-developed specimen. Slight obesity, but not your standard cardiac candidate."

He looked through his notes. "I took a swab from what was left of the brain man's nostrils. Analyzes for erythroxylon. Cocaine."

CHAPTER TWENTY-SEVEN

At the bottom end of the Miami city limits near Coral Gables, O'Doull found the district of Coconut Grove. The area was mixed ritz-hip. The Mangrove Arms Hotel was outwardly sedate, apparently luxurious.

A young woman in a tight dress sat in a corner of the lobby, her legs crossed. She looked poised for action.

The clerk wore a shirt open three buttons from the top. A gold chain was twined among the dark hairs on his chest.

"I'm a police officer," said O'Doull. He did not show identification. Explanations of his exact status would complicate things. "It's about the murders in the penthouse."

"You're kind of late," the clerk said. "Everybody else left twelve hours ago."

"You were on duty last night?" O'Doull asked.

"Found the bodies. You got my name? It's J.R. Peabody. A lady called, switchboard put her through to me, told me I'd better check the penthouse. An emergency. Then clicked off."

O'Doull pulled out the duplicates of the police reports, showing, for the benefit of J.R. Peabody, the printed name of the Miami Police Department. "That checks out," he said. "Did you see anyone go up the elevator or come down from it around two o'clock?"

"People come. People go."

"Girls?"

"Girls, boys, women, men. I don't notice."

"I guess you're not supposed to notice."

"What does *that* mean?"

"It means this place looks as if it runs a call-girl service."

"This is an expensive hotel, officer. We cater to a lot of businessmen on expenses. We look after them. Valet parking, twenty-four-hour room service, anything they want to order up. If our customers want a girl in their room, we don't make a habit of complaining about it. The company that owns the hotel also owns an escort service. Everything is honest, and everything is discreet."

This kind of operation was something new in the ken of Theophile O'Doull. He was trying to be cool and worldly, but he felt like a yokel just in from the farm.

"'Everything is discreet,'" O'Doull repeated. "I suppose that means you are not going to tell me if you *did* see a woman go up or come down the elevator." The woman who phoned the desk *had* to have been in the room.

The clerk answered the ringing phone, then scribbled a number on a piece of paper. He motioned to the woman who had been sitting in the lobby chair. She came over, took the note, and disappeared in the direction of the elevators. Peabody didn't look O'Doull in the eyes.

"Did you send a woman up to the penthouse last night, Mr. Peabody?"

"No."

"If you're lying, I'll have this place closed. You'll be charged with keeping a common bawdy house." It was a desperado tactic, O'Doull knew. He had no idea what the Florida morals statute said.

"No," the clerk repeated. "I'm being level, officer. No. For sure. I don't know all the girls. If a lady walked off the elevator, I might not know her. I can't remember."

O'Doull guessed he was lying. "I want to go up to the room," he said.

There was a slight sheen of dampness on Peabody's forehead. "You can't," he said. "I want a search warrant."

"If we come back with a search warrant, we'll tear the place apart room by room and take you in for questioning, Peabody." O'Doull tried to imitate the voice of a made-for-TV-movie cop.

The clerk's voice dropped. "Look, detective, if I send you up there, my nuts are on the chopping block, and you'll be putting yours up there beside them. The boss sent a guest up to the penthouse. He's a VIP."

"Just a minute," O'Doull said. "You mean your boss is letting someone use the *same* suite where two people were killed not twenty-four hours ago? Did anyone pause to clean up the blood?"

"This is a hotel. Empty rooms lose money. It's spic and span. The cleaning lady went through it. You fellows left a mess."

O'Doull muttered a soft profanity. He hoped the cleaning woman had not wiped the phone.

"What about Mr. Escarlata's personal effects?" he asked.

"What about them?" Peabody said. "You guys have them."

"Oh, yeah, I forgot," O'Doull said. "Is there a woman up there now?"

"Yeah." Peabody narrowed his eyes and grinned darkly at O'Doull. "Maybe you better decide to wait until tomorrow. The man ain't going to let anyone in unless I phone ahead."

"He'll be in bed."

"Yeah," said the clerk, "he'll be in bed."

Okay, O'Doull thought. That lessened the chance of the man further smudging the living-room phone. "I'll be back. I'm going to call headquarters."

"Pay phone's around the corner."

There were two coin phones and two house phones. The

234

switchboard operator put him through to the penthouse. O'Doull knew there was another phone in the bedroom.

The man who answered conveyed his irritation in two words. "Hello. Yes."

"It's Mr. Peabody at the desk, sir. Would you care for any refreshments? Compliments of the management, of course." He affected a high voice, similar to Peabody's.

"Send up a cold pitcher of Margueritas, and a couple of good cigars. Good cigars. Bering coronas in the aluminum casings."

O'Doull waited until Peabody's back was turned, then slipped into the stairwell. He took the elevator from the second floor to the top.

A heavy man in a robe opened the door. He looked puzzled. "Are you room service?"

O'Doull gently shouldered his way in, flashed his RCMP badge quickly, and, before the man could focus on it, announced he was O'Doull, from the police. "I won't be long." He went to the living-room phone and dusted it with print powder.

"What's going on?"

"There was a murder here last night," O'Doull said.

The man's eyes popped; his jaw dropped.

O'Doull found seven possibles, and lifted them from the phone. He was looking for finger and thumb impressions around the earpiece or mouthpiece, where one would normally grasp a dangling phone to return it to the hook. There were two prints from the earpiece.

"Have you used this phone?" O'Doull asked.

"No."

"What about whoever's in the bedroom with you?"

"Got here before I did." O'Doull made for the bedroom.

"Please don't go in there, officer." O'Doull opened the door.

"I am telling you *not* to go in there." O'Doull went in.

The two women did not bother to cover themselves.

O'Doull saw one of them hide something under the mattress. A rubber dildo, he thought, and a short leather strap. He was smiling bravely.

"Have either of you used the phone in the other room?"

Both of them shook their heads. One was dark, possibly Latin, and wore black stockings hooked to a garter belt. The other was blonde and flat-chested, and wore nothing.

O'Doull, feeling silly, peeked under the bed, as if he might find a murderer hiding there. Or, he told himself, an overlooked weapon.

"There's just the two of us," the blonde said. "Ain't nobody under the bed, officer. You busting us or something?"

"*You* could use a bust, Cherrie," said the dark-haired woman.

O'Doull was about to leave the bedroom, when he turned around. "Do you girls work this hotel regularly?" he asked. "The hotel, the street out front?"

The Latin woman shook her head. "I work up in Lauderdale. Cherrie called me in for tonight. She needed an extra."

"Yeah, this is my territory," Cherrie said. "You're on the murder team, huh? I split right out of the hotel when the cops came by last night."

"Where were you just before that?"

"Fourteenth floor. For a couple of hours. Eighth floor after midnight for an hour, hour and a half. I wasn't nowhere near the floor, if that's what you're asking, and I didn't see nothing."

"At two A.M., where were you?"

"Lobby. Cocktail lounge."

"See anyone come down in the elevator? A woman?"

She looked at him for a long time. "I ain't going to court. I ain't keen on giving evidence, you know."

"No court. This is just for me. It's important."

The women's trick came to the bedroom door, interrupting. "Look, officer, I've just phoned the desk. They tell me

236

you don't have a search warrant. Get out of here, or I'll have you on report in ten seconds." He was red and shaking.

O'Doull stood his ground. He stilled his nervousness, and smiled at him. "I don't think you want to do that, sir," he said. "After all, if I *did* have a search warrant, I might have to seize the evidence." He reached under the mattress. His right hand pulled out the strap and the dildo. The man opened his mouth, then closed it without saying anything. He backed away from the door.

O'Doull's left hand had found something else, small, cylindrical, soft, slightly damp. He pulled it out. A string dangled from it.

"Did you put this in here?" he asked the women.

They shook their heads. They were both giggling.

"What is it?" Too late, he knew the answer. He was blushing.

"Tampon," Cherrie said. "It looks a little used."

"Right, right," O'Doull said. "Of course." He slipped it into an envelope.

"You asked me if I saw a lady in the lobby around two o'clock," Cherrie said. "I *did* notice someone walk out the front door about ten or fifteen minutes before the police came. Not a regular. A real good looker, I hate to say. I always look the competition up and down pretty good. She was high class."

O'Doull felt a little knot of unhappiness. "Blonde?" he asked.

"Yeah. About my height. Short hair. She wasn't dressed up or nothing, and I thought that was weird. Just jeans and a shirt, no heels, no makeup even. Didn't see her eyes. I think she took a taxi. She had a travelling bag with her."

"Would you recognize a photograph of her?"

"Yeah, maybe. If she's trying to work out of here, she better clear it with a few of us."

He arranged to meet the prostitute back at the hotel the next evening, before she went on shift.

It was two A.M. Twenty-four hours since the murders.

O'Doull was watching a whodunit on the late show. At the end, annoyed, he flicked the set off. He had guessed wrong. The murderer had turned out to be the woman, the mistress of the rich industrialist.

The murderer is always the person you don't *want* to be the murderer, he thought. That's the way they construct these damn movies. They set you up.

For about the tenth time in the last hour and a half, he studied the photograph.

Marianne Larochelle, smiling at him.

CHAPTER TWENTY-EIGHT

"You're good," she said. "How did you know where to find me?"

"I knew the hotel is full of stewardesses, and people on the run like the comfort of familiar surroundings." He smiled. "It was cyanide trioxide, wasn't it? Paralyzes the heart muscles, then disappears without a trace."

"You *are* good." Her .357 Magnum was pointed at his gut.

"You sprinkled it into his bag of pot. All it took was one toke." He moved closer to her, his eyes looking deeply into hers. "You won't kill me," he said.

The gun fell to the floor. She was in his arms. He felt her hands tug at his zipper, and her warm fingers curl around his cock. . . .

But it was O'Doull's own hand. He withdrew it, lay sweating on the bed, counting slowly backwards from a thousand. Then he got under a cold shower.

Before going down for breakfast, he called Meyers' home number.

"I didn't wake you," he said.

"Of course not. It's my practice to fall asleep every night exactly at midnight, and to wake at six o'clock. Six hours sleep. A disciplined, regular routine. A precise order of habit patterns gives a continuity to life, Theo."

"I'll have to try it."

"Do you need a ride to your plane?" Meyers asked.

"Not yet. Are you sure Marianne Larochelle is on the ship?"

There was a silence. "What do you have in mind, Theo?"

"I have in mind she's not. Still here, or back in Canada."

"What makes you say that?"

"I'm just covering the bases."

"Maybe you're onto something, O'Doull. The dame who called the desk at the hotel – could be her. And she *was* laying Escarlata. Maybe she couldn't get enough of it. I hear he was quite a cocksman. Anyway, we'll find out when the ship pulls in. If you've got some theory, you should talk to Detective Braithwaite about it."

"I don't think he's interested in theories. They clutter up his simple case."

"What's *your* theory?"

"Assuming for the moment that she's involved, I would guess she would hang around here, lying low, waiting for the heat to die."

"If she's doing that, she's picked the perfect part of the world. There are five hundred hotels in Miami Beach alone, maybe another two thousand apartment hotels. And they're all empty in April."

O'Doull stopped off at the police station and gave the fingerprint lifts to one of the officers working on the file.

Braithwaite scowled at him when he walked into the homicide office.

"Look, O'Doull, I know what you've been up to. My phone has been burning off the hook over the business at the hotel last night. I'm up to my armpits in shit over it."

"The guy in the hotel room," O'Doull said. "He complained?"

"He's a circuit court judge down from Tallahassee. He was there sawing off a quiet piece of ass. You bust in like you own the place. No search warrant. No goddamn authority whatsoever. A cop with – what is it you've got, an Irish accent? – that's what the state attorney's office said. I covered as best I could, said it was some dumb rookie. Get the hell out of this country, O'Doull."

"I'm on official business, detective. It's cleared with the DEA." He hoped. "Check with my boss in Canada, or check with Jessica Flaherty."

"I damn well will. I thought at first, okay, you can snoop around. You're not costing the U.S. taxpayer a nickel. Who knows, maybe you'll find out there's someone else implicated. Instead, you've been running around like some cockass Sam Spade."

"I picked a couple of things up –"

"If it's not going to grab me, don't tell me. Don't give me theories. We've got a reputation for unsolved crimes around here we'd like to ignore. This one is solved. Don't try to add to the list."

"Dr. Benitez –"

"I'm up to here with Dr. Benitez. Everything's the crime of the century when Benitez gets to carve up the body. He's got some grandiose delusion he's a two-fisted coroner out to expose lazy cops. The lazy cops around here are working triple overtime for piss-all. Don't give me complex theories, O'Doull. It always turns out the right one is the logical one, which was the obvious one all along. If you kick a guy's nose into his brain, you're a candidate for heart seizure."

"There was no blood on Kelly's boots. Where's the murder weapon? Dr. Benitez says it would take something as heavy as a crowbar –"

"Dr. Benitez! Don't give me any more Dr. Benitez!"

O'Doull went to the airport to pick up the tape, then phoned an electronics firm and arranged to rent their laboratory facilities. "I'm working for the U.S. Drug Enforcement Administration," he told them.

Then he checked in with Operation Potship.

Braithwaite *had* contacted his boss.

"O'Doull, I warned you not to play detective," Mitchell shouted at him. "You're going to cause a goddamn international incident. Get back here, before you get charged with impersonating a police officer."

"I'm coming, I'm coming. I don't think Larochelle is on the ship."

"What?"

"Nobody saw her leave on the ship."

"Theo, leave the heavy stuff to the Miami police. I want you back to help us land our fish. On the double, O'Doull."

O'Doull made inquiries at Air Canada to find out where its stewardesses stayed in Miami, then rented a Dodge Dart and drove to a hotel near the airport. It was a hunch.

"I'd like to look at your check-ins Tuesday, after midnight. I'm a policeman."

O'Doull was handed registration slips. A Mr. and Mrs. Nesbitt from Ohio checked in just after two A.M. A Mr. Schaffer at two-fifteen. A Gabrielle Hubert several minutes later. No one after that until the dawn hours. Gabrielle Hubert was from Montreal. Someone had marked "Air Canada discount" on the slip. Room 714.

"Do you know if she's in the room?"

"You can phone her."

"Do it for me. Ask her if she's planning to stay another night."

There was no answer from the room.

O'Doull went to the bar and had a rum and soda. In an hour, he returned to the desk. "Can you try again for me?"

Again, no answer.

"Can I have a key to the room?" O'Doull asked.

"No."

"I'm investigating a murder."

"May I see your identification?"

O'Doull hid in the corner of the lobby until the clerk took a coffee break. "I'm afraid I left my key in my room," he told the relief clerk. "Room 714. My name is Gabriel Hubert." O'Doull crossed his fingers. The clerk gave him the key.

There was a "Do Not Disturb" card dangling from the doorknob of 714. O'Doull put his ear flat against the door and heard a soft sound of voices.

He put the key in the lock and quietly pushed the door open.

The room was empty. The bed was mussed and a soap opera was playing on the television set. He stepped inside and closed the door. The air seemed to cloy his nostrils.

"I have a gun on you," a voice said. "I will kill you."

CHAPTER TWENTY-NINE

O'Doull walked straight ahead, towards the bed, past the wan-looking version of the woman whose eyes had so often peered at his through the glossy finish of a colour photograph. She was standing by the bathroom doorway with a gun in her hand.

"My name is Theophile O'Doull," he said. "I am a policeman." He put a hand into his inside jacket pocket.

"Don't," she said faintly.

"I am going to put my wallet on the bed, open to my badge and to my identification. Then I will back away and you can look at it. I don't have a gun."

He went to the window, and turned to watch her approach the bed. She looked drawn, fragile, and the green of her eyes was subsumed in the darkness of hugely dilated pupils.

O'Doull had an urge to touch her that was almost overwhelming.

" 'Sergeant O'Doull,' " she read. " 'RCMP.' God, I've got it coming at me from every side." She put the gun in her purse. O'Doull saw it was a snub-nosed revolver, a .32. "I bought it in a store yesterday," she said. "A woman can't be too careful in Miami. Sit down. I can't offer you anything. Unless you'd like to do a little cocaine. I've been tooting it, smoking it. Christ, if I had an outfit, I'd be cranking it. Getting myself so goddamned wired I can't stop moving."

Her motions were jerky, her speech choppy and quick.

On the bedside table was a package of cigarette tobacco, a mirror, a razor blade, cigarette papers, a small test tube with a cork stopper. It was half filled with white powder.

"You're late," she said, pacing. "I've been busted already and let go. You know all about it, I guess. I was on the ship. I went along for the ride, and the ride got a little too wacky, so I got off."

Larochelle was wearing blue jeans and a loose blouse. There were dark areas under her eyes which to O'Doull seemed extravagantly beautiful.

"I'm not co-operating," she said. "I'm not giving statements. The people are friends of mine. I wish them luck, but I'm not a part of it any more. I can't be arrested twice for the same offence, right? That's the law. How did you find me? You must be pretty smart for a narc."

She sat on the edge of the bed, then stood up and walked to the window. "You're not going to turn me in for nose candy, are you? Only a couple of grams left. You won't bust me for that." O'Doull just stood by the window. "Doesn't look like you're planning to, anyway."

She went to the bed table, pulled a pinch of tobacco, and rolled it between her palms, and into a cigarette paper. Then she began hunting frantically around the room for matches.

O'Doull pulled a penny pack from his pocket, struck a match, and held the flame to her cigarette. She placed a trembling hand on his while she lit it. O'Doull felt a shiver run through him at her touch.

She shut off the television set. "I usually don't watch this crap," she said. "I'm bored. Any sort of low-level diversion will do." She paused, steadying one hand with the other as she held the cigarette to her lips. "So, a cop walks into my life. He adds more drama to it. What do you want?"

"Why weren't you answering your phone?"

"Too busy trying to stay loaded to chit-chat with anyone. But you are here, Sergeant O'Doull. We are chit-chatting."

"You registered under a false name."

"What do you want? I'm sorry, would you like a cigarette? I didn't think."

"No, thanks." Then, "Okay, yeah." O'Doull rarely smoked, but he was feeling jangled. Larochelle's pacing was unnerving.

She rolled up another cigarette. "Do you turn on? I could put some pizzazz into the cigarette. Ever smoke a bazooko? They're usually made with coke base. You can guess why they call them bazookos. Look, don't just sit there staring at me like a puppy dog. What do you want?" She put on a deep voice, "Like, what's happenin', man? What's shakin'?"

"Why are you staying on in Miami? For a holiday?"

"Yeah, I love airport hotels. The sound of planes out the window makes me happy. What do you want, Sergeant O'Doull?"

"You may be implicated in a murder, Miss Larochelle."

Her face turned white. "Holy mother of God," she said. For a while, the only sound was the whirr of the air conditioning unit.

"I'm not very good at this end of the police business, Miss Larochelle. I'll tell you what I know, and you can decide to talk to me if you want. Oh, I forgot. I have to give you a warning. You don't have to say anything, and anything you say can be used against you."

"You have got to be kidding." There was a catch in her voice.

"Two nights ago two men were found dead in the penthouse suite of the Mangrove Arms Hotel. Kevin Kelly, Augustin Escarlata. I think you are acquainted with them." He felt he sounded pompous. Larochelle sat down heavily on the bed, took a deep pull on her cigarette and blew out a stream of smoke.

"I believe you were in the hotel around two A.M. I believe you made a phone call to the lobby reporting the deaths."

She shook her head.

"I think you were in the room when they died."

This time there was no reaction. Her eyes were large and damp.

"We have your fingerprints on the telephone." It was a small lie, but O'Doull was sure her prints were there. "Also, you left something under the mattress in the bedroom." He cleared his throat. "I think it is possible that you removed a tampon and inserted that test tube of cocaine in your vagina before you left." Again, he cleared his throat.

Her smile was unexpected. It was a flicker of a smile, and quickly disappeared. Ash from O'Doull's cigarette fell on his knee.

"Escarlata was killed with a blunt instrument. I'm not sure about Kelly. A heart attack, they think."

Larochelle took a deep breath. Her words came softly. "Do you think I murdered Augustin? With what you call—a blunt instrument? Do you *think* that?"

There was a smile again, a sad one. Her lips were pale.

"Do you think that, sergeant? Would I have murdered someone, and then phoned the hotel to report the murder? Did your witness see me walk out of the hotel with my blunt instrument?"

Her eyes were blinking rapidly.

Suddenly tears were streaming. She didn't wipe the tears but let them run, her hands still on her lap.

"Help me," she said. "Please help me."

O'Doull clung desperately to his chair, holding himself back.

"I'm afraid. Oh, God, I'm afraid."

"What happened, Miss Larochelle? What are you afraid of?"

"Meyers. Rudy Meyers. Oh, God, he's trying to kill me, too."

CHAPTER THIRTY

O'Doull went to the bed, and was at her side. She was sobbing brutally.

"They've been watching the hotel," she said. "They work for him, I'm sure of it. He's hunting me." She held his arm. He could feel her fingernails digging into the muscle. "It's not just the cocaine. I *know* they're out there."

"What happened?"

"I'm sure he killed them. I saw him in the lobby. He was coming off the elevator. I didn't think he had seen me.Then I went up to the room, to the penthouse . . . I saw them, dead . . . Oh, God . . . I was panicking, I freaked . . . I came down with my bag . . . I went out. He was there, following me. He had blood on his sleeve. I got a taxi, and came here. He must have traced me here somehow."

O'Doull felt a spasm of shuddering run through her body. He knew he should be making notes, but there would be time later to get a statement. He wanted desperately to believe her, and although he felt he heard truth in her voice, he knew he had nothing to corroborate the presence of Meyers in the hotel that night. Meyers had told him he slept from midnight to six A.M. A disciplined routine, he had said.

"Did anyone else see him?"

"Yes, of course, the clerk. The night clerk."

"Anyone else hanging around there? Any girls?"

"A pross, you mean? I . . . I think so. Maybe."

"Miss Larochelle, the clerk didn't mention anything about a man in the lobby around two A.M."

She drew back and stared at him. "My God, you don't think I'm *lying*, do you? The night clerk saw him. That pimp! He *saw* Meyers. He said hello to him. Oh, God, please believe me!"

O'Doull tried to remember. Had he *asked* about a male person? Or had his mind been fixed upon a woman, the woman who phoned? But Meyers had no reason to kill the two men. Not Escarlata certainly, his own informer.

Larochelle took his shirt in the ball of her fist. "Please, Sergeant O'Doull, help me. Get me out of Miami. I've been sitting here going crazy. I went out once . . . for the gun . . . I'm sure someone was following me . . . Meyers . . . I don't know. God, when you opened my door, I was in hysterics. I thought it was him."

"Why did you run away from the murder scene?"

"Oh, Christ, I was just thinking: murder, police, I'm going to get busted again if I stay. I grabbed my bag from the bedroom. I knew I was going to need the cocaine. I traded it for the tampon. Oh, God, I just ran! . . . I can't remember. I must have phoned the hotel about the bodies. I shouldn't have, maybe."

"What were you afraid of?" O'Doull asked.

She wept quietly for a while. "I was high. I panicked. Coke twists your head. You know what I do for a living. The flight attendant thing – that's just a sideline. I can't afford to be around bodies. I just wanted to get home, back up to Canada. That's all I was thinking."

"Do you know why Meyers would want to kill them? What do you know about him?" He felt he was asking too many questions at once. But it was important to get what he could from her now, while she was vulnerable, while she was talking.

She drew away and looked at him. "He's working for *you*. He's a narc, isn't he? Boy, you guys have a tiger by the tail."

"He's helping us, yes . . ."

"That's why he killed Kevin. Kevin blew his cover!" She spoke slowly, then accelerated. "I went out that night to score a little dust, and Kevin was coming in. He said: 'I got the inside scoop on Meyers.' That's what he said. He said: 'I was right all along.' I don't know how he found out. He was in a smoke-easy, he said. They have these underground bars in Miami, where you can smoke dope. He must have met somebody on the inside, somebody who knew. He had always suspected. But that night he was certain. Jesus Christ, I need a hit."

She got up, went to the night table, and chopped two lines of cocaine with the razor blade.

"I guess he went up to the penthouse and confronted Meyers. Meyers killed him. Somehow. How did he do it? And Augustin. Oh, God." She ran to the bathroom. O'Doull heard her coughing and spitting. She probably had nothing in her stomach by now, if she had been throwing up like this all day. After a few minutes she returned, and rolled up a bill, and snorted the two lines.

"You're sure that's wise?" O'Doull said.

"I'm not looking for wisdom. I'm looking for escape."

"Why would he kill Augustin?"

"I don't know, I don't know. Kill one, kill two, what's the difference?" The coke, strangely, seemed to calm her. "Jesus, you guys are going to be doing some fancy covering up on this one." She sat beside him again. "God, two days in Miami and my world has fallen apart. Can they charge me with anything? In Canada? I *did* leave the boat."

"No," O'Doull said. "Unless you try to meet the ship when it comes in."

"Take me back to Canada with you. I'll try to co-operate. I'll give a statement. Not against the guys on the ship. But for the murders." She began rolling another cigarette.

"They'll never charge Meyers, will they? They'll cover it up, maybe try to pin it on somebody else. Or just write it off as another unsolved crime. Oh, shit, get me out of here. Take me back to Canada!"

"I'm not going back just yet," O'Doull said. "Maybe not for a day or two. But I'm going to take you with me now."

"Where?"

"We're going back to the hotel, and I'm going to ask a few more questions."

"I *know* the clerk saw me, sergeant. Peabody. He introduced himself to me."

"We'll see."

She smiled a little. "Am I your prisoner?" She started undoing her blouse. "I'm going to have a shower. If I'm allowed."

She went into the bathroom, and O'Doull waited until he heard the sound of the shower, then he began to go quickly through her handbag and travelling case. The gun he put in his pocket. He found some loose marijuana in her purse. It smelled sweet and powerful. In the travelling case: clothing, jewellery, travellers' oddments. He carefully removed some undergarments and probed around with his other hand.

"Are you going to try them on, or what?" She was leaning against the bathroom doorway, watching him. He realized he was holding a pair of bikini panties in his hand. "Is there anything else you want to see?" she said. "Just ask; I'll show you." She let the towel slip from her body, then disappeared behind the shower curtain.

The bathroom door was open. O'Doull knew that if he remained standing by it, he would see her stepping out of the shower. He took a deep breath, forced himself away, and opened a window, letting the warm air fan him.

He heard the shower turn off, and heard her voice behind him.

"If you're shy, don't turn around. Do you buy dinner for prisoners? Should I wear a bra?"

O'Doull pretended to be interested in the Eastern Airlines jetliner that was passing outside, accelerating noisily as it climbed over Miami.

"The gun isn't loaded, by the way," she said. "I didn't even buy any bullets for it. I don't know anything about guns. It was just to scare him off."

He turned around. She was standing in the middle of the room, watching him. She was wearing a simple green dress, no makeup. She had not even tried to cover the darkness under her eyes. It gave them a soulful quality.

"I'm ready," she said.

O'Doull noticed the cocaine was gone, packed no doubt in her nightcase which he, gallantly, was carrying for her.

As she paid her hotel bill, O'Doull glanced about the lobby and outside, through the windows. He saw no one who looked as if he might be one of Meyers' crew. He led Larochelle to his car.

"We have a few hours to kill," he said. He looked at his watch: three o'clock. The night clerk would not be on duty until about seven. "We'll take a drive."

He followed a map to the West Dade Expressway, then turned south, to the Keys. Larochelle didn't speak, but seemed to be getting nervous again. She was fidgeting.

They were ten miles down the expressway. "What are you looking at?" she said. His eyes had been studying the rear-view mirror.

"The panel truck behind us – I passed it a few miles back, and now it's just sitting there, a hundred yards back." In the left lane, a Ford station wagon accelerated past him about fifty yards, then slowed to O'Doull's speed. "And that guy was behind us almost all the way from the hotel. Watch for a third vehicle."

O'Doull knew that experts followed in three-car teams, trading positions to avoid detection.

After a while, the third vehicle appeared, an Oldsmobile, moving between him and the panel truck. There were two men in it. There were also two men in the station wagon. He had seen only one in the panel truck.

O'Doull raised his speed by eight miles an hour and held it for six miles. The vehicles in front and in back of him maintained their distances. Then he slowed by fifteen. The Oldsmobile raced past him, ahead of the station wagon. O'Doull got a glimpse of the two men in the Oldsmobile. The driver was black, the passenger looked Latin. The panel truck remained behind him.

O'Doull's car followed the station wagon over the bridge to Key Largo. As they drove through Islamorada, O'Doull spotted the Oldsmobile sitting by a roadside café. It began to follow them again. The panel truck had now disappeared, but the station wagon was still in front of him.

They pulled into a hamburger stand. O'Doull saw the Oldsmobile drive past, without slowing. Then the panel truck. The driver had a hand microphone raised to his mouth.

After a few minutes O'Doull pulled out and carried on a little farther on the Key West highway. He saw nothing following them. O'Doull began to wonder if he had been daydreaming again. Perhaps he *wanted* to believe Larochelle's story about people following her, wanted to believe the business about Meyers.

They were on Grassy Key when he next saw the station wagon, coming up from behind them. O'Doull spun off the highway onto a gravel driveway, did a backwards U-turn, then returned to the highway, going northeast, towards Miami. The station wagon, then the Oldsmobile, swished past in the opposite direction. Again, O'Doull caught a glimpse of the driver of the Olds, and there was something familiar about him.

"Did you see them?" he asked. "Did they look like the men who had been following you?"

"I think so. I can't be sure. What should we do?"

"Well, one thing we *shouldn't* do is try to outrun them.

This isn't a movie, and I don't have a fast car. In fact, the last thing we should do is convince them we know we're being followed. That's an edge we want to keep."

The Oldsmobile was behind them again. O'Doull took an alternate route from Key Largo to the mainland, off the Number One, onto the 905. The pursuing car remained half a mile behind them. They had been driving for three hours, and dusk was falling.

For the first time since O'Doull had become a policeman, he was feeling a rush of danger. He wondered whether he should try to confront the men in some place public. But if in fact he were dealing with men from Meyers, it was too early to do that, maybe too dangerous.

"Put what you absolutely need into your handbag," he told Larochelle. "We're going to leave your overnight case behind."

"Cocaine, pot, toothbrush, and a spare pair of panties," she said. "Okay, now what?"

"We're going to pull into that Shell station, and I'm going to fill up. You go in like you're going to the washroom. I'll leave the car at the pump with the motor running and go in, too. I'm sure there's a back door, into the alley."

"You're going to leave the car behind?"

"I'll phone and explain, pick the car up later."

It turned out to be easy. The alley was deserted. They skipped between some buildings, onto a dark street, then across somebody's yard to another lane. O'Doull decided to stay there, behind a garage, for fifteen minutes.

Nobody came down the alley.

The air was sultry. Larochelle was standing close to O'Doull, and he could feel her warmth. Be dispassionate about this, he told himself. But he wanted to believe her.

CHAPTER THIRTY-ONE

Larochelle smiled at the night clerk as they entered the lobby. "*Buenas*, Mr. Peabody," she said.

The clerk looked at her, then at O'Doull, then grinned crookedly.

"You know her," O'Doull said.

"Sure, he knows me," Larochelle said. "He wanted to make out with me."

Peabody showed many teeth in a large, strained smile. "This is the girl you were asking about, officer," he said. "Now I remember her. She walked out with a little suitcase. I remember thinking she might be skipping her bill."

Larochelle took O'Doull's hand in a gesture of closeness. "He thought I was a working girl. Didn't you, Peabody? The girls have to pay him off to work around here. He thought he was entitled to something free from me."

"Look," O'Doull said, "I asked you some questions last night and you were so concerned about protecting a call-girl operation, that you couldn't seem to remember a goddamn thing."

"Some things come back. Soon as I saw her, I remembered. She was here that night."

"If he saw me," Larochelle said, "he saw you-know-who."

"A man," O'Doull said. "Walking through the lobby. To

the elevator, or from the elevator. Or both."

"People come and go, like I say. Let's see, there was a guy. Walked through here like an arrow, out the front door."

"Give me a description."

"Only saw the back of his head. Can't remember what he was wearing." Peabody studied the ceiling. O'Doull felt there was something unnatural in the way the man seemed to draw on his memory. As if he were deciding how much to tell.

"Hair?" O'Doull asked.

"Short."

"Short?" said Larochelle. "It was a –"

"Don't," O'Doull said.

But a woman's voice from behind him completed Larochelle's sentence.

"It was a brushcut. Military moustache. Average height. Chunky. Round face. He's a vicious fucker. A killer in bed."

It was Cherrie, the blonde prostitute who had been with the judge in the penthouse. O'Doull guessed she had been standing behind him for a few minutes.

"And this is the girl I saw," Cherrie said. To Larochelle: "I don't mean to get you in trouble, dear." She sounded insincere.

But there was a triumphant expression on Larochelle's face. "She saw him!"

"A killer in bed?" O'Doull repeated.

"I hope I don't mean it literal. But he was savage. He took me upstairs once. I thought he was a cop. Packed a chunk, anyway. Didn't take his jacket off, and I'll tell you, I got a five-inch bruise from the gun. He rents rooms here a lot, for clients, I guess, I don't know what for. Peabody here knows him, don't you, sweetie?"

Peabody had a blank look. Then his face seemed to fill with light.

"Oh, *Rudy*, sure, sure."

"What about Monday night?" O'Doull asked.

Peabody's eyes looked like those of a small, hunted animal. They were flickering about the lobby. O'Doull's patience left him.

"For Christ's sake, just do me a favour and come up front with me for a few minutes. You'll do yourself a favour, too, especially if you want to avoid being an accessory after the fact to a murder."

"Oh, *yeah*, Rudy was here. He often comes by. He went up to one of the rooms for maybe five minutes."

"What room?"

Peabody spoke in a hushed voice. O'Doull began to realize that the man was afraid of Meyers. "I'm not here to get anyone into trouble. I think he went up to the penthouse; I'm not sure. He goes up there once in a while. Friend of the guy there. The guy that got killed."

"Was he up there after midnight?"

Peabody's eyes switched from Larochelle, to O'Doull, to Cherrie, back to O'Doull. "Around the time I seen this lady, I guess. Maybe two A.M.?"

"Two o'clock," Cherrie said flatly. "If I had known you were asking about a guy, not a lady, I'd've told you."

"Did you see him *before* you saw me, or after?" Larochelle asked.

"Uh, after, I think," the clerk said.

"Before," Cherrie said. "He came out. In a hurry. You came down, and walked out. In a hurry."

"Okay, folks," O'Doull said. "I'm going to write out a couple of statements now, and you're going to sign them."

"Like I say, Mr. O'Doull, you've got a tiger by the tail. What are you going to do about it?" Larochelle and O'Doull were sitting in a dark but friendly restaurant in Little Havana. Three guitarists were singing sad songs on a stage.

What, in fact, *was* he going to do about it? Should he talk to Braithwaite? Or get on the blower to Mitchell? Those were uncomfortable alternatives. He didn't feel ready yet to put Mitchell in the picture. He thought about going to Jess Flaherty, who might be more receptive. It was obvious she hated Meyers. There were other things to check out, too. The fingerprints on the phone. The tape. He would try to spend some time on it tomorrow.

"Okay, don't answer," Larochelle said. "The bigger question is, what are you going to do with *me*?"

"Maybe we can find a little hotel for you out in Miami Beach."

"Don't tell me I'm not your prisoner any more? I think I'd rather not be free."

"What does that mean?" he asked. He felt hypnotized by her eyes. A languid, erotic energy seemed to flow out of them. Maybe it's the wine, he thought. They were on their second bottle.

"It means I'm scared shitless. It means that maybe I'd rather shack up with you for the night."

O'Doull could feel his cheeks reddening. He cleared his throat.

"If you're afraid of me, I'll sleep on the floor," she said.

"We'll work something out," he said. He felt weak.

O'Doull had always been fascinated by the women of Montreal. On weekends, he had often escaped to there from the ennui of Ottawa, the boredom of those countless husband-seeking secretaries, so yearning, so lonely. The women of Montreal, by contrast, were elegant, *soignée*, possessed of a cosmopolitan confidence, a chic. But never had any of those alluring canadiennes given O'Doull even an eyelash flicker of hope.

Much more than a flicker of hope was offered by the eyes of Marianne Larochelle – here, in this hot and humid little restaurant; here, in candlelight that seemed to flicker to the beat of guitar and marimba, to the musical poetry of José Marti.

O'Doull's eyes were swimming in hers.

The ship whore, Meyers had called her. O'Doull's gut

twisted in silent fury. At the same time, her amorality made him wary of her, caused him to withdraw. She was liberated, he supposed – although several years ago, before the dawn of the New Woman, he might have thought of it as looseness. He decided to keep a warning light burning somewhere within him.

Tonight, a serenity had replaced the terror that had been in her eyes when they first met. There was a calmness, a sense of self-assurance.

And there was something else in her eyes that he could not read. They were as green as a forest in summer, and as inviting, but they spoke mysteries. Behind the eyes, he felt there was something dark, hidden, trapped.

Nervously, O'Doull began talking about himself, although he suspected there was little enough in his past to excite the imagination of this jet-set cocaine smuggler. But he wanted her to know him better, and talked about his boyhood in the little outports of Newfoundland from which the route to anywhere was by sea. He talked of his loneliness, of the long, empty spaces in his life when as a boy he surrounded himself with his crazy machines, his inventions, his books, his experiments. He talked a little of his father, and of the pain he felt for him.

Through all this, her lips were parted with a gentle perfect smile. After a while, she placed a hand on one of his, and leaned towards him.

"You're nice," she said.

CHAPTER THIRTY-TWO

The air conditioning had been left on in his motel room. It was cold, and he switched it off.

It was one-thirty. O'Doull was feeling tipsy. "I guess you left your pyjamas in your nightcase," he said.

"Pyjamas?" She laughed.

There was one king-sized bed in the room. O'Doull was sitting on the corner of it, watching her.

Larochelle began rolling a joint.

"Just think," she said, "there's another fifty tons of this on the ship. Do you think you'll find it? Do you know where it's coming in?"

O'Doull warned himself to be careful. He hadn't told her about the satellite tracking. Mitchell would explode if he even suspected he was sharing a motel room with her.

"Not talking, huh?" Larochelle said. "You don't trust me; I don't blame you. What will the police do with the pot if they seize it? They'll steal some of it, I guess."

O'Doull was offended. "They'll burn it. At a municipal dump."

She sighed. "What a shame. What a waste. What a world we live in. A fifty-ton bonfire of one-toke dope."

"What's one-toke dope?"

"This stuff." She wiggled the joint at him. "One toke is all you need. One toke and in five minutes you're Mary Poppins, floating on top of the world. *Sinsemilla.* Female flower." She smiled. "The female is deadlier than the male, Theo." She held the joint up to him, with a question in her eyes.

"No, thanks. It doesn't do anything for me."

"And it's against the law, isn't it, Theo? Well, I wouldn't want you to break any laws. I might have to turn you in."

She lit it, and drew on it. O'Doull could smell the heaviness of it in the air. He had tried low-grade Mexican when he was a kid, and had often caught a floating whiff of marijuana here and there during parties in Ottawa, but this seemed different. Larochelle was standing near him.

Then she kneeled in front of him, putting her hands behind his neck, drawing him to her. She placed her lips on his, bringing his mouth open with her tongue, and exhaled. His lungs filled with the smoke from her mouth. He did not withdraw from her, was unable to. Her tongue danced within his mouth. Their lips seemed to hold together forever, fixed with sweet glue.

When she released him, he had to blink the stars away. Tiny swirls of smoke came from his mouth and nostrils. He hoped it was the marijuana. Otherwise, he was on fire.

Larochelle half-closed her eyes and peered at him. She smiled. Her right hand gently stroked his cheek; then she touched her fingers to his lips so lightly he felt only a tingle. With her hand she guided his face to hers, again with a touch so light it seemed to O'Doull that he was being drawn forward by a force that was outside her, but that she controlled. She touched his lips with hers, withdrew, touched again, withdrew, and touched again. Each time, O'Doull felt a flow of energy, an electric pouring-out.

Her eyes had been closed as she kissed him. As she withdrew a little from him, they opened, and O'Doull felt a great pulsing. He was spellstruck, possessed. Her eyes mesmerized him. There was something of a proud, wild animal in them. A cat, a leopard.

She sprang lightly to her feet, and swirled around the room like a ballerina, flicking light switches off. Then in the glow from outside – the Miami moon – she emerged from her dress, a butterfly. The dress twirled around her fingers and floated over her head like a sail.

It came suddenly to O'Doull that he was blasted.

Larochelle's panties fluttered like a leaf to her feet.

O'Doull's mouth was dry and his palms were wet.

She came to him, touching her lips to his ear. "I'm going to take you to places you've never been before," she said.

It was half-past four in the morning.

O'Doull emerged from his motel, onto the street, dizzy, awed. The street was deserted. The lights glowed like saints with haloes. O'Doull was trying to digest the sensation of being this stoned, and was having difficulty relating it to anything in his experience.

An hour before, Larochelle had rolled another joint, and O'Doull, totally abandoned by then, smoked it with her. As they began to make love again, she had started to cry, and held him tightly with her arms and legs, the muscles of her vagina holding him like a vise. After that, she turned cruel, making love to him viciously, causing him pain. She told him she wanted him to hurt her, too. He could not do anything like that. She called him obscene names, in English, in French, in Spanish.

His complaint of dizziness had been an honest one, and he excused himself to walk in the fresh air.

He did not wobble. He was steady on his feet. In fact, he felt light, as if he were weightless in space, or as if his feet were springs. He drifted down the empty streets of the city, along Biscayne Boulevard, up Flagler.

He stared in shop windows and saw small, strange faces staring back. Coloured lights bobbed and blinked in the back of the stores. The air seemed to buzz. An old bum, shoulders slouched, passed him on the street, his shoes

262

making a soft pat-pat as he went by. O'Doull fished a ten-dollar bill from his wallet, called him back, gave it to him, then walked on.

A patrol car cruised towards him, and slowed as it went past. O'Doull waved at the men inside with a smile. They don't know I'm stoned, he thought.

After a while, he stopped walking. He stood on the sidewalk, struck by something that was in his mind, something that he couldn't make out, but which was sending him a signal. He stood for a few minutes, touching his fingers to his forehead, his eyes closed.

Then he began to retrace his steps. He went back half a block, and studied the sign on the door.

"Joe Mitsui," it said. "Martial Arts Studio." A smaller sign described Mitsui as a master of Shotokan karate, a sixth dan "shihan." Tae Kwon-Do, third dan. He looked at the photographs for a while, then returned to the motel.

CHAPTER THIRTY-THREE

Joe Mitsui looked about thirty-five. He told O'Doull his age was fifty-four.

"I was born in California," he said. "I'm American in my bones, but I like to think my spirit is in the East. After the war, I studied in Japan and in Korea. I spent twenty years learning. After all these years, I know a little, but it is very little. I describe myself as a master, but that is just arrogance and conceit. There are teachers in Japan who would toss me in circles. I would be a three-year-old in their eyes, taking my first stumbling steps. Let me close out this class, and then we can talk."

There were six men and two women in the class. They wore white, yellow, and green belts.

"Open your eyes," he said. "Now touch one another. Touch your fingers upon each other. Touch the face. Smile at each other. Thank you. Practise the breathing methods for next week, my friends. Thank you. Thank you." He bowed, and they bowed and left for the dressing rooms.

O'Doull was feeling flabby, un-toned. And exhausted. After he had returned to the motel, Larochelle had given him a final burst of strength and they had stayed awake for another hour before releasing themselves to sleep.

"Some come here seeking an experience, a new religion," Mitsui said. "They are looking for titillation. The martial arts are spreading like junk food through America. We westerners are always seeking newness, and so the martial arts become a fad. But the truth of karate is zen, and the aim of zen is satori, enlightenment, the unifying of the spirit. I fear that America is not yet ready for such enlightenment."

Mitsui smiled gently, somewhat wistfully. "It is so easy to sell out to the values of this country. I have done so. When I came back from Japan, karate and kung fu were catching on. Heck, I just climbed on top of the wave and surfed right into a comfortable business. My capitalist heritage took over. I have a boat, an acre on the water, kids at university, too many comforts."

He offered O'Doull a hard chair, and took one himself. "You want to know about commando karate. That kind of business, we don't teach. We are not interested in death; we are interested in life." He shrugged. "But I know the movements, the killing touches, the thirty-seven kyusho points. You learn them in order to avoid them."

O'Doull described the condition of the bodies of Kelly and Escarlata. Mitsui nodded from time to time, without change of expression.

"Let me instruct you," Mitsui said. "Westerners often express disbelief. They are not ready to accept the possibilities. Let me explain first that we are all surrounded by energy fields. Force fields. There is skill to organizing these fields, amassing their energy, directing them. There is a life force, *ch'i* which, when concentrated, focussed like an electric beam, can split a ten-foot block of ice, can drive spikes into concrete. I'm not talking about any strange psychic power, sergeant. It's in all of us, but few of us learn how to use it, and it is in knowledge, not strength, that the power lies. I am a humble beginning student when I think of the knowledge of others." There was a hint of Oriental lilt to his voice, as well as a warmth.

"There are practitioners of such subtle ability they can touch a man at a certain time and certain place, and two weeks later that man will die. This is called the delayed death touch. There are those who can fog your vision. There are those who can create a wall with their mind through which no blade can penetrate. These are the masters, the artists. Those versed in the so-called art of commando karate are merely butchers. Cave men."

As he took this in, O'Doull was trying to amass his own personal force field to beat back his fatigue.

"The West often seizes upon something that is good, as I say, and corrupts it. War then corrupts it even further, twists it, and makes it evil. This is how commando karate was born – through war. It is karate without the centring of the spirit, without love of your fellows, without a soul. There is only the idea of the kill. The kill is everything. And, of course, it is quite easy. The ability to make swift killing moves is nothing, and can be learned by the meanest of men. I could come up to you, Sergeant O'Doull, and touch you in nine different places and cause you instant death. It would be play."

O'Doull urged a smile.

"Any black belt – it matters not how high a dan – can make the kills that are trained in commando schools. The two deaths that you described do not involve any extreme level of expertise, although admittedly one was more subtly engineered than the other."

"Okay, start with the man by the door, with his face smashed," O'Doull said. "There were some broken face bones."

"A basic commando kill," Mitsui said. "It is done with either a middle knuckle fist or with a palm heel, up and in and twisting, so the nasal bones will rip the brain tissue." He demonstrated with his arms and hands. The movement was sharp, snapping, so fast that O'Doull almost missed it. Mitsui repeated. His arm shot forward like a steel coil suddenly released, his fingers bent at the middle knuckles, his hand twisting.

266

"If you have control over your energy field, there is much more power, of course. The other fellow, as I say, his case involved some more technique, but it is in the repertoire. The knuckle of the middle finger is extended so, straight in line with the forearm, and all the strength and energy of the arm muscles is focussed there, and passes through it into the body, into the heart." Mitsui demonstrated a hard jab, his arm reaching full extension, the middle knuckle of the middle finger protruding like a stubby dagger.

"With the right motion, the arm is like a battering ram, and you can transmit as much force as if you are swinging a hammer over your head. Directed perfectly, you will stop a man's heart, destroy it. And the bruise will grow from inside, not the outside, so one does not detect external injury. Directed imperfectly, the blow might, as in this case, cause superfluous damage. Such as a collapsed lung." He sighed. "Commando karate is a black art, Sergeant O'Doull. No one who believes in the teachings would practise it."

"But there are those who do not believe in the teachings," O'Doull said. "Who, Mr. Mitsui? Who is an expert?"

"There is a man named Hernandez in Tampa. He teaches commando karate. Also, a Simon Hawthorne in Key West, an Englishman. Here, in Miami, there is Rudy Meyers. He is a black belt."

CHAPTER THIRTY-FOUR

O'Doull didn't return immediately to his motel, but went to the Budget office. They had picked up the Dodge Dart he and Larochelle had abandoned at the gas station. Her bag was still in it. He drove west through the city, past the Palmetto Expressway to the Koger Executive Centre and the Drug Enforcement Administration offices.

Flaherty asked her secretary to leave, and closed the office door so they were alone. She gave him a big smile, as if they were old friends.

"Nice to see you," she said. "You look frazzled."

"I want you to tell me about Meyers."

"He's a prick, for starters." She folded her arms, still smiling. "Why?"

"I think he may be involved in these murders."

Flaherty didn't blink. "Wouldn't surprise me."

"What about him?"

"He's good. That you know. He gives value. I don't think he's psychopathic, but he's close to it. He *has* a morality of sorts, the kind you find all wrapped up in the flag. He's a Spartan. He could afford to get fat; but he doesn't."

"What about his little Cuban army? All these people he's training?"

"The CIA folks are quite content. Reagan's people at best turn a blind eye, at worst give the wink and the nod. It's not

268

just the Cuban votes down here. They'd *like* an incident. The whole thing scares me. I don't want some turkey who's got it in his mind he's some modern-day warlord out to restore America's greatness dragging me into an international scenario involving Fidel and some nervous nuke-fingers in Russia."

"He's serious?"

"Sure. This time they're going to try to avoid going in by the Bay of Pigs, but they're going in just the same. Castro may be sorry some day that he emptied the prisons and sent all these people up here. They may come back to haunt him. Meyers' staff of so-called private investigators and security guards, they're all tinpot ex-soldiers and gangsters who didn't fit into Castro's plan for a socialist state. They're Meyers' field staff. He has another four or five hundred regulars that he trains just south of here near the Homestead Air Force Base and I don't know how many reserves he can call up. He's out there every evening. They call the group the DSA. After *diez y siete de abril*. They remember April 17, 1961, the Bay of Pigs. They had an anniversary wake not long ago."

"How do they raise their money?" O'Doull asked.

"There's some they get from the Somoza estate, I think, and maybe a bit comes from the odd contributor in Texas, but mostly it's from the Cuban colony. Little Havana and Cuban groups upstate and in the North. Every refugee with a job is expected to donate. It smells of a protection racket. There's a big Colombia dope connection, too. You guys, the Canadian government, you're contributing to the cause, because of the deal Meyers made with your man Mitchell. Meyers wangled a good one there."

"How do you mean?" O'Doull had not heard about this.

"Half a million dollars. You didn't know? Half a million if Meyers gets the ship, contents, and culprits to Canada with a case for conviction. Nothing if he doesn't."

O'Doull just stared.

"Why have we got Meyers on contract, Jessica?" he asked. "*You* recommended him. Why?"

"The inspector wanted the best. Price didn't matter. I've got no love for Meyers, but he's a good one. Mind you, if he's left some bodies lying around, Mitchell may find that his precious little Operation Potship is a game that isn't worth the candle."

"Did you have any other reason for suggesting Meyers to us?"

She smiled. "Naw. Keeps him out of trouble as much as possible. I'd rather have him working for you guys than for the Colombian Mafia." She looked at the clock on her desk. "I've got a lunch date. I can talk to you later. I'm wishing you good luck on your theory."

"Kelly used to be a friend of mine."

"I heard, I heard. Is that what is keeping you overtime down here? You're not out on some little self-serving mission of vengeance, are you? I hear you've been stirring up a few red ants, and got a few people upset. Watch your step. This can be a dangerous town."

They got up to go.

"It's funny," she said, giving him a sharp sideways look. "Talking to Mitchell, I had a different picture of you. Some absent-minded police misfit who couldn't tie his own shoe-laces. He was lots of laughs about you." She grinned. "I suppose he expected you to bumble around for a couple of days, get in everyone's way, and come back with a piece of bullshit that keeps Operation Potship on line. I wonder if he suspects something deep down in his gut about Meyers, and refuses to accept it as truth. He assumes you're not going to destroy his illusions, Theo."

At Miami police headquarters, O'Doull went straight to the identification section, hoping at all costs to avoid Braithwaite.

"You've got Rudy Meyers' prints?" O'Doull asked. "With his application for a private investigator's licence?"

The clerk went to look for them.

O'Doull spent the rest of the day in the electronics laboratory of an audio tape company.

Then he drove west, to the training camp of Diez y Siete de Abril.

CHAPTER THIRTY-FIVE

"Well, O'Doull, you were brilliant. You have caught me in a tissue of lies, as they say, a tissue of lies. You have proof that I was at the hotel. Who have you talked about it with, this evidence you have?"

"No one." O'Doull wondered if Meyers would make a move. If he did, that would ice the cake. He knew he had been a fool not to have brought bullets for the snub-nosed Smith and Wesson .32. He would have to be cool, and bluff.

"I killed them," Meyers said. "It doesn't matter that you know. Because in thirty seconds you will be dead. Faster, if you try to reach for the gun. Enjoy the last few seconds of your life."

O'Doull kept his eyes on Meyers' hands. He would have time for one block, a hard Rising Block against the striking arm. He *might* have time to get away a Knife-Hand to the throat. But it had been years since O'Doull had won his belt.

The heel of Meyers' right hand came slashing through the air, towards O'Doull's nose. . . .

O'Doull blinked away the fictions of his mind, sat with the engine idling, and stared up at the wooden sign suspended above the driveway of the old army camp. The sign bore the words, "Diez y Siete de Abril," and below, in English: "Remember the Seventeenth of April."

O'Doull wondered whether he should confront Meyers

directly in the hope he would blurt some statement – either an admission of guilt or some obvious lie. O'Doull was wired, and had a receiver-recorder hidden in his car.

He understood that a main weapon in the arsenal of a detective was surprise. He had not attempted to alert Meyers of his coming.

He stopped the car near a large barracks, with an office at the side. Nearby was a hangar large enough to serve as a gymnasium, and beside it was a track and playing field, with goal posts at either end.

O'Doull stood for a while and watched Meyers, whose back was to him, working with about twelve men. Another forty men at the other end of the field were paired off and sparring.

"Varques," Meyers shouted. A man came forward and picked up what looked like a bayonet. He took up a stance. *"Me mata*, Varques," Meyers said. "Kill me."

Varques circled, then darted at Meyers. Suddenly the knife was flipping harmlessly through the air, followed by Varques. Meyers seemed not to have moved. "Kill me, Varques." The trainee picked up the bayonet and charged Meyers once more. Meyers blocked the thrust with one arm and slammed his other elbow into Varques' midriff, doubling him up.

Meyers told the men to spar, and turned and walked towards O'Doull.

"That last little demonstration was intended for your enjoyment, Theo. I assure you, they are not all as bad as that fellow made them look."

He took O'Doull by the elbow and gently directed him towards the barracks office.

"In six weeks, he *will* be able to kill me. At that time, I will not be attempting that type of exercise with him." He laughed. He was looking at O'Doull carefully as he opened the door and they entered.

"I hope this is important, Theo, because I really dislike

being interrupted when we are doing exercises. These men give up most of their free evenings to come here. They are all fervent anti-Communists. It is a passion. They want to learn. The defence department sold us this land. It was used to train reserves. It's not much, it's a start." He stared out the window. "There will be an army of freedom soon. I will have three thousand men, each worth twenty of Castro's."

He plugged in a hot plate. "Tea?"

"No, thanks."

Meyers put a kettle on. "I keep a stock of herbal teas. I avoid caffeine. It's as poisonous as any drug. You seem nervous. Uptight, as they say, uptight."

There was sweat rolling down the sides of Meyers' face. His tunic and sweat pants showed patches of damp.

"Watch the kettle, will you, Theo, while I clean myself up." He pulled off his tunic and stepped through a door. O'Doull heard the sound of water running. For a few seconds he just sat there, feeling his advantage fast falling away. Then he looked around for Meyers' pager, found it hanging from his belt, quickly took it apart, slipped into it the small transmitter he had originally designed for Kerrivan, and closed it again.

Meyers came out, naked, whipping a towel across the back of his shoulders. He was huge across the chest, bull-like but with muscles that seemed loose, not rigid. O'Doull watched as Meyers, with the towel tied at his waist, removed the kettle and picked a few pinches of tea from a jar, put them in a teapot, and poured the steaming water into it.

"Peabody, the night manager of the Mangrove Arms Hotel, saw you walking out of the lobby at about two in the morning, the night before last. So did a woman who was there. Cherrie."

"The one is a pimp, the other an incompetent whore. What else is worrying you, O'Doull?"

"Marianne Larochelle also saw you at the hotel. She saw

blood on your sleeve. You have had your men following her. And for a time they were following me as well."

There was no expression on Meyers' face. "Go on."

O'Doull opened his briefcase, took out his portable Uher tape recorder, and plugged it into a wall socket. He played the tape of the ship-to-shore telephone call between Kelly and Kerrivan.

Meyers' expression remained bland throughout. The tape ended: *"I am sorry. Your party does not answer."*

Meyers sipped tea.

"This is a duplicate," O'Doull said. "The original is secure, with instructions. What you heard is virgin. In about fifteen seconds, you will hear it from the beginning, only this time most of the high-frequency wave lengths will have been filtered out."

Kelly's voice was clear: *"Just a minute. Stay with me. Hang on. I'll be back to you."*

There had been some muffled, distant sounds on the original tape. Now they assumed the form of voices, still distant, still unclear.

"I isolated that eight-second gap," O'Doull said. "Quite frankly, I was surprised at the pickup, but I knew that eight seconds of pure static was impossible. There *had* to be voices. The machinery is voice-activated. Everything clicks on when human voice frequencies come through the radio. I worked around with loudness variables, tried different frequency filters, and managed to clean it up pretty nicely, if I do say so. This, coming up, is the gap, with lots of volume.

The spool of tape slowly turned. Meyers' eyes were fixed on it.

The voice's pitch was a little high and slightly flat, blurred, and wavering. But it was unmistakably the voice of Rudy Meyers.

"I'm sorry, I was . . . Augustin. Who are you phoning? I don't want you using the phone."

There was a strong note of anger.

O'Doull said, "A few words are missing still. 'I was coming to meet Augustin'? The point is, it's *your* voice. You were there. In the room. Kelly was trying to warn Kerrivan. He was telling him to dump the cargo." O'Doull rewound the tape and replaced the machine in his briefcase. "What do you say?"

"Is that everything?" Meyers asked. His pager beeped. "My office is calling. I'm very busy. You'll have to go."

"Somebody hung up the phone after the killings. The tip of your left index finger shows up on the receiver. At least eight points of similarity, enough points to qualify for court."

"I don't understand what the problem is, Theo."

"Come on."

"Of course I had been in the room. I told you that, didn't I? I had popped in to look for Escarlata. Kelly told me he wasn't there. I left."

O'Doull looked at him with disbelief. "You told me you were asleep. Midnight to six A.M. 'A precise order of habit patterns,' I believe you said."

"I certainly did *not* tell you I was asleep at midnight that night. I was working. I was to meet with Augustin. Where do you get these ideas? Of course my fingerprint would appear on the phone. I used it that day. As for Marianne, she is lying to save her own skin. Blood on my sleeve – that's a little too much, Theo, a little too much. Congratulations on finding her. She's the murderess, of course. Excellent work in that regard, Theo. Where do you have her? She must have been hiding in the bedroom when I came to the door."

The scene was not being played as O'Doull had scripted it.

Meyers began to walk towards him. O'Doull stiffened, but Meyers carried on, into the shower room. He emerged, slipping on a jock strap and a clean pair of sweat pants. "I think I need to work out some more."

276

O'Doull was guarded, ready to pull out his gun if necessary.

"Mitchell warned me that you were a dreamer, Theo. I really don't like you." He walked past O'Doull again, picked up the phone, and gave a credit card reference and a long distance number to the operator. "I suppose your reveries have Rudy Meyers, his black deeds bared, becoming a desperate man at this juncture. He is about to deliver a killing blow to your spine and you, anticipating this, suddenly pull out the firearm that weighs so heavily in your pocket. Perhaps you would find the strength to shoot me. I don't like you, Theo. You are a romantic, and you are absurd, and you are so neurotic that you are dangerous to yourself and others."

He spoke into the phone. "Inspector Mitchell, please. It's Twenty-Nine G-K in Miami. Harold? Sorry to bother you."

O'Doull, wearied by a long night and a long day, felt his energy slowly seeping from his pores.

"I have your man O'Doull with me," Meyers said. "He is compromising the operation. Get him out of Miami. I don't care if you have to send an armed escort, get him out. Get him out before I send him away myself, on the end of my foot."

O'Doull took the phone. "Inspector, there's some bad business going on here. I think I had better fill you in."

"I'll fill *you* in if you don't get your fucking ass up here by tomorrow morning."

"Inspector, things have kind of blown up—"

"We'll discuss it here! Get back or you're under suspension for insubordination. That's *all*, Theo." He clicked off.

Meyers' smile was especially frigid. He showed O'Doull to the door.

CHAPTER THIRTY-SIX

There was a late flight to Montreal on Air Canada. O'Doull rushed back to the motel and began sticking his things into his suitcase, as Larochelle leaned against the window ledge, her arms folded. She was wearing only bikini panties. A Ravel piano composition was coming loud from an FM station.

"I'm liable to get kicked off the goddamn force if they don't believe you!" he shouted.

"What do you mean?" She moved away from the window and did a few ballet-like twirls.

"He's very neatly changed his story. He says he *was* in the hotel before the killings. *Just* before. You're going to St. John's with me. I'm going to get you to talk to Mitchell."

"Are you kidding?" She went to the radio and turned the sound down. "I'm not walking into that wasps' nest. If I go in there, The Bullet will grab me. For something, I don't know what, but he's ruthless. Everybody tells me that."

It was hard for O'Doull to look at her. His eyes kept wanting to slide down to her chest, to follow the trickles of sweat that ran down it.

"There's nothing they can charge you with," he said. "You were already cleared down here. The judge wasn't involved in that charade in court, so the dismissal order is valid. You can't be convicted twice of the same offence. Double jeopardy."

All this came back to him from a course on the law that had been a part of his training.

"Anyway, you stopped short of breaking any law in Canada. You've got nothing to worry about. If you come with me you may indirectly help the guys on the boat. Mitchell *has* to scrap the operation, it's too badly tainted. The newspapers would create havoc with us."

"I'm not so sure, Theo. Maybe I'm cynical. I trust *you*, Theo, but I don't trust *them*."

"I know something about how these things work, Marianne. Nobody's going to think of hassling a C.I., a co-operating individual."

"*Co-operating?*" She shook her head firmly. "Darling, just because I made love to a policeman doesn't mean I'm one of your 'co-operating individuals.' There is absolutely no way I am going to assist in your Operation Potship. Mitchell will try to get me to say where and when the ship is coming in. God, you're innocent for a cop."

"We know when the ship is coming in. Or we will."

"What do you mean?"

"I'm just telling you that you've got to come with me. I . . . can't arrest you."

"I suppose you *would*! God, I thought you were different, but down inside, you're just pure cop. I guess you have to have that attitude if you're going to be a cop. Duty before feelings."

"That's kind of a low blow. You have alternatives – you can come with me, or you can stay here." He was speaking more coldly than he intended. "I told Meyers you were my primary witness."

"Jesus! Did you also tell him where he could find me after you've gone? You're a ruthless kind of bastard!"

"You *said* you wanted to come back up with me."

"Home to friends, not to bloody Inspector Mitchell." She bit her lip. "Oh, God, what have I got myself into?"

She seemed suddenly very fragile and haunted. O'Doull walked over to her, touched her face, and she came to him, burying her head in his chest. He placed his hands on her back, and it felt damp and cool. "We have forty minutes before the plane," he said.

"Okay."

It was after midnight when they landed at Mirabel. They had gotten slightly drunk on daiquiris. Larochelle had been playful, pretending she was a prisoner, asking his permission to visit the washroom, answering questions only with name, rank, and serial number. She threatened to go to the cockpit and have the plane redirected to Cuba.

O'Doull felt woozy at the customs counter. The customs officer, smelling the booze on his breath, started going through their bags, so O'Doull showed him his badge and the man apologized and waved him and Larochelle through.

He stood with her at the taxi line, uncertain about what to do next, where to go. He looked at Larochelle and she smiled at him.

"I know a nice little hotel," she said.

Larochelle pushed him gently onto the bed and slowly undressed him. He felt her lips touch his belly, and felt the tip of her tongue slide along it, down through his hair, to the base of his penis.

"Are you married?" she whispered.

"No."

"That's nice."

She nibbled at the head of his cock, then brought her mouth wet over it. He felt explosions.

Later, as he was thrusting inside her, her voice began to

rise urgently. "Oh yes, oh yes, oh God, don't stop. Oh my God!" She shrieked it. He felt her nails biting into his shoulders. "Oh, Theo, what have you done to me? I feel strange. It's never been like this before. God, I think I'm falling in love. Hold me, stay inside me!"

When he woke up, she was gone.

PART FOUR
How Brain Damage is Caused

CHAPTER THIRTY-SEVEN

Johnny Nighthawk

Jimmy Buffett's voice sounds as wrecked as we feel. We left the speakers on the deck one night, and it rained. Now all the music we play sounds rasping and hollow.

We are three strangers on a ship, human machinery, oiled and greasy, stained by sweat and bile and lubricant, stinking like dead animals, fuelled upon Spam and beans, unwarmed.

The romantic life of the sea smuggler.

We are strangers in that we do not speak to one another, or even make polite sounds. We pass each other by noiselessly, not daring to look into one another's eyes for fear of seeing truth in them.

The truth being, perhaps, that Kevin Kelly's urgent radio message of many days ago has been too easily dismissed. "Jettison the cargo," he had said. "Deep-six the ship."

"Aw, it is Kevin freaking out again," said Pete, and we all wisely agreed.

"Stoned out of his tree, he was," said Pete. And we nodded our heads. "He must have been falling down loaded and dead to the world when we tried to phone him back." Billy Lee and I solemnly agreed that this was the fact.

But we dared not look at one another in case we might recognize the doubts that our eyes spoke.

And the worst of us is Billy Lee who is smoking fifteen J's a day, to the point that he has built himself up to peak tolerance level, where life is a stoned blur, where you are at a point that you never really get off any more. He goes at it like a junkie, his face is grey and sad, and the dope is bringing him down, and never, never does he look at Pete or me. . . .

●

"Sir, it's the Prime Minister's office. I . . . I think it's the P.M. himself. Unless someone's playing a joke."

O'Doull tucked the phone between his jaw and collarbone as he continued typing his report. He planned to release it to the media that evening, and a fifteen-minute slot had been arranged for him on CBC "Newsmagazine."

"Yeah?" he said.

It was no joke. "Sergeant O'Doull, I am personally directing you to lay off, do you understand?"

O'Doull swore softly as he misspelled a word, corrected it.

"There are sensitive interests involved. Very serious international implications. I am not at liberty to discuss them with you, sergeant."

"I'm sorry, sir, I have issued warrants for two members of the Cabinet and five high-level members of the RCMP."

"Look, you jerkwater twerp, if you say one more thing to the press, I'll have *you* charged. With treason."

"When I joined the force, sir, I swore an oath of allegiance to my country. I am acting because I believe in my country –"

O'Doull's door crashed in and three uniformed members of the assault team started to come towards him. . . .

O'Doull unashamedly luxuriated in thoughts of his own imaginary heroism, then yawned and stretched to clear his head, and returned to his typing. He had finished thirty-five pages and was nearing the end of the Epic of Operation Potship. He intended to have it on the desk of the Solicitor General of Canada on the following morning.

Nothing else had seemed to work.

Three days later Superintendent Edwards was alone in the bullring with a raging minister of the crown and gingerly side-stepping.

"O'Doull! O'Doull!" the Solicitor General was shouting. "Who is this crazy man? Is he trying to destroy us? What is he, a malcontent? A subversive? Get rid of him."

"We can't. He'll go to the newspapers."

Lessard, behind his desk, looked like a cornered bear. He riffled through O'Doull's forty-page typewritten report, then opened it at a random page, hoping to discover that he had misread it the first time.

His voice came in a hiss. "Five hundred thousand *dollars*? For what? An informer? An agent provocateur?" His eyes seemed to recede behind the bush of his eyebrows and when he spoke again his voice was quiet. "I saw no such number on a budget."

"It wasn't spelled out in black and white, Mister Minister. As I recall, you didn't want to get into specifics." Edwards pointed to the marble monkey paperweight. "Hear no evil, you said." Edwards was determined he was not going to carry the can alone on this one. The budget for Potship *had* been approved by the minister. In general form.

"No, Milt," Lessard said. His voice was strained but steady. "There was no five-hundred-thousand-dollar fee for an undercover agent on the budget you showed me. I saw no reference to a contract with this man Meyers. Don't try to pull that old game on me. Pass no bucks to Jean-Louis Lessard, my friend."

"You remember the meeting, sir. You approved the budget. You chewed the ass off Mitchell."

Suddenly Lessard turned red with rage. "Mitchell! That son of a bitch! Don't mention his name! I'd like to kick his ass right into Hudson Bay!" He seemed to subside, and he spoke with a quieter voice. "O'Doull says this agent, this man that you and Mitchell hired—not me, nobody mentioned his name to me—has murdered people, Milt. To protect a contract that you and Mitchell made with him. If this comes out, they won't vote me in as county chicken inspector."

"Ah, it's bull," Edwards said. "We're checking it out. It's bull. Meyers is innocent." But there was uncertainty in his voice.

"O'Doull doesn't think it's bull, Milt. He's made a credible case. I'd convict on it."

"It's all bull."

"It is bull such as this that causes ministers of the crown to suddenly lose their jobs. Now, you are going to have to shut up this man O'Doull. And I mean shut him up." He laid emphasis on the last three words.

"It's not going to be easy. He is a very strange bird. And he is hot about this."

"It stinks," Lessard said. "The whole Potship thing. It stinks." He leaned forward on his desk, clasping his hands and leaning his chin on them. "Edwards, you are going to do a job on this one. I want the clamps on. Everything is going to be tight and buttoned. Do you understand that?"

Edwards puffed his cheeks and blew out slowly. "Mister Minister, let me lay out for you the whole Greek tragedy. Right now these smugglers are sitting two miles off the Canadian limits waiting for the night to fall." He checked some numbers on a piece of paper. "Forty-six degrees, thirty-one minutes latitude, fifty-five degrees, eight minutes longitude. In their holds they are carrying three hundred million dollars' worth of narcotic. Now these fellows are going to get arrested. And they are going to get a lawyer. And that lawyer is going to get the whole story. And he is going to scream to the press. 'RCMP Agent Kills For His Fee, Lawyer Charges.' In court, this lawyer is going to make high-camp melodrama out of this thing."

The minister shook his head firmly. "We can't have a trial, Milt."

"What do we do? We can't just sit on our rears and let them *land* the dope. What do you think the media would say if they learned we turned a blind eye to the biggest drug operation in the history of the oceans? We're damned either way."

His head clasped between his hands, Lessard let out a long, low moan. "Jesus, son of Mary," he said, repeating it three times. After a while, he looked up. "Okay, get Knowlton Bishop."

Edwards nodded. He felt a release of tension.

"I don't care what he has on his plate," Lessard said. "I don't care if you have to yard him out of the middle of a ten-day argument to the Supreme Court of Canada. Get him."

"Can I turn the whole thing over to him?" Edwards asked, a note of eager desperation in his voice.

"The whole thing. The whole can and all the worms in it. Tell him no publicity. None. He can quote his fee, any fee, we won't argue. And, Milt, if no publicity means no trial, then no trial. Arrest these guys, seize and burn the drugs, but no trial. And if it involves letting somebody go, that's the way it will have to be. And it's got to be fast, before anyone has a chance to think. When is this ship coming in?"

"We've intercepted a radio message," Edwards said. "Tonight at midnight. Where they're planning to land, we don't know, but they're coming in," he checked his watch, "in fourteen hours."

"There's no chance we might lose them?" Lessard said. His tone suggested he hoped they might.

"No. We have the little magic box. And if that fails, we have something else. Double coverage."

"Get hold of Bishop."

•

Johnny Nighthawk

I am a prisoner of the machines, shackled to them. I work a fifteen-hour watch. I nap and Pete takes over. I work another fifteen hours. I come up for air and it is night. I come up again and it is day. I settle into a drifting state of semi-consciousness.

I am doctor and nurse to these engines, lover and mother and stern, demanding friend to them. I cajole, I threaten. I whisper words of charity and caring, and tell sly untruths to encourage them, to make them believe they are healthy and have many years to live.

Through it all – and there have been crises – the screw turns and the propeller bites the water, and the *Alta Mar* carries north into the grey, cooling ocean.

It is day twelve of the run to Judas Bight. I *think* it is day twelve. I keep no time or an engine log.

The crises.

Number One: the fresh-water pump for the starboard plant broke down, and we shut the engine before it cooked itself, and we drifted dead in the water, picking it apart and finding, to great dismay, that the shaft had stripped some splines. We have jury-rigged the toilet pump to run the engine cooling system, and now we cannot use the head. So we swing teetering from the rail and hang moons over the side of the ship in the lee of the wind.

Number Two: a water hose broke and flooded one of the main generators with salt water, shorted out a major terminal block. The gyro nearly exploded before we could lock it. All the fancy gear on the bridge lost their reference

290

points. For hours we drifted, drying out.

Day twelve, and we are well within the two-hundred-mile fishing zone and worrying about fisheries patrols. Marine radio gives us the best news of the last two weeks – cloud to hide the moon and fog to hide the *Alta Mar*.

Yesterday we patched a coded message through to Bill Stutely in Newfoundland with the aid of a CB operator, and we let Stutely know, and he will let Kevin Kelly and the other boys know, that we are coming in tonight.

"We're bringing the baby to town for the birthday party, Uncle Bill. Arriving late, midnight. Over."

"Ten-four Eleanor," said Stutely. "Over and out."

Now we are waiting nervously for the evening to settle in. The radar flickers with shadows of distant boats coming in from the Banks. A drone of aircraft fades away into the distance.

Eight o'clock. I am with my engines. We have slowed to about three knots, and the engines chug softly and hiss, like a diesel train at rest.

I am sagging, bent by the burden of tired flesh, and I feel aged. A pair of pressure gauges stare malevolently at me from the control board.

Crisis number Three. The bells clang. It is Pete from the bridge.

"Yeah?"

"Johnny, you better come right up here. Billy Lee is holding a gun on me."

CHAPTER THIRTY-EIGHT

O'Doull sat hunched, nervous, tight, studying the man in the armchair who was studying him. They were in the Hotel Newfoundland, in the suite of Knowlton Ogilvy Bishop, Q.C., a tall, confident man with a rich and vibrant voice, a great burden of white hair, and smiling, shrewd eyes.

O'Doull knew the old man's reputation: a courtroom magician, a smooth gunslinger, adviser to Her Majesty's government on all matters grave and solemn that involved the application of the laws. At a retainer of five hundred dollars an hour. He sat regarding O'Doull with the relaxed assurance of a man with easy access to power brokers.

But in truth Bishop was masking his fatigue this evening. He had met with Edwards at noon; they had been taken to the airport armed with O'Doull's and Mitchell's reports, and had been flown to St. John's on a Department of Transport jet. Bishop had excused himself to Edwards, had dinner in his room, and spent the early evening organizing this mess in his mind, trying to put together a strategy. Every such crisis seemed to slow his body more, and with every crisis he renewed a promise to quit the hard business of the law, and always the promise was broken.

He had been about to say no to Edwards, but the superintendent made it clear there were distasteful implications to this. Such as murder. Murder in the name, it might be argued, of Her Majesty the Queen. Bishop had insisted upon a free hand, and both the Solicitor General and the Minister of Justice had granted it. The only ground rule was no publicity. Keep the lid on. Bury the corpses quickly.

That meant controlling O'Doull. And it meant controlling Mitchell as well. Soothing him. Appeasing him somehow with a taste of victory. He had invited both O'Doull and Mitchell to his suite to look them over, get a fix on them.

Bishop watched them interact. O'Doull looked at Mitchell with contempt. Mitchell looked at O'Doull with a simmering hostility.

Either of these two men could loosen the lid from the kettle, and O'Doull had clearly threatened to. He was problem number one, a brush fire that had to be dampened before it spread into the political forests.

"I have been appointed an inquiry commissioner," he said. "That gives me the power to subpoena records and witnesses. I am not anybody's servant. I am playing footman neither to the government nor to the RCMP."

That was for O'Doull. Bishop had to have his confidence.

"Let me begin by congratulating you, sergeant," he continued. "I doubt that anyone else has had the courtesy to do so."

The territory seemed friendlier than O'Doull had hoped. He had expected an inquisition, with Mitchell whispering venom into the inquisitor's ears. The fact that Bishop had been hired, that the government had not sent a stooge, was a sign to him that he was not going to be written off as a mere annoyance.

"Inspector Mitchell thinks you were out of line," Bishop said. "That is a point of view. Another might say that you were exhibiting a rare quality in police officers. Enterprise."

"Have you read my report, sir?" Mitchell said. "I have another word for it." O'Doull saw there were veins standing out on his forehead. His hands were clenched into fists.

Bishop studied Mitchell with a puzzled expression as if he were a piece of abstract art. "I have read your report, inspector. I have reviewed the whole of Operation Potship. I am not impressed." It was sad that he had to do this, Bishop felt. The man no doubt was a dedicated officer, although wrongheaded. He would worry later about mollifying him. He turned back to O'Doull.

"Maybe you are also owed an apology, sergeant. I know you feel this inquiry was a long time coming, and I know you feel, to use the current expression, that you were being stonewalled. But your report has been reviewed by the minister. And I am here to assure you that we intend to get at the truth."

O'Doull nodded.

"Naturally, the minister hopes that things will not go beyond this stage, that matters will not be discussed outside the four walls of this inquiry. We don't have to hang our dirty clothes on a public washline."

"It's him who's been threatening to go to the press," Mitchell said.

Bishop kept his eyes on O'Doull as he spoke. He was hard to read. It was difficult to know what tack to take.

"I am sure Sergeant O'Doull understands his duty," he said. "As a servant of the government he has taken an oath of secrecy and he knows the penalties that apply to a breach."

O'Doull was impassive. Bishop had hoped for at least some gesture, a nod of the head.

"The key to this thing is Meyers," he went on. "You believe, sergeant, that he committed a murder in the course of his, if you'll pardon the expression, duties on behalf of the force."

"Two murders."

"The Miami police say homicide and heart attack. They do not accuse Meyers."

"He was in the hotel room," O'Doull said. "I have his

294

voice on tape. Before I confronted him with the tape, he had denied being there."

"That's b.s.," Mitchell said. "I'm sorry, sir, but that's exactly what it is. I won't dignify it with another expression. Meyers never denied being in the hotel room. He was there well before the murder. It's in Detective Braithwaite's report. Braithwaite interviewed Meyers after the bodies were found."

O'Doull's mouth fell open. "That *can't* be right. Braithwaite made no mention to me of that at all. I have his xeroxed reports."

"Braithwaite gave O'Doull some stuff just to get him off his back. I've talked to him, sir."

"His voice is on the tape," O'Doull repeated. "Just before the murders."

Bishop seemed to think about it. Then he said, "But the taping was voice-activated, sergeant. You know much more than I about such things, but let me ask you: would it not be hard to tell from your voice-activated tape just how much time elapsed between Meyers' arrival and the occurrence of the deaths?"

Of course, O'Doull thought, that would have been Meyers' *ex post facto* offering. Meyers *could* have left the room. The tape conceivably *could* have stopped running. The deaths *could* have occurred some time later. He felt himself sagging a bit. Meyers and Mitchell had really worked on this one, hunting for holes.

Bishop was content for the time being to let the argument settle in with O'Doull. It was important to try to instill doubt in the man's mind about the strength of the case against Meyers.

"Marianne Larochelle," O'Doull said. "She saw him leave the hotel. He had blood on his sleeve."

That brought Mitchell to his feet furiously.

"Marianne Larochelle! He's asking you to take the word of a known dope dealer, a pusher, a whore, over the word of a police agent. Where *is* she? *She's* really interested in helping out, isn't she? Where is she? She's on the run, that's where she is. Let's see *her* come forward like Meyers and take a lie detector test. If she's got the guts."

"A lie detector test?" O'Doull asked.

"If nobody told you, O'Doull, I will," Mitchell said. "Meyers volunteered for one and he passed."

"He could lie about his own name and pass a polygraph," O'Doull said. "He is a psychopathic liar."

"What the *hell* are you trying to do to me, O'Doull? Have you any *goddamn* idea of what you're trying to do? You go to the newspapers or to some damn politician, and you'll blow up Operation Potship."

Mitchell hovered like a standing bear over Bishop, talking loudly. "Can't *you* see what he's doing? He's *friends* with these people, with Kerrivan and the rest of them. He's got together some bullcock to attempt to embarrass us into pulling back from the operation. I'm not going to stand for it, goddamnit!"

Bishop's voice was hard and commanding. "You *are* standing, inspector. I am going to suggest that you either sit down or leave this room."

"You're going to let him get away with this?" Mitchell was shouting now, and seemed to O'Doull to be nearing a state of hysteria. "My *God*, Mr. Bishop, you've got my report! That bitch suckered O'Doull right into a bed with her. Maybe that's something that's not in *his* report!"

O'Doull went red.

"She was screwing his cock off in Miami. We found out they were staying in his motel room. I don't know what happened when they got to Montreal. He probably blew her a kiss, patted her on the ass, and sent her off to hide out!"

"Inspector—" Bishop began.

Mitchell interrupted, ignoring him, turning to O'Doull. "If you tie the can to my back end over some misbegotten theory of yours, I'm personally going to get you drummed out of the force. What happened to your old man is nothing compared to what I'll nail you with, O'Doull. Nothing! You've been fucking the ass off–"

"Inspector!" Bishop's voice boomed through the suite. "You're not in a barracks room. Control yourself."

Mitchell, sweat streaming down his bare head, moved towards the door. "You've got a nut case on your hands, Mr. Bishop. I'm telling you, he's dangerous!" And he strode outside.

There was a long, turbulent silence. O'Doull was staring at the floor.

"I did sleep with her," he said, finally. "I didn't mention it in my report."

Viewed with the perspective of the passing days, those two fervent nights with Larochelle had taken on a manic hue. It seemed now he had been utterly crazy to have shared a bed with her, and yet he remembered the time as being magic. For the last week and a half his sleep had been thin, her presence overpowering in his dreams. A passing infatuation, he kept telling himself, a wave that had burst upon him and that should subside and wash back to the sea. But the surge kept coming, kept coming.

Bishop, studying the man in front of him – hunched over, head bowed, hands clasped – realized now that he had the key to O'Doull. Marianne Larochelle. That odd sexual episode had not been some mere haphazard plunge by O'Doull. He was not the cold or corrupt policeman who would take advantage of an attractive woman in distress. The woman was the key to controlling O'Doull. He was in love with her.

"Meyers passed a polygraph test?" O'Doull said softly.

"It was inconclusive. They couldn't prove he was lying, couldn't prove he was telling the truth. As you say, the machine doesn't work well with some people."

O'Doull looked up and fixed his eyes hard on Bishop. "I know he killed them, sir. And I think the Miami police

297

know it, too. There's a game being played down there, a mini-Watergate. The DEA team leader, Jess Flaherty, has been kept on the outside, too. I think the U.S. State Department or the CIA is behind it."

"Sergeant, in my time I have prosecuted two hundred murder trials. I will be blunt. I think it doubtful that a jury would convict on the evidence you have gathered. It is impressive, but it is not enough. In any event, the problem belongs to another country."

O'Doull shook his head. "I have never been so certain of anything as I am that Meyers is a murderer."

"Okay, you're right. He's a killer. Let's assume that. Where does it get us? Does that excuse these fellows of the crime of importing drugs? I'll be frank, sergeant, I think Operation Potship reeks. But there is still the question: does improper police behaviour justify excusing the importation of nearly a third of a billion dollars' worth of illicit narcotics? It's a hard question, isn't it? A disturbing one. But I think you know the answer."

O'Doull said nothing. The dilemma seemed to muddle his mind.

Bishop tightened the pressure. "You have feelings for Kelly. I understand that. But you are a police officer and you know what your duty is."

O'Doull found himself nodding.

"And you have a duty to the police force you represent. The RCMP, like any police organization, is made up of human beings, and human beings are frail. But it is a proud force with a proud history. I think you and I would both hate to see all of its pride sapped."

O'Doull shook his head quickly as if to clear it out. He took a deep breath. "Mr. Bishop, I *have* pride in this police force. I am going to do my best to maintain that pride."

Smiling, Bishop made an expansive gesture with his hands as if to say that they were of one mind about the important things.

"And the best way to maintain that pride," O'Doull continued, "is to root out such things as cause us to feel shame. I can't sustain pride if I play a role in a . . . cover-up." He had said the forbidden word.

Bishop sat back and let a cloud of fatigue wash over him. This was going to be very hard, after all.

"I am prepared to breach my oath of secrecy, Mr. Bishop. If that means breaking the law, then I will break the law. I don't know who is giving Detective Braithwaite his orders, but if he does not arrest Meyers and charge him with murder, I will personally go down to the state attorney's office and I will lay a complaint. And if that does not work, I will go to the press and embarrass a murder charge out of the Miami police."

After O'Doull left, Bishop met with Edwards.

"Arrest the girl," he said. "And arrest her right now. I don't care where she is hiding – Montreal, Toronto, or Moose Jaw, Saskatchewan. Arrest her."

In his darkened office at Potship headquarters, Harold Evans Mitchell stood staring bleakly out a window into the grey, unmoving nothingness of fog, his right hand clenched upon a large tumbler of scotch and water.

One of his men rapped softly on his door, opened it, and cleared his throat.

"Problem, sir."

"Problem?" Mitchell's voice was husky with drink.

"We've lost them."

CHAPTER THIRTY-NINE

Johnny Nighthawk

I am panting hard. I have chuffed up to the bridge as fast as my legs will go.

"I been meaning to have this talk," Billy Lee says, motioning to me to sit down. He makes the motion with a .32 revolver, one of the chunks that Meyers had left with us. In case of pirates.

"I'm the man," he says. "I'm the fuckin' *man*." He snorts. "Ah, Jesus, can you believe it?" His chest heaves with silent, dry laughter.

Pete is wilted, collapsed, sitting by the wheel and staring blankly at Billy Lee. He looks like he did when Marianne walked out with Escarlata. Only worse. As for me, my brain has locked up.

"It's got so I can't handle this no more without talkin' about it," Billy Lee says. "So I want to talk." He is not wearing his shades, and although all the ship's lights have been doused, I can see his face from the twinkle of the lit dials on the control panel. His eyes seem socked back into his head. He is studying the gun as if curious to find it in his hand.

"Sorry about the firearm, man. Sorry about the whole scene. It's the way it is, you know." He is wrecked on weed and his Alabama drawl is stretched and pained.

"Ol' Rudy. He kinda has a gun on me, too. Lemme jus' talk about it. We met in 'bama, Rudy and me. Like I told y'all, only different. I am flyin' in carrying half a ton. Comin' in on Mary Jane, my ol' B-26. I guess I told you it was broken down. It ain't, and that was jus' a ruse, an excuse to go on your ship. Anyway, never mind. I am comin' in, and ol' Rudy-Tootie is waitin' for me at the field, after chasing my people away. I mean, he squeezes me, man. He's got my buddies' names and licence numbers and pictures and he takes samples of dope from the plane, and he's able to turn us all over to the narcs. I'm lookin' to fifteen years in the joint, man. Plus whatever else for the desertion rap."

"He's working for Meyers," Pete says to me, explaining the obvious. "And Meyers is working for The Bullet. And Meyers bought Billy Lee with his own planeload of dope."

Billy Lee can't look either of us in the eyes, and he is still looking down, studying the handgun. "It's a real tight squeeze play, jus' so y'all unnerstan'." With his free hand, Billy Lee turns an imaginary screw, putting body English into it. "Real tight, man." He is really wigging out.

I think: I could jump him. He is so torn up on weed he might not see me coming. But I am so weary, so depressed. And Pete would be no help.

"Wal, ain't it the shits," Billy Lee goes on. "Anyway, lemme talk this here thing out a bit. Don't nobody get strange. Jus' lemme talk. I been meanin' to have this talk, man."

I have shut the engines down completely, and we are sitting in the fog, enveloped in it, enveloped in a silence that is disturbed only by Billy Lee's soft voice.

"That plane that was settin' up there earlier, before the sun went, that was an Argus. That means Coast Guard."

"You been talking to them, Billy Lee?" Pete asks wearily.

"Naw, naw, nothin' so blatant. You see this here countermeasures pod that's supposed to jam the enemy radar? It don't work. What they got, built right into it, is a kind of like a bumper-beeper, only we got it antennaed right up to – now, y'all ain't gonna believe this, man – right up to a NASA satellite. I mean, this is *high* technology. This fuckin' boat is wired up like the *Starship Enterprise*. The S.S. Sittin' Duck. They're gonna track us right into Judas Bight. They're gonna bust you guys, bust the whole landin' crew. Bigges' fuckin' bust in history, man. And I'm the cops' main man, and I got a free ticket after it's over."

"You're a shithouse rat, Billy Lee," Pete says. He does not raise his voice. Just a low, even tone.

"Yeah, well . . . you know." His voice drifts off, and he swallows. "Lemme work this out, man. Lemme jus' talk a little. Miami. That scene was all bullshit. *Pura paja*. They sent you up the Florida Strait so they could pull you into Miami, stage that phoney courtroom drama, all jus' so's they could install this here satellite bug."

He waves the gun at the navigational equipment. "All this here hardware, this is all jus' decoration to make it look good. Remember when we was taken out separately for questioning? I said to Meyers, what the fuck are we doin' in Miami, man? He said we been hookin' you guys into a satellite. Real military operation."

A hoarse laugh. "I mean, man, *what* an operation. It's been a setup right from go. Meyers, he got Ugarte to blacklist you in Bogota, told the ol' bastard some lies about y'all payin' off the cops in Canada, stealing his dope, man, and sellin' it. That's 'cause Meyers and the cops had some- thin' bigger in mind for you. Paez. The *sinsemilla*. They didn't want to catch you in no penny-ante deal. The narcs want you real bad, Pete."

"It's a fixed game, hey, Billy Lee?" Pete says. "Mitchell sends the plays in. Meyer runs them. You steal our signals. I never knew you played that game. I always thought you played honest with friends."

"Stacked deck, y'know. You're a gambler, Pete. You know about a stacked deck."

The fog seems to grow denser. It encases us like a heavy wool quilt.

Billy Lee sighs. "I did a readout half an hour ago. We're still a mile off Canadian waters. Damn, I'm beat." He looks down at the .32 and he looks disgusted with it.

There is a silence.

"What are you thinking, Billy Lee?" I ask.

"Wa-a-al, I'm thinkin' I could use another toke. Shee-it, this is fine smoke. Jus' so fine." He pulls a number from his shirt pocket and wets it with his lips. "Three thousand bucks a pound is what *I* figger. We're sittin' on a hundred thousand pounds, an' it seems like the whole world is sittin' on top of us."

He sticks the joint into the corner of his mouth, strikes a wooden match against the barrel of the gun, and holds a wavering hand under the J until he finally gets a light. I am thinking, one more of these and he will pass out.

"Toke?" he says, passing it to me. I shrug and drag on it, just a little. Pete takes a hit, too.

"Perfect, ain't it?" Billy Lee says. "The night. The fog. You know this here coast like your hand, Pete."

"This is where I live, Billy Lee. My back yard. I'm almost home."

"Almos' home," Billy Lee repeats. "Aw, man, if you was to get this sucker in behin' some rocks, man, I bet they couldn't get no fix on you." He takes the joint again and does a long suck on it. "You figger that ol' man's boatshed is big enough to hold all this stuff?"

"Yeah. Is that where the cops are waiting?"

"Well, actual, I made like I didn't know." He is talking tight, holding the air in his lungs. "So d'you think we could unload this here ol' beater an' take her out and sink her?" He blows out the smoke, and studies the fat roach. "I mean,

Jesus, man, when am I gonna get a chance ever again to put three hundred million dollars' worth of pot in the ground? Never again in this ol' boy's lifetime."

And Billy Lee squints at the counter-measures pod. He fires six bullets into its eye.

"Yeah, Pete, y'all claim to be a gambler." He looks at me, then Pete, and spreads his hands wide apart. "Well, let's go for it, man."

CHAPTER FORTY

Johnny Nighthawk

The radio is bubbling like a coffee pot. There is a great deal of rapid-fire conversation. Fishermen. Hundreds of them, it seems. Out on the Grand Banks chasing an enormous school of cod. At eleven o'clock at night? Yes, at eleven o'clock at night.

There is an edge in their voices, often a frantic sound.

We are doing maybe three or four knots, going as close in to this deserted shore as Pete dares. We can't *see* the shore. We can't see the sky or the ocean. We would be completely blind without the tools that Meyers provided us with.

From the portside radar unit, Pete picks out the images of known – at least to him – landfalls along the coast. Pete uses the depth sounder as a navigation device as well. He knows the soundings through here, and needs no chart. This is his world. He had helped old Captain Pike carry rum and brandy through here when he was a kid.

I should be in the engine room in case Pete suddenly has to call down a reverse engines, but I think he wants an audience.

"I know these waters, boys," he says, smiling, "like a French chef knows his kitchen."

The fog is as thick as jelly, and darkening with the night.

Pete is dodging behind the sunkers like a soldier running from snipers. A few degrees east, a few degrees west. A wide sixty degrees to port, and I watch the fathoms tick off: nine, eight, four. A long three. Then five. And then deep water again, and Pete takes her around the other way, to starboard.

"We just came through the Devil's Coffin there," Pete says. "Right between two brandies not forty feet apart. You can see their tips at low tide, and you have to ease in just gentle between them. They've taken out fifteen, twenty boats, mostly people not from around here. That's why we call these rocks sunkers."

Pete is rambling on, happy as a porpoise. He is in control. He is Peter Kerrivan of the Butter Pot leading the English squadron a merry chase. He is feeling good because we have reversed Mitchell's scam right back on itself. The odds do not seem overpowering in our favour, exactly, but maybe even. Eleven-to-ten and pick 'em, as Pete puts it.

And that is enough to make us feel very alive.

Pete devised his own scam, and it might work. A scam that might suck away this Dunkirk armada which is noisily spreading a net of patrol boats along the coast. After Billy Lee shot out the satellite transmitter and before we set off for Captain Pike's, we slung thirty million dollars into the sea – we cleared the decks of the bales that were under the tarps, threw them into the ocean, and watched them catch the current and run away.

The last bale to go was the crippled one, the *bulto* that had been sliced open by the U.S. Coast Guard. Billy Lee stuffed his pockets full of flowertops, then we heaved it overboard in a cloud of dust and resin. High-energy food for the cod-fish and mackerel.

"High tide coming in, boys," Pete had said. "It drives a current east through here, a current like a river." The current would carry the floating *bultos* down towards Fortune Bay.

"A false trail," Pete exulted. "Just the way the Masterless Men did it!" Pete loved to tell the stories about how his eighteenth-century namesake and his men cut false trails through the caribou bushlands near the Butter Pot, enticing the pursuing English marines down dead ends that petered out in bush and swamp.

When the police find the floating bales, I am thinking, there will be an uproar. But, God, if they find them too soon, they will be sweeping all around here with radar, heat sensors, noise detectors, who knows what. From all the voices on the radio, they sound like they've got every RCMP patrol launch in the Atlantic out there, plus the Coast Guard to boot. It's like a naval blockade.

A few hours have passed, and now it is time for Stage Two of Operation False Trail. "Okay," says Pete, checking the clock. He plugs into the emergency channel.

"Fire!" he screams. "My God, we're going down!" He yells out a pair of false co-ordinates. "May Day! May day! Abandoning ship!"

That is all. Brief, before they can triangulate on us with shoreside radio direction finders. The position that Pete gave them over the radio is the point which he estimates the bales will have reached in about two hours.

The radio is now like a beehive. Some stupido loses his head and blows their code, forgetting that we are supposed to be a school of cod. "*Alta Mar*? *Alta Mar*? Are you on fire?"

Everybody is jamming the emergency channel – a half hour of pure chaos before clear directions are given for boats to head out to the position in Fortune Bay that Pete had announced.

We turn the volume down to help Pete concentrate. "Judas Bight," he mutters, "where are you?" He licks his lips, studying the radar and the fathometer. "Okay, this has to be Little Boot Tickle. We're going to have to wiggle in here, boys, just so fine. Bad reef in here. The boys call it the

Grim Reefer. Anyone hear any noise, that's me scraping along a rock."

We are almost on top of a blue light when we see it. A ship's lantern.

Dit-da-da. "W" in Morse Code.

And "W" in our operations is the first letter of Welcome.

It is Bill Stutely in his Cape Islander, and a couple of the boys are with him.

"My compliments to the captain, sorr," Bill calls up to me, "and would ye kindly tell the captain that knowin' as I do he's a poor excuse for a sailor and as like as not to stay lost in the fog all night, we t'ot we'd come out and lead ye's in."

●

At Potship offices, it seemed to be all crew and no captain. Mitchell was standing at the edge, watching and listening to the turmoil, but giving no orders. He had heard the distress call, played back to him on tape. There was no question it had been Kerrivan's voice.

The chief radio operator was trying to clear the channels, trying to co-ordinate a search for Kerrivan's ship in an area concentrated around the co-ordinates he had broadcast. "Sir," the operator called, "they've picked up some floating bales. Not far from the May Day."

The Coast Guard commander went up to Mitchell. "They've probably taken to the longboats. The fire must have blown the Sat-Track transmitter. But, shit, if the bales have floated off the deck, the *Alta Mar* is probably at the bottom now."

Mitchell spoke slowly. "Commander, I want all boats to return to their stations."

"Inspector, it was a May Day! Lives are in danger. We have no choice."

"It's a con job," Mitchell said. "We've been double-crossed by Meyers' so-called failsafe device. I know Pete Kerrivan."

"Inspector, I can't break the law. It's a May Day."

"Your people are under my orders tonight," Mitchell said. "I'll take responsibility for the law. Put the net back together."

"Inspector –"

"Put the net back together."

CHAPTER FORTY-ONE

Johnny Nighthawk

The boys swarm onto the *Alta Mar* like pirates. There is no time to be wasted, little enough time for greetings. We have to be out of here well before the dawn.

There are a few quick handshakes for Pete and Billy Lee and me as we scramble wearily onto the dock. It takes the boys only seconds to open the holds and start the crane. They are experienced fellows: Dave Doncaster, Artie Bland, Wilbur Scathe, Stutely, and six others.

Pete heads for a man who stands by the boatshed with a brier pipe ablaze. "I could smell that terrible concoction from halfway out the bay, uncle."

"Y'er a foine quare sight, Petey," says Captain Pike. "And ye smells yerself, loik a mess o' rottin' gurry."

But despite that he hugs Pete hard in his arms. Pete introduces us and he grasps us with a leathery hand.

"Ah, it's loik the auld days," he says. "And would ye takes a little drap o' stuff?"

Cups are passed around, and Captain Pike pours into them from a flask of warmed brandy. A pot of simmering fish and brewis sits on the planks and we go to it like starving wolves.

"Some Mounties from Sin Jan's come callin' a few days

back, Petey," the old man says. "Checkin' out on yer auld acquaintanceships, they was, but I says to them, I says, six year gone by since I last set eye on the loiks of Peter Kerrivan. We drank a little tay and they went they ways. They was foine b'ys."

"Where's Kevin?" Pete asks.

"And ain't he with you, Petey?"

Oh, no, I think.

"Like as not he stopped off somewhere before going home," says Pete. But he looks worried, and I am feeling a little tight button of doubt.

We have no time to reflect on Kelly. I jump over to Artie Bland's herring seiner and help him get his block and tackle set up to assist in hauling the shrimp-net slings from our holds.

We dump the slings at the door to the boatshed, where some of the boys are hauling and piling, back-breaking work. I take some turns with them, and after some hours of this, I feel torn and wasted, my muscles screaming. Twice nets break and once a couple of fellows had to dive into the cold water to retrieve some of the bales, tie up the nets, and get a grapple on them. No wet suits, either.

The grind and clank of the cranes seems deafening to our ears, but the noise is muffled by the fog.

By five o'clock in the morning, the thousand bales are in.

"Mr. Stutely," Pete calls.

"Sorr!"

"Lock up the shed, Mr. Stutely."

"Aye-aye, sorr." The shed doors close, and we hear the sweet clink of the padlock.

"Gentlemen," says Pete, standing on some piled dories, "the Queen."

We all raise our cups of brandy into the air. Some of the guys are roaring with laughter. This is a smuggler's finest hour.

Captain Pike gives Pete another hug as we clamber back

aboard the *Alta Mar* to take her to the sea and scuttle her.

"We'll move the goods out in a couple of weeks, uncle, after the heat simmers down," Pete says. "If anybody asks around, you've seen no one, and you haven't unlocked the shed in six months."

Old man Pike sounds cross. "Petey, b'y, for shame. Me pore moind ain't gone loik ye t'inks. I knows how to handle the b'ys when they comes to visit."

He passes us up the rest of the flask of brandy, and we are off. On the way out, we unslip the longboat from its cradle and hang it over the side, so we can be away and gone in the time it takes to slash a knife across the lines.

I remember thinking we have moved a long ways from Peddigrew's original plan to bring the ship into a wrecking yard in Halifax, where his so-called clients are supposed to be waiting for it.

I am up on the bridge. The radio is crackling as busy as ever, describing our configuration and our colours. The police have dropped all pretence, and they are calling on civilian craft to look for a ship called the *Alta Mar*. As to locations, there are lots of wild guesses.

"Believed now to be moving south towards the high seas," is what their traffic co-ordinator suggests.

"Then let's not go to the high seas," Pete says. He brings her around, towards the Devil's Coffin. "There's deep enough water just around here."

The marine weather report makes an ugly promise: a fine, sunny day, and the sun will burn away the fog. Already puffs of twilight wind from a land breeze are beginning to stir the soupy air, to ripple it.

Without warning, the ship explodes into a great open gap, and we are surrounded by a brightness that seems nearly blinding. The eastern sun is reflected back on us by a bellying bank of fog, and we are in the open, naked.

"Jay-sus!" Pete shouts, and sends me scuttling down to

the engine room to crank it up full speed ahead, into the next fog bank.

The light through the porthole dims, and I sigh with relief knowing we are again in heavy mist. But the wind has started to rise, and the fog is rolling and beginning to clump up like swatches of cotton candy. Pete rings me, and I bring the engines to slow, and go topside again.

"It won't be long before we're an ugly sore thumb on the ocean," Pete says. "What do you think?"

"I think we open the cocks here," I say.

Pete nods. "Open them up, and I'll take her in a bit where it's thicker, up into the bay behind the sunkers."

Billy Lee and I open the sea cocks and water comes pouring in.

With a rushing tide, we creep in dead slow between the horns of the Devil's Coffin. Four fathoms, three fathoms, and we watch the floor of the sea sliding beneath us. Then we are through, into the deep water of the bay. I go below and bring the engines to a clanking halt.

It is time now to say a prayer on behalf of the *Alta Mar* to the Old Man of the Sea, before his arms envelop her. *Alta Mar*, alias *Mayor Juan Atrapa*, we have been through much together, and I am unhappy that I maligned you and called you down and described you in obscene ways. May you sleep and dream of us.

We fill glasses with brandy. "May the seas always be high above you, you dirty, beautiful old queen," says Pete. We toss back our drinks, and we remember that Davy Jones likes a tipple and we toss him one, too.

Except for the sound of water gurgling into the holds below, the air is as silent as the moon. But there is something distant within the silence. A muffled shout? A laugh? I look at Pete. He is squinting into the fog.

And as we stand at the rail, straining, the fog rolls gently away and spots of sunlight dapple the decks, and the waters of the bay open up around us.

The sound again. The shouts of men.

"I got a bite! A big one!"

A flash breeze combs the mists from the far side of the bay, and we can see. Three hundred yards away, emerging out of the mists like some ghostly galleon, is a forty-foot anchored RCMP patrol boat.

A couple of guys in toques and heavy sweaters are out on the deck with mugs of coffee, jigging for cod, and one of them is yelling and pulling up his line, hand over hand. He obviously has a big fish on the hook end.

"Get the net, get the net," he yells.

"Johnny," Pete says softly, "go down and get the engines rolling. Billy Lee, get in the longboat and go the opposite way. You got extra gas and rations." Billy Lee hesitates, but Pete presses into his hand a thick bundle tied with rubber bands – about ten thousand bucks from the stake that Peddigrew gave us.

The generator balks for several agonizing seconds. I am frantic here, and there is water up to my ankles. It finally fires into action. Pete orders reverse, and takes her into a bootlegger's turn, back and around, then forward full speed ahead.

The fast little police launch will take just minutes to climb right up our stern end. Pete is going for the fog.

CHAPTER FORTY-TWO

Meyers was awakened by the dogs barking and snarling outside. Then the buzzer rasped. It was five-thirty in the morning. It would be the man from Switzerland. He opened the front door, whistled to bring the dogs away from the fence. A station wagon, with its lights off, was idling by the gate.

Meyers turned the switch which released the gate, and through the leaded-glass windows he saw the man move his car into the driveway. Meyers turned the switch again, and the gates swung shut.

A couple of his men came running from the guest house. "Take the dogs in," he said to them in Spanish. The dogs were police-trained. Working as a pack, they would kill.

The arms dealer climbed nervously from his station wagon and went quickly up the stairs to greet Meyers.

"This is a palace," he said.

"It belongs to a client," Meyers said.

The man, who was known to Meyers only as Kurt, stood quietly as if waiting to be asked into the house. But Meyers said, "We'll do our business outside. What do you have with you?"

Kurt led him to the back of the wagon and lifted a cloth wrap from a pair of shiny, oiled, and deadly-looking pieces of military equipment.

"The automatic rifle is a Heckler and Koch G.3, much better than the Belgian FAL, I assure you. West German. And this, the sub-machine gun, is Swiss-made." He spoke with pride. "A SIG MP .310. Nine hundred rounds per minute. They are in short supply, now. But I have the contacts, of course."

Meyers picked it up and cradled it in his arms, feeling its weight.

"Made with traditional Swiss attention to detail," said Kurt.

Meyers fondled it, turned it about. He would have loved to fire a few rounds into the swamp, but there were neighbours half a mile away.

"A hundred of these," he said. "Two hundred of the other. I have already looked at the specifications."

"And arrangements for payment?"

"Cash on delivery."

Looking over his shoulder, Kerrivan saw the two men on the RCMP launch scramble wildly to stations, turning the engines over, winching up the anchor. The *Alta Mar*, recalled from the dead, grunted heavily forward.

Billy Lee Tinker's longboat was in the water and its outboard engine, cold, coughed several times before Tinker, with a frantic heave on the cord, brought it alive with a burst of smoke, and began racing away into the mist, towards the shoreline.

"Come on, my darling," Kerrivan whispered to his ship. "Give it some juice." The *Alta Mar* took on speed before a churning white wake.

There was a rolling hump of fog by the pass, between the sunkers. He would be taking the Devil's Coffin at full speed on a dropping tide.

The patrol boat was coming now, and it fired a warning shot from its seventy-six millimetre cannon and a green fountain burst a hundred feet to starboard of the freighter.

Kerrivan took the *Alta Mar* hard in, close to the northern horn of the Coffin and prayed, glancing at the fathometer. The floor of the sea climbed towards the ship like a rising giant, and the rocks were only a few feet from the keel. The tide was pouring through the gap like a river after spring break-up.

Not quite through the pass, not quite into the fogbank, Kerrivan heeled the ship hard to port, tacking like a sailboat, and the old coaster rolled so hard that Kerrivan almost lost his sea legs.

There was this chance: the operator of the patrol boat, lacking local knowledge, being too harried to glance at the charts, might cut too quickly to port in his effort to shorten the angle between him and the *Alta Mar*. That, at any event, was what Kerrivan was inviting him to do.

It worked.

A scream of metal on rock. A snap like a thundercrack. A wild churning and gushing and frothing of water.

The cutter had been sweeping through the sea at close to thirty knots when it impaled itself on the left horn of the Devil.

The *Alta Mar* began to slide into the roiling mists and Kerrivan looked back and saw the patrol boat listing gradually to its side. Two men were in the water and a third was throwing lifejackets and ropes to them.

Nighthawk came aloft.

"Wasn't *my* fault," Kerrivan said. But he wasn't smiling. He felt drained and light in the head—all the tension, and the many sleepless days and nights. "Get the other dinghy ready, John," he said.

Nighthawk didn't move. He was staring at the radar screen.

"Pete, either that's an iceberg, or the *Île de France* is out here lost in the fog."

Kerrivan's eyes bugged.

The *Alta Mar* emerged from the fog and found herself

dwarfed beneath the towering guns of the *HMCS Mackenzie King*, 426-metre DD 280 Class destroyer, flagship of Her Majesty's Royal Canadian Navy in the Atlantic fleet.

A voice bellowed at them through a bullhorn.

"Welcome to Canada, you poor mother-fuckers."

James Peddigrew, on a day free of trials, was studying the weekly newsletter from his investment counsellor. He had asked his secretary not to disturb him, and he scowled when the door clicked open, and a woman slid inside and closed it softly behind her. He did not recognize her at first.

"James," she said, "this is the shits." She took off a pair of horn-rimmed glasses and slipped them into the pocket of a bulky, ill-fitting coat. It was Marianne Larochelle, and she was a brunette.

"What in hell are *you* doing here?" he said, getting up.

"How did I let you talk me into this thing?" she asked.

Peddigrew locked the door. "Why didn't you phone? How do you know they haven't followed you?"

"Don't be stupid. I've been holed up in the Laurentians for the last ten days, in a little ski cabin." She cleared a space on the corner of his desk and perched on it, shrugging off her coat. She had lost weight and looked drawn. "I finally ran out of nose powder. I had to get out. Do you have any idea what has been going on? *Any* idea?"

"They've picked up the ship. Busted Pete and Nighthawk."

"This morning, yes. It was on the news."

"But they don't have the dope."

"Never mind the dope, what's going to happen to *me*, James? You had better start thinking about saving my ass." There was a threat in her voice.

"Your ass is in pretty good shape."

"Only figuratively, James."

"There's nothing they can do to you. They don't know you were a part of this."

"Oh, but they do. They had undercover on us the whole way."

"What do you mean?"

"*Do* you know what's been going on? They killed Kevin, for God's sake!"

Peddigrew went white. "Maybe you *had* better tell me what's going on," he said slowly.

"Act like a lawyer," she said. "Give me some damn advice. I've had some dealings with a Canadian cop. Cute but dumb. He says they can't charge me with anything. Is he right?"

"A cop? Maybe you better stay in hiding a while longer."

"Is he *right*? If he's not, I'm leaving this country on a rocket."

"Keep calm, Marianne. Give me a little time. I have to figure out what's been going down."

"What about the guys? What are you going to do?"

"I already have a plane reservation to St. John's." Peddigrew managed a stiff smile. "Things could be worse. I guess we've got the cargo, and we've got the ship."

"*They've* got the ship. The cops."

"We can get everything released to us by court order, like the last time."

"Don't you think you should get things into gear, James? And go and see Pete before Mitchell takes a turn at him?"

"Let's not worry about Pete. Let's worry about us. Now start from the beginning."

When Peddigrew showed her to the door twenty minutes later, a young woman and man in the waiting room stood up to meet them. The woman showed a badge and handed Larochelle a blue sheet of paper entitled Warrant.

"My name is Constable Ewers," she said. "This is Constable Daniels. Miss Larochelle, you are under arrest upon a charge of conspiring to import marijuana into Canada. You need not say anything but anything you do say may be used as evidence at your trial. Do you understand?"

Larochelle seemed to go limp, and she staggered back a step.

"What's all this about?" Peddigrew said. His throat had gone dry; his voice sounded frayed.

Ewers looked at him with a bland smile. "They told us you were her lawyer. We've been staking out your office building in case she showed up here. We're taking her to St. John's."

"Staking out a lawyer's office – this is outrageous!"

Ewers shrugged. "I have a message for you, Mr. Peddigrew. Before you go out to Newfoundland to see your clients, you are to call Mr. Knowlton Bishop in his office in Ottawa. Collect, he said. He wants to meet with you." She smiled again. "Come along, Marianne."

Flaherty was in Detective Braithwaite's office in the Miami police building and she was making a pitch to extend the deadline.

"You still got no word?" Braithwaite said, glowering. "You really screwed it up, didn't you?"

Flaherty tried to look apologetic. "Just give me a few more days."

"No." Braithwaite sat behind his desk with his arms folded. He wondered why he had listened to this broad in the first place.

"Four more days. That's all I'll ask."

"It ain't going to be you who's going to be caught in the wringer, Jessica."

"Four more days."

"Two."

"Three?" She stuck out her hand to shake on the bargain. Braithwaite kept his arms folded.

"Get out of here," he said. "All right, three. Three. Period. That's it."

CHAPTER FORTY-THREE

"Hullo, Theo," Kerrivan said, looking up at O'Doull through glasses that hung cock-angled across his face, broken at the stem. His face was a mat of bruises.

The guard let O'Doull into the cell and left.

"We got fighters in the navy, boy," Kerrivan said. "We can be proud of them. I guess I'm lucky. Two hundred years ago, they'd have hanged Peter Kerrivan from the yardarm."

"I hear you started it, Pete."

"So they claim. How's Johnny? I hear he lasted nearly ten rounds out there."

"One broken jaw, a ruptured spleen, five cracked ribs, a broken right hand."

Kerrivan groaned. "Is he in hospital?"

"Those are the *navy* casualty figures," O'Doull said. "All except for the right hand. Nighthawk is getting a cast put on that. We think Tinker has gone for a hike in the bush somewhere. He'll give himself up after a few cold nights in the Newfoundland wilderness. By the way, Inspector Mitchell will be coming to see you. He wants to talk about the pot."

None of this was really what O'Doull had come to talk to Kerrivan about.

"So, Theo, are you part of this rat's nest? This NATO military exercise, or whatever it is?"

"Operation Potship. I'm a technical adviser." O'Doull,

uncomfortable, wanted to say what he had come to say and he was having trouble getting it out.

"I don't hold it against you, boy. I guess you had no choice."

"That's about it."

"You always wanted to be a cop, Theo. It's a curious type of obsession, I'm thinking. You get it from your dad?"

"I've been depressed about this whole thing, Pete. Really down." Come on, he told himself. Get it out.

"I feel for you. I get that way myself sometimes. Especially looking down a fifteen-year-long tunnel, and you can't see the light. They haven't got you out here to do a number on me, Theo? You're not playing the friendly cop to soften me up for the hardnose who's going to work me over?"

"I'm not playing cop here at all." O'Doull nervously rubbed his palms together, and wet his lips. "Pete, they tell me you don't know about Kevin." Kerrivan's face went dark. Blurt it out, hard and fast. "He's dead."

Kerrivan was on his feet, clutching O'Doull by his lapels. "What? How? Who?"

O'Doull backed up a step. "I think he was murdered."

"Goddamnit, how?" It was a shout that echoed down the jail corridor.

"Meyers. In Miami."

"Meyers . . . Miami." Kerrivan blinked and his pupils fuzzed over.

O'Doull put his arm around his shoulders and eased him down to the bench. They were both shaking badly.

A shadow fell through the bars.

O'Doull, his arm still around Kerrivan, looked up to see Mitchell glaring at him.

"Get out of there," Mitchell said.

"Fuck off," O'Doull said softly. "Sir."

"I'll have them drag you out, O'Doull."

Kerrivan looked up at Mitchell with red eyes. "If you

want to talk with me, inspector, I want a witness. I want Theo to stay."

"Where was the drop?" Mitchell asked. "You know we'll find it. We have boats going inch by inch along sixty miles of coastline. We've already found Tinker's longboat. On a rock, near the road at Hermitage, under some broken boughs."

Kerrivan glared malevolently at him. "Are you going to offer me a deal, inspector? I help you find some marijuana, you drop the charges against me. Is that it? Haven't I heard that before some place? Wasn't that the deal you offered Kevin the last time? And what a wonderful grand deal it was that Kevin just bought from you *this* time! I'll tell you where I hid the pot, inspector. I stuffed it up my anus, and you can stick Operation Potship up yours!" He flew at the bars, screaming. "You hear me? You can stick it, you bastard, you whore-mother, you cocksucker!"

Mitchell didn't back up. They were nose to nose eight inches apart. "Kerrivan, this time we're going to throw away the keys. Dope or no dope. We've got you photographed and tape-recorded forwards, backwards, upside-down, a thousand ways to Sunday."

"Meyers better be hoping I get nailed with a *lot* of years," Kerrivan hissed. "Because every year I'm in the box is one more year he'll live."

"I didn't hear that, Kerrivan. Now listen to me, I *am* going to make you a deal, and O'Doull is your witness, and you listen to me carefully. You tell me where the drop was, we'll stay the importing charge and take a plea to something less. Conspiracy to traffic. You've got exactly one minute to decide."

"Where's my lawyer? He was supposed to be here this afternoon."

"He's got other business this afternoon," Mitchell said. "That's the deal. Take it or leave it."

Kerrivan looked at O'Doull.

"Don't take it," O'Doull said. "Talk to your lawyer."

Mitchell's voice was icy. "Get back to the lab, O'Doull. Clean out your desk. Close everything down. You're suspended indefinitely from the force."

Just then, a voice came to them from down the hall.

"End of the road for you, old man."

Two uniformed RCMP came smiling down the corridor. Between them, handcuffed to one of them, was Captain Pike.

"Inspector," one of them called, "what do we do with fifty tons of grass?"

Mitchell's face stretched wide into a gleeful smile.

"You take it somewhere and burn it, constable."

CHAPTER FORTY-FOUR

Peddigrew had to shout into the telephone. Kerrivan was in a screaming rage.

"Calm down, damnit!" Peddigrew yelled. "I'm in Ottawa. I'll see you tomorrow. I'm with the government's number-one man, and I'll be doing some fast talking. I'll have their heads spinning before I'm through."

Peddigrew was making his call from the lobby of Ottawa's Renfrew Club, a refuge for the wealthy and for the mandarins of the civil service.

Knowlton Bishop, who had arranged to have the call put through for Peddigrew, had decided on his club for the meeting because it represented a homefield advantage in what promised to be a hard-fought match. Peddigrew was known to him as a wily advocate and, worse, a headline-hunter.

And Bishop was going in there with the worst of handicaps: he had no weapons and no protective gear. No trial, the minister had said. No publicity. Jean-Louis Lessard was worried about his job. And maybe he had reason to worry.

What price would Peddigrew exact? Fortunately, the man had no idea of how far down the page the government had drawn its bottom line. The bottom line was simply this: no bodies. Take no prisoners if it came down to it. It was almost a no-win proposition for the government – there would be as much hell to pay if the prosecution came out of this imbroglio without a single conviction as there would be if the press picked up the stink of Mitchell's overdone operation. And the smell of Rudy Meyers which seemed to pervade this whole thing.

The dilemma was compounded by the fact that Mitchell had hinted that if Kerrivan were not sentenced hard, the inspector himself would raise an uproar, intended to embarrass the minister. Somehow Mitchell would have to be paid off with a big jail term for Kerrivan.

So Bishop would have to bluff it out. He would do what he could: wheel and deal, trade bodies, move whom he could through the courts, pre-packaged and stamped. But in the end—no trial. If Peddigrew called the bluff, Bishop would have to retreat in ignominious defeat, fold the government's hand, give up the chips, drop all charges.

He watched Peddigrew walk towards him, looking jaunty and confident, decorated like Christmas with diamonds on fingers and tie pin. Bishop felt stuffy and unkempt in a worn English wool suit that had fit him ten years ago.

Peddigrew took a cue from the martini glass sitting on the table in front of the old lawyer.

"Dry martini with a twist," he said to the waiter.

"Gin or vodka, sir?"

Peddigrew laughed. "Gin, of course." He smiled at Bishop, who would appreciate that Peddigrew was quite in tune with the fact that vodka in the Renfrew Club was just a little crass.

"I'll take another, Fred," Bishop said.

"One gin martini," said the waiter. "One vodka martini."

"Can't stand gin," Bishop said. "That lingering sweetness."

Round One.

"I hope you don't mind this little side trip to stuffy Ottawa," Bishop said. "I would have gone to Toronto, but that city is too fast for an old man like me."

326

The waiter brought the drinks.

"To your health," Bishop said.

"To yours, sir."

"I thought we should have an early chat. Time, trouble, and expense can usually be saved by a quick clearing of the decks, as it were."

Peddigrew nodded. He planned to play it close, wait for the first offer.

Bishop waved to a florid man at the next table who pushed his chair back and came over.

"How are you, Jeff?" Bishop said to him. "You fellows still working on that damn provincial resources referral? I thought you'd be back in three minutes after you finished slicing me up in there."

"We didn't want to embarrass the other side by being too easy on you, Knowlton."

"Mr. Justice Jeffery Forrest, James Peddigrew from Toronto. One of our bright up-and-coming young legal lights."

Peddigrew stood up and grasped the judge's hand. "A fantastic pleasure, sir. I read your dissent in the Jacques Sawchuk sedition case. You had *me* convinced."

"Too bad I couldn't convince those other eight buggers." He went back to his table.

"Everyone says that's where you should be," Peddigrew said to Bishop. "On the Supreme Court of Canada."

"Turned it down. Not going to spend the rest of my life closeted in a smoky room debating constructive trust in impugned wills. I prefer trout fishing." His laughter was gentle, rolling, and unaffected. "Mr. Peddigrew, I know something about your reputation. I've been following the report. I read the newspapers. I'm *paid* to do so as part of my annual retainer with the federal justice department. Advise on possible appointments to the bench, that sort of thing. I don't know – I suppose I'm just another voice in their busy ear, but sometimes they go along with me."

It was all grease, Peddigrew knew, but flattering nonetheless.

"Let's see if we can't cover a little ground before lunch," Bishop said. "I know you're not the kind of fellow who likes to waste time. We can parry about for half an hour or so, but we both know what we're here for. I think we can consider that we are unabashedly plea-bargaining in the Renfrew Club."

He waved for another round of drinks. Peddigrew's head was already light from the first one. He wasn't used to hard alcohol.

"Now what do you want, Mr. Peddigrew?"

"What do *I* want?"

"Let's turn our cards face up. We've given you all the facts, the best and the worst of them. Tell me what you want. If you've got something we can live with, I might even decide to go with it."

Peddigrew was taken slightly off base. The usual opener from the crown attorney sought at least a token sacrifice of blood.

"I won't pussyfoot, Mr. Peddigrew. We're willing to pay a price. The government is embarrassed about the case. The RCMP staged this operation a little close to the shady line. I'm not saying *over* the line, but close. And personally I think close is dangerous territory for a police force."

Peddigrew figured he might as well stick the knife in hard and early. "If a government hireling commits murder, that's *close* to the line? The papers could be nasty."

Bishop felt his stomach muscles tighten, and this time his laugh was a little forced. "Oh, God, that's *all* we need. No, we even sent a man down there to check it out. It's a drug murder, heart attack, and the Miami police have closed their file. Sad business, though." He looked intently at Peddigrew. "Actually, there's a bit of a theory that one of your clients, Miss Larochelle, might be implicated. But that's not our concern, is it?" It was something to back Peddigrew off.

"What do *you* want, Mr. Bishop?" Peddigrew understood that there would be no first names for a while yet.

"Let's get down to the bones, Mr. Peddigrew. We have four persons under arrest. They comprise the North American end of one of the biggest drug rings in this hemisphere. Single richest drug cargo I've ever seen recorded. *That* is headline material, too, and not stuff that will afford aid and sympathy to your clients. Perhaps the public at large – from whom we choose our jurors – will understand the need for aggressive police action when dealing with such a sophisticated syndicate."

Peddigrew returned Bishop's smile. "My clients and their sophisticated syndicate were introduced to this record shipment of drugs by a man under contract to the RCMP. If it hadn't been for the police, my clients would have returned to Canada empty-handed. The newspapers might find *that* the more interesting news item."

"Mr. Peddigrew – is it James or Jim?"

"James."

"Quite bluntly, all four of them are dead on the facts. This fellow Pike is found sitting on nearly fifty tons of drugs. Kerrivan and Nighthawk imported it. The girl conspired to bring it in. All the headlines in the world aren't going to change those facts. Let's think about time. Kerrivan, as the leader, will get fifteen years. Nighthawk, with his terrible record, will get no less. Pike, well, he's getting on and I suppose we'd settle for the statutory minimum of seven."

"What is your offer, Knowlton?"

"I know that in an all-out war we will take our scars. But I do not intend that the government take any of them on its backside. We'll fight if we have to, like a damn tiger. Four convictions are certain. Five when they find Billy Lee Tinker. And *I* will be doing the trial."

"What about Marianne Larochelle? What do you see her

getting?" Peddigrew realized it was a flub as soon as he'd spoken. He should not have expressed an early interest in her.

"Why should she get less?" The old lawyer narrowed his eyes. There seemed to be a softness here, an opening that he could breach. "She made a confession to a policeman, then made a fool of him by slipping away."

Peddigrew studied his hands, then looked up. "I'll have to check that out," he said. "It sounds as if that episode – or that *relationship* – might yield a few nuggets of gold along the way."

Bishop was unhappy that Peddigrew seemed to guess too easily where his own areas of weakness were. Peddigrew would have to be kept away from O'Doull at all costs.

"What is your offer?" Peddigrew asked again. "Your down-to-the-bones offer."

"I've been wasting time, haven't I?" Bishop said. "Too much talk. It's a bad habit of old tired trial lawyers." He was silent for a moment. He had been going to suggest letting the girl off easier, but he decided to include her with the others. "We'll take seven years each."

He rose and led Peddigrew into the dining room. "We can meet with the judge in his chambers before sentencing and let him know we are of one mind," he said, as the waiter put menus before them. "I see no purpose in stating our positions in open court, in front of the world." Bishop looked at Peddigrew with a straight face, but there was a twinkle in his eye. "We'll let the editorial writers blame the *court* for its excessive leniency."

Peddigrew was quietly exulting. He knew there was more meat yet to be carved from the generous ham bone the government was tendering.

"That's a deal you'll never see again," Bishop said. "And I mean that literally. The deadline is tomorrow. At two P.M. In front of the provincial court judge in St. John's. We'll have a quick burial."

"That's rushing things a little."

"A *quick* burial, before the rot sets in."

Peddigrew studied the menu, thinking furiously.

"I don't like to rush you, James, but it seems appropriate to have your reaction."

"Let's order first. We can chew on it. As it were."

"As it were."

The waiter interrupted and took Bishop to the phone at the desk.

"Knowlton, it's Milt Edwards. I thought I should bring you up to date. This is the story on Billy Lee Tinker. He got lucky while he was hitching a ride, got picked up by one of Kerrivan's boys in an old restored Packard. We checked out the plates: a Dave Doncaster. I assume he was down on that part of the coast as part of Kerrivan's landing crew. Doncaster took him all the way to Gander, to the airport."

"Yes, I have that so far," Bishop said.

"He managed to get a flight to Sydney with a connection to Fredericton, and we found out he has reserved a charter to Houlton, Maine. That's at the New Brunswick border."

"Is there any chance the U.S. officials will detain him?"

"No, we contacted Flaherty and she says she has nothing on him. There's a desertion charge, but she's going to ignore it. It's our show, she says. Unless we get an extradition warrant."

"I wouldn't dream of it, Milt. There's no danger our immigration people will do anything?"

"They've been instructed to let him through. I have a feeling he'll lay low in Alabama for a while. The thought that we may be looking for him will be enough to keep him from surfacing, and if he stays out of sight, that's one headache out of the way. How are things going at the legal level?"

"Peddigrew hasn't said no to anything yet. I think he wants to make a deal."

Following food, coffee, Courvoisier, and the obligatory conversation about the future of confederation, Peddigrew leaned forward and said, "Let's work out the minor clauses first, then we can get to wages and hours of work."

"You've done some trade union law, James."

"I've done a little bargaining in my time, Knowlton." Peddigrew had gotten over his initial nervousness about Bishop, who was not the shark that they claimed. The man was going to be easy.

"Money," he said. "Crass as the subject may be, money is what puts meat and potatoes on the table. Nearly sixty thousand dollars was seized from Kerrivan, another five thousand from Larochelle. I would like those sums released to me in trust."

Bishop had forgotten about the money. "No problem, no problem." He was jolly.

"Fees, you understand."

Sixty-five thousand dollars: a nice fee for a day's work, Bishop thought.

"All the equipment aboard the ship," Peddigrew said. "There is about fifty thousand bucks' worth of gear."

Meyers could take the loss, Bishop thought. Out of his five-hundred-thousand-dollar fee. "You can have everything," he said. "From the coffee cups to the Mae Wests. Except the Sat-Track and the marijuana, of course." They laughed. After a few samples were taken for court, the marijuana had been reloaded onto the *Alta Mar* by a navy crew and burned at the Halifax city dump that morning. The *Alta Mar* was now tied up at the Halifax naval yard.

"All I need is a release from your clients," Bishop said. "Is there anything else you want?"

"One more thing. Marianne Larochelle. She was just along for the ride. Drop the charges against her."

Bishop couldn't believe it. The government was getting off cheap. He wondered if he dared push this a little farther. Larochelle was the obvious key.

"We can't just drop the charges against the woman," he said. "It's still eight months before Christmas. No, I think we'd be prepared to take our lumps before we let her go completely. Of course, if you were to agree to a bit of a stiffer sentence for Kerrivan and Nighthawk, I might be able to give some more thought to the girl's case."

Peddigrew shrugged a nonchalant shrug. "They're expecting at least fifteen anyway. Well, let's say fifteen for Kerrivan, fifteen for Nighthawk, and we drop against the girl."

Bishop was impassive. "Done," he said. He raised his glass. "To justice, James. May it be done, may it be seen to be done."

"To justice."

They clinked glasses.

CHAPTER FORTY-FIVE

Johnny Nighthawk

Fifteen years. I can handle it. I can handle it. I am saying that to myself, over and over, as we wait for court. Fifteen years. Do not start thinking about hours or days or months. I can handle it. Keep telling yourself that, Hawk. Keep afloat. The world seems to have imploded in on itself. I tell myself: keep afloat.

"Otherwise, it's probably seventeen or eighteen years for both you and Johnny, maybe ten to twelve for the old man." Peddigrew is explaining it all again to Pete and me. "And you've got to think of Marianne. *She'll* get at least ten. This way she's free as a bird."

I think of a bird.

"Johnny's willing to take fifteen years," Peddigrew goes on. "He's an old con, and he knows he's got a good deal. Fifteen years — it isn't the end of the world, is it, Johnny?"

"No." It is not the end of the *world*. I think of a bird in the sky.

"Okay, Pete? We've got to see the judge in half an hour. It's going into court as a package."

A package. Sealed and tied. I think of this image.

"Go back and play some poker," Pete says.

Peddigrew's mouth sags open. He has the look he had when he caught Pete fucking his wife. I am thinking: why so surprised? He knows Pete.

"Pete, for God's sake, I've wrung them dry. Come to your senses." His voice is brittle.

"Look, James, I'll take the whole hit," Pete says. "The whole hit. It's *me* they want. Go back and tell this Bishop guy I'll do the fall, but Uncle Pike and Johnny walk out of this."

Pete is lounging on a wooden chair, bruised up but cool. Two bones in my right hand are broken, and it is aching, and this pain helps me deal with the fifteen years.

"Pete, I know my business," Peddigrew says.

"What business is that, James? The law business or the ship salvage business? You know something about the business of locating old ships in Colombia, I'll grant you that."

Peddigrew looks wildly at Pete and makes large motions with his hands to tell him to lower his voice. He scribbles a note on a writing pad: "This place may be bugged."

Pete ignores that, and goes on in a conversational tone. "I want you to go back to that guy and I want you to save my friends' necks." He takes Peddigrew's pen and scribbles this: "And your *own* neck, too."

Peddigrew is flushed and looks ready to storm out, or maybe have a tantrum. "Pete, goddamnit, I squeezed the last corpuscle of blood from them. Come *on!*"

"They're scared, boy, and you know it. They know you thrive on those big newspaper headlines. Now I'll tell you what I'm going to do, old son. If you don't save John and the captain, I'm going to fire you, and I'm not going to sign this release." Referring to the paper in his hand. "And you won't get the money and the stuff from the ship. And I won't be copping a plea. I'll be handling my own defence."

Pete lowers his voice a little.

"I could say a lot of interesting things in that courtroom,

James. The prosecutor is going to ask me to name names. And I'd be in contempt of court if I refused to give those names. Wouldn't I?"

Peddigrew is like a cornered raccoon.

"Go back," Pete says. "Talk to that dumb old lawyer you think you conned so bad, and really take him to the cleaners this time. Wring him dry. You claim to be the best tongue in the business. Strut your stuff."

•

Bishop knew it had been too good to be true. He had been so pleased with himself. The fifteen years for Kerrivan was just enough to mollify Mitchell. Freedom for Marianne Larochelle was enough to satisfy O'Doull, to buy his silence. No trial and no publicity: that would satisfy the minister.

But here was this unethical excuse for a lawyer telling him the deal was off. Kerrivan had vetoed it. Was it a ruse by Peddigrew to bang out a better bargain for his clients on the courthouse steps? Probably not, he decided. Peddigrew had seemed too pleased yesterday over lunch.

"What does he want?" Bishop asked, calm but with a hard border to his voice. "Does he want less time?"

Peddigrew's brain had been working frenziedly for the fifteen minutes between leaving Kerrivan and meeting with Bishop.

"You have to understand that he's a Newfie, Knowlton. He doesn't reason things out the same way you or I would. He says he doesn't care about his own time. All he wants is the charges dropped against Pike and Nighthawk."

Bishop realized it wasn't a catastrophe after all. He could live with it.

"Look," Peddigrew continued, "the old man is like a father to him. Kind of adopted him after his own father died. Pete just won't see reason about him. Doesn't want the old man to live his dying years behind a prison wall. I

mean, if you look at these things with a little compassion . . .
Hell, I'll even tell the court Kerrivan *used* the old guy, so
that will seem to justify your dropping against him."

"You'll say that to the judge."

"Sure. Pete says he'll do the whole rap. And Nighthawk—hell, he's just a stooge, a dumb Indian that Kerrivan
has literally got hypnotized into believing he's some kind of
saint to be worshipped. I don't think he has an I.Q. higher
than a goldfish." Peddigrew was talking rapidly, urgently,
in one of the hardest submissions he had made in his career.

"I'll say Kerrivan used him, too. I'll say Nighthawk was
only going to get a few bucks out of this, and all he'd do is
spend it on booze."

"He has a couple of previous traffickings, already got
seven years on one. I can't conceivably drop the charges
against this man. I'd be laughed out of the profession. The
old fellow, okay, although I always thought that leniency
was the prerogative of the courts, not the prosecutors."

"No, it has to be Nighthawk, too."

"He's dangerous. You heard what he did to those sailors.
How can I let him loose on the streets?"

"For God's sake, Knowlton, he's charged with marijuana,
not attempted murder."

"I thought we had a deal, James. The judge is waiting to
see us. This is very awkward." Don't push it too far, Bishop
told himself.

Peddigrew moved to Plan Two.

"Well, God, I don't know what we're going to do." His
face had the expression of one lost in thought; then it
brightened. "All right, here's an idea—let's assume you *can't*
just drop the charges against Nighthawk. Let me run this by
you." He hesitated as if unsure how to put it. "Let's assume
I make a bail application for him. So he can be released on
his own recognizance, without sureties. Let's assume that
you, on behalf of the crown, consent."

Bishop coughed. "Bail! He's an American, no fixed address, lifetime criminal and dope dealer, fluent in Spanish. He'd be just about as good a candidate for bail as the Ayatollah Khomeini would be for President of the U.S.A. He'd be gone and out of here forever, in about two seconds after leaving court."

Peddigrew just looked at him.

After several seconds, Bishop said, "Okay, I have your point."

The provincial court judge was a solemn-looking man with a broad heavy face. There were no crinkles by his eyes and no glint of humour in them. To Bishop, he looked somehow friendless. He was a rookie judge, and that made Bishop nervous. His scouting report told him that Judge Squires had been a small-town conveyancer of properties and a Lions Club booster before his recent appointment to the lower-court bench, a political pay-off.

But Judge Squires was writing everything down and seemed to be getting it straight.

He read it out. "Larochelle, stay of proceedings. Court doesn't have to do anything. Pike, stay of proceedings. Court doesn't have to deal with him, either. Nighthawk, his own bail, and the court adjourns his case for a month. Kerrivan pleads guilty. Court gives him at least fifteen years."

He looked at Bishop suspiciously. "You say you're working directly for Ottawa, Mr. Bishop. We don't usually do things this way. Not that I've heard."

"I'm appointed by the minister himself," Bishop said. That seemed to impress the judge. "Just to keep the record straight, the crown isn't *asking* for these dispositions. It is not opposing. The defence makes the application."

Bishop realized the subtlety of that was lost on the judge.

"The crown doesn't ask, doesn't oppose," repeated Judge Squires. "But that is what you're agreed on."

"The fifteen years," said Peddigrew, "we're not asking for that. But I agree to say that anything less might be regarded as an unreasonable sentence. In the circumstances."

"In the circumstances," Squires repeated. "You're asking for that, and the crown is not opposing."

"No, the crown asks for that, and I'm not opposing."

"But you're not consenting." There were beads of sweat on the judge's forehead.

"Well, we're not consenting, but we're not *not* consenting, we're not saying anything but what I've said we'd say."

For the judge it was, as Bishop's teenaged daughter would say, confusion city. There was despair in the man's face.

"Except," Peddigrew continued, "I'll make the usual submission. Then we leave the sentence up to the court. In its discretion," he added nervously.

"The usual submission?" said the judge. "Is there a usual submission? I don't mind telling you boys that I'm a little new at this."

"The submission as to character," said Peddigrew. "The good character of the accused."

"That being . . ."

"Kerrivan."

"And that's before I sentence him."

Bishop and Peddigrew were both feeling little flutters of panic.

"Well, I know about Kerrivan," Squires said. "I know about his character, all right. I have a niece went out with him."

Peddigrew felt himself relax, but it was just for a moment.

"He got her all screwed up on drugs. She's never been right since. Moved out to the West Coast. Living with a bunch of dope fiends in a commune, is what I hear."

Peddigrew tried to catch Bishop's eye. But the prosecutor was studying a watercolour of a sailing ship running into the sunset. Peddigrew said, "Of course Your Honour being a well-known jurist in these parts . . ."

"No, I don't fancy I'm well known," Squires said. "I'll be

frank, I've got a lot of learning to do yet."

"Yes, yes," Peddigrew said, "but you do understand, of course, that what you have personally heard, which is hearsay after all, can't be an influence in sentencing." He said loudly to Bishop: "I'm sure the crown agrees with that."

"Yes, of course," Bishop said heartily.

"Oh, I understand I can't base my decision on pure hearsay," Squires said. "I have to take account of what happens in court. But it's not hearsay, either, Mr. Peddigrew. I saw her with my own eyes. All screwed up on drugs. Giggling and smiling. She was up her tree."

"The prosecutor is not insisting on more than fifteen years," Peddigrew said.

"No," said the judge, "but not opposing neither."

Outside in the hallway, Peddigrew spoke to Bishop in a hushed, urgent voice. "I don't like this."

"We don't have time to go judge-shopping," Bishop said.

●

Johnny Nighthawk

In court, light-headed, fuzzy, trying to focus, I fix my eyes on the judge. He is blinking his eyes around the courtroom, as if he is surprised to find himself there. I am minutes from breathing fresh, free air, as soon as my bail papers are drawn up and signed. I am as close to being long-time gone from Canada as I am to the St. John's airport.

Mitchell sits stolidly at the back, a stone lion guarding the door.

The prosecutor is a grandfatherly type, who seems okay, not beating any drums in here. Peddigrew, as is his habit, is preening and showing off with a long, windy speech about Pete's good background, although he is heaping the offence up on his shoulders alone.

Old man Pike is sitting there nervous, but he is a free man, as is Marianne, who sits poised and beautiful as ever, with that soft inner smile. I notice her hair is dyed black. Pete, however, seems unable to look at her.

The judge waits for Peddigrew to sit down, then begins to read off a piece of paper something he wrote up, I guess, after the lawyers met with him.

"It is my duty to sentence you, Peter Kerrivan." The voice sounds sonorous, like that of a preacher at a funeral. "I have taken into account all the things that have been said about you by your lawyer, which is a lot. He has made an excellent submission and he has said everything he could possibly think of on your behalf." He clears his throat.

"I have to take account of the protection of society and the vast amount of drugs that you have brought into Canada for illicit sale and consumption. That is the main thing. The amount. There is no way to estimate the millions of minds that might have been crippled if the RCMP had not caught you and all the drugs. I have heard a lot of people gripe about the police, these days, but it is only through their hard work that this vast and massive shipload of narcotics was consti . . . confi, confiscated." He turns the page.

"Now the other thing is deterrence. I have to impose a sentence that will deter you, and those of like mind, from doing this again. I have let one of your gang out on bail and two of you have got off altogether, so there is not much deterrence there. The minimum sentence for this is seven years. I can see a point to seven years if you were bringing a small amount across the border for your own use. But I have to think of this massive shipment of drugs in terms of all the young people in this country whose minds are prey to them. Peter Kerrivan, will you stand up and be sentenced."

Pete shambles to his feet.

"I sentence you to life imprisonment."

CHAPTER FORTY-SIX

Theophile O'Doull stormed through the operations centre like a Nazi lieutenant, bawling orders, swearing, slamming boxes shut, sweeping papers and tools from his work table.

"Clean up and get out. We're closing shop. Get your damn reports in. Come on! Move it! Move it!"

He stopped by the desk of the fingerprint man. "Where's your report? I haven't seen a single fucking print sheet."

"Jeez, sarge, the case is over. What's the point of finger-prints?"

"Get off your ass, tab the prints, and close your file."

The print man sulked. "There ain't gonna be no trial."

"Do it!" O'Doull screamed at him.

He stomped down the hall to the chemical lab and threw open the door. The analyst, Wegthorne, was so startled he dropped his paperback on the floor. O'Doull glared at him with eyes like hot coals. "Are your reports in?" he said, his voice barely controlled.

The toluene and petroleum ether solutions for the Duquenois-Levine and thin-layer chromotography tests were still in their flasks, sealed, the marijuana samples still in exhibit envelopes.

"Hey, Theo," Wegthorne said, "how are you doin'? Guess you and I can go back home."

O'Doull had recruited Wegthorne from his lab in Ottawa

with the thought that he might be able to dump him permanently in Newfoundland.

"*You're* not going home until you've done the analysis and signed your certificates."

"What's the point, Theo? There ain't going to be a trial. Kerrivan copped a plea."

"You're the laziest goddamn chemist I have ever encountered. Do your job!"

Wegthorne slowly removed his feet from the table and turned to face O'Doull. "I don't know if you've got the right to order nobody about, Theo. Being that you got your ass suspended by the inspector." His lips curled up in a smirk, but he didn't look O'Doull in the eye. "Speaking of ass, that cute Frenchie dame – I hear you got a little bit. That's what the boys are saying. How was it? I hear she's got a box about as big as an open-pit mine, and just as busy."

O'Doull swung his fist almost as a reflex action. Two seconds later, blinking his eyes, he realized Wegthorne was sprawled on top of the table, blood pouring from his nose.

He wheeled around, strode down the hall, told the receptionist to make plane reservations for him to Ottawa, then took a taxi to the airport, where he began to drink a lot of dark rum while he waited for his plane.

The last two days had been the blackest period of his life. The suspension. The blackmailing by Bishop. The life term for Kerrivan. The cold, cold shoulder from Larochelle outside the courtroom.

O'Doull, unable to marshal strength enough to watch the proceedings, had stayed outside the courtroom doors. Earlier, in the subtlest of dialogues, Bishop had bought O'Doull's silence with a promise of freedom for Larochelle.

The thought of her spending ten or fifteen years in the Kingston Women's Penitentiary had caused flutters of nausea in O'Doull's stomach. He had had sleepless nights over it, rolling and tossing in agony, blankets and sheets balled up and crushed and damp with his sweat.

The first person to come out of the courtroom had been Mitchell. Mitchell with a smile, clenching his fists in front of him as if he had just coached his team to a narrow win.

But it was Larochelle he had been waiting for. All his dreams, waking or sleeping, had converged into a dream of Larochelle. One more night with her had been all he dared to pray for. One long, rich, fulfilling night that might set him free of her.

And when she came out, she had given him a look that froze him.

"You bastard," she hissed. "You lying *bastard*! I really believed you, and you were trying to set me up all along."

He had tried to move to her, but Peddigrew had blocked his path.

"Keep away from her, O'Doull. You'll be happy to know that you helped get your old pal Kerrivan a lifer in the pen. Does it feel good?"

O'Doull's stomach had turned to acid, and he had stood there, feeling it burn, long after Peddigrew had taken Marianne's elbow and led her out of sight.

●

Johnny Nighthawk

I do not have a chance to put my head together before I am dog-trotted from there by Peddigrew. I had wanted to talk to Pete, I had wanted to touch him. But only our eyes touched, and mine were wetly out of focus, and his seemed empty.

Peddigrew began grumpily thrusting money at me, three or four thousand dollars American, telling me the fastest way to get to the airport is by running down the street to the nearest taxi stand, a couple of blocks away.

"Dorchester Pen is a hell-hole, Mr. Peddigrew," I am saying. "They will break a guy like Pete. They'll put him in the

344

damper and they'll break him. He'll end up on the spike, wired on jailhouse smack. What are you going to do about it, Mr. Peddigrew?"

"I don't think we can win an appeal. I'll agonize over it, but the main thing now is for you to heel out of here and go into hiding."

I am a blur of feelings right now. I have to get away by myself. I shake his hand – he has done well for me – and move on down the street, up a few blocks to where my old Ford pickup has been sitting for the last month. I wiggle the ignition key out of the ashtray. The engine does not turn over, so I ask a guy for a boost, then head down to the Blue Boar to seek the company of the boys.

Jimmy Arthur is polishing the bar. None of the boys are in here.

"Congratulations, Johnny," he says. But he looks a little down. For Kerrivan. The word has got out fast. "What will you have?"

"A double rye on the rocks. I am going to get drunk."

Comes a familiar voice from behind me. "We got other things to do first, John." It is Crazy Dewey Fitzgerald, second bike of the Phantom Riders, a guy I remember beating on during the brawl down here the night Pete and Kelly got acquitted. This, I am thinking, is all I need. Some asshole from a former grievance wants vengeance in a bar. I note that Dewey has a serious expression. Not fighting serious. Serious serious.

"Down the drink," he says. "My chopper's out on the street. You follow along behind. Try to keep up." That's all. No explanation. He leaves. I follow. I am too tired to try to figure out what is going on.

Half an hour later, I follow him off the Trans-Canada Highway, onto a long gravel road that winds in among a grove of grungy little spruce.

There are a couple of cars outside and about eight or nine bikes sitting there. An old farmhouse, club rooms of the

Phantom Riders. I can hear laughter from inside.

Dewey takes me in. At the head of the table is Midge Tobin, head honcho of the Riders. "Okay, gentlemen, last order of business," he is saying. "We talked about it in executive session. The motion is we volunteer two outriders. Behalf of the executive, I so move. I see a seconder, Ned Noseworthy. Discussion – we ain't got much time. Okay, all in favour. Carried."

The club members are sitting around a long table. On a chair against the wall is Dave Doncaster, looking sombre. A few days earlier Dave and I were laughing our heads off at Captain Pike's boatshed. Dave is one of Pete's most loyal boys. Later, I learned he picked up Billy Lee Tinker a few days before and helped smuggle him out of Newfoundland.

"There being no other formal business, I will entertain a motion for adjournment," says Midge Tobin. "Moved by Noseworthy, no seconder required, no debate on a motion to adjourn. All those in favour, signify. Motion carried. Hi, Johnny, me old trout, this is going to cost you. We ain't doin' it for love." He turns to his members. "Two volunteers, boys. I recognize my own hand up first and . . . I pick Dewey, thanks anyway, Barney and Horse."

Midge pounds out of the building like a rhinoceros, followed by Crazy Dewey Fitzgerald, and I hear their bikes starting up outside. My head is whirling.

Dave grabs me by the elbow and hustles me outside. I should have noticed his car. It is a classic old Packard, nicely restored.

"Far out," Dave says, "you brought your dirty old truck. That's just the ticket. I *ain't* gonna let the boys use this baby." He pats his car on the hood. "Follow along behind me, Johnny. The rest of the boys is waitin'. We got ground-to-air radio, and the cops is gonna be leavin' the lockup soon if they're gonna get Pete to the ferry. We got to time this to the split second, boy."

CHAPTER FORTY-SEVEN

Two uniformed guards held Kerrivan, one on each arm. He was handcuffed, looking straight ahead. They put him in the back seat of the cruiser, alone. The rear doors were locked from the outside.

Night was falling. They drove to the Trans-Canada Highway, moving fast in order to make the late ferry from Port-aux-Basques to the mainland, and to Dorchester Penitentiary.

"I hope you guys made a reservation," Kerrivan said after a while. "I'd hate to miss it."

There was no response.

"Could I have a smoke?" Kerrivan asked.

One of the guards pushed a lit cigarette through a hole in the screen.

An hour later a big Harley roared past them, going in the opposite direction. Then a few minutes later it was behind them, on their tail. It moved up slowly alongside them, sitting square on the centre line of the highway while the driver peered into the cruiser.

"Get off of there or I'll *blow* you off of there," the guard-driver said. The bike swept ahead of them, accelerating to a hundred and fifty kilometres an hour.

"Did you get his plate?"

"Naw, it's smeared with mud."

Half an hour later, in the middle of nowhere, in the empty Newfoundland forest, they came to a sudden halt.

"Jesus!" the driver said.

A tall spruce had fallen over the road and was sitting on the cab of an old pickup truck. The headlights were on; the horn was blaring.

"There's gotta be somebody in there!"

"I guess we better try to get him out," Kerrivan said hopefully.

"Don't try anything smart, Kerrivan. Just sit tight." One guard picked up a sawed-off shotgun and got out of the car. His partner glanced back at Kerrivan, then got out, too.

Kerrivan saw shadows drifting among the trees beside the road.

"This tree's been *cut*," one of the guards yelled.

"There's nobody in the truck," shouted the other. "Something fishy here."

The sound of Kerrivan's boots punching at the metal screen was masked by the blare of the horn. The fastenings were starting to give.

From the corner of his eye, Kerrivan saw two huge swatches of herring net swirl through the air, weights tied to the sides. The netting fell on the guards, taking them off their feet.

Kerrivan got enough of the screen open to jam his body through, and he squeezed out, still handcuffed, and somersaulted out of the passenger door, onto the road's shoulder and into the ditch.

The guards were by now screaming panicky curses. Of the boys sliding out from behind the cover of the trees, Kerrivan could make no one out for certain. Their faces had been blackened by charcoal.

He saw headlights snap on by a side road. Two men raced up to the cruiser, and one yelled, "Where the fuck is he?" Bill Stutely.

"I'm down here, b'y," Kerrivan called. "Getting some air."

"And would ye be good enough to stay there, captain, sorr, while I signal our radio man to send the word." Stutely pulled out a flashlight and clicked it on-off three times, then repeated the signal. His companion, slightly built – Kerrivan guessed it was Tommy Hogan – got into the front seat of the jail escort car and began cutting out the wires to the ignition and police radio with a fish knife.

The guards were by now tangled hopelessly. Kerrivan's rescuers continued to throw nets on top of them.

Kerrivan had no trouble recognizing the form that now came hurtling down the slope of the ditch towards him, high on his Harley 1600. Midge Tobin, built like a buffalo, looking like Zeus in his full brown beard.

Kerrivan swung up behind him. "Where's my helmet?" he said. "Isn't no helmet against the law?"

"Ain't against my law, Pete. Hang on."

Kerrivan did. The bike spit gravel until sparks flashed, swinging deep into the ditch to avoid the top branches of the fallen tree, then it accelerated westward towards Gander.

A few minutes later, Dewey Fitzgerald's bike pulled up alongside them. On the back, grinning at Kerrivan like a lunatic, was Johnny Nighthawk.

"The pressure can be enough down here to cave your face in," Dr. Jan Bjarling, the team leader, warned.

"I know."

"You may black out for a little while."

"I can handle it. I've been down to five hundred metres."

But this was seven hundred. Even Levontov of the crack Soviet navy team had not been able to handle anything under six hundred.

It was starting to hit him. After fifteen minutes he would

enter the cockpit of the bell jar. And then he would have maybe eighteen minutes to get the bell jar into the Ryuku Trench, perhaps seven minutes to dismantle the neutron device. No more.

O'Doull *had* to get back up. He had, after all, made that promise to Suzanne, the medical student, who was waiting up top. Suzanne, with the sea-green eyes . . . .

In the airport bar, O'Doull slowly plunged his stirstick into the deep recesses of a tall glass of rum, into the trench between the ice cubes, down, down, to where his face was about to cave in.

"Paging Sergeant O'Doull."

He heard his name being called from someone up top. It was not the voice of Dr. Jan Bjarling.

"Paging Sergeant O'Doull of the RCMP. Would Sergeant O'Doull *please* go to the RCMP office near the west door."

O'Doull, somewhat impaired, slid off the bar stool, and found his way to the airport detachment where a uniformed· man passed the phone to him.

Wegthorne, the analyst.

"All right, Wegthorne, I'm sorry. I just lost control of myself."

"I did the analysis."

"All I can do is apologize."

"It took a little longer than I expected."

"What took a little longer?"

"The analysis."

"You paged me to tell me you did the analysis." O'Doull looked hard at the receiver as if Wegthorne's face might be seen there, and could be studied.

"Actually, Theo, to tell the truth, none of the samples analyzed out."

"The samples . . . give me that again?"

"It's all alfalfa. Hay. It took me a while to pin it down. Alfalfa *smells* like pot, especially when you burn it."

"*Alfalfa?*"

350

"Alfalfa."

O'Doull slowly put the receiver back on the hook. He stared at the floor, frowning, then walked to the Air Canada counter. "I want you to reroute me," he said. "Miami. The fastest way I can get there."

"You may be a little late getting out. They're holding up all flights to Eastern Newfoundland. There's some kind of kefuffle up at Gander International."

They hit a hundred and eighty kilometres an hour, the bikes thundering like an artillery barrage. Kerrivan had his arms around Tobin's great belly, his eyes smarting from the whip of the air rushing by. They moved like bullets past cars and lumbering trucks, taking the curves with a list that made his stomach churn.

Tobin spun off onto the airport road east of Gander, glanced at his watch, and shouted back to his passenger, "We got two minutes. We ain't gonna stop at no gate."

The bike crashed through a wooden barrier and through the gate. The watchman rushed outside his guard house, yelling and waving, then leaped for his life as Fitzgerald's hog came screaming through the gate.

There was chaos in the tower. The air controller was shouting through an airport-wide system. "Get those guys off the field! Alert all aircraft! Get those assholes out of there!"

"Oh, *Jesus*, there's something coming!" his assistant yelled.

It was on the screens – and it was out there to the south – and it was all lit up and forty feet above the runway and coming down.

"Looks like a goddamn B-26!"

•

Johnny Nighthawk

We run for the plane as it brakes and wheels about, and we are up the ladder before Billy Lee has finished his U-turn.

The two-wheel boys are still running patterns on the runway, and there are so many sirens and flashing lights it is like a travelling carnival.

Billy Lee guns it, playing chicken with an oncoming police car. Billy Lee wins, the car goes careering away into the mud.

"Git up, sweet baby, git up! Git up, Mary Jane!"

His beautiful old bomber skims over the trees and settles into an altitude which is no more than two hundred feet above them.

"Man, am I tired," Billy Lee says. "I been flyin' all day. On uppers, lid-proppers. Didn't have no time to say hello to the folks back home. Jus' put a couple of bladder tanks on the wings and flew like crazy." He blinks his eyes and stretches.

"I worked this here out with one of your boys on the way out of here. Knew I'd have to time that little ol' touchdown to the second. I mean I ain't even *stoned* – I had to be *that* sharp, man."

He lights a big joint that is sitting in the ashtray. "At last, man," he says. He takes a deep draw on it, holds his breath, then blows out. "Ah, man, this here shit is jus' so *fine*. You guys know some friendly place over on the mainland where we can gas up?"

"Northern Maine," says Pete. He picks up a chart and shows the spot to Billy Lee.

"And where do you reckon we should go after that, Pete?"

"Miami." Pete says it ever so softly. . . .

●

Mitchell, alone in his hotel room, was on the telephone with

Wegthorne. "Somebody did a switch on you," he said.

"No, sir, no way. I have the only key to the locker."

"O'Doull has a key."

"No, sir. Standard procedure – one key. Also, the initials of the members who took the samples were on the seals on the envelopes. What does it all mean, inspector? What happens to Kerrivan now?"

Mitchell spoke slowly. "I guess he . . . goes free. We'll get the conviction quashed."

Mitchell let the phone slip into the cradle. He poured himself a large tumbler of scotch and water. He looked like an ancient stone fortress fallen to ruin.

The phone rang again. It was from the Gander airport detachment.

CHAPTER FORTY-EIGHT

Jessica Flaherty leaned from the driver's seat and smiled amiably at O'Doull from the passenger window. "You came all the way back down here just to see little old me? Nice."

Flaherty did find him attractive. Gentle, perhaps a little too earnest. But attractive.

O'Doull slung his bag into the back, got in, and she drove off.

"If it doesn't sound too obscene, what's up?" she said. "A mysterious call from the Miami airport. A quick clandestine meeting at Concourse B. A handsome Canadian Mountie. A sexy female narc. Let's find a sleazy motel."

O'Doull glanced at her. Sexy she was, sexy in a low style. She was in faded jeans, high leather boots, and a T-shirt a size too small. On it were the words "Blow it up your nose" and a comic face with straws sticking out of both nostrils.

"I'm undercover," she said. "Do you think it's too obvious?" She looked at his heavy tweed jacket. "You're going to die in that thing."

O'Doull shrugged it off and threw it over the seat. "I didn't have time to change," he mumbled.

They drove in silence. She took an aimless route, the expressway to the west, then Highway 27.

"What am I supposed to do to make you talk?" Flaherty asked. "Put splints under your nails?"

"We've been had, Jess. Duped and diddled."

"Stung, stuck, swindled, and screwed," she said. "Is it a word game?"

"There's an old con trick," O'Doull went on. "The gypsy switch. That's what Kevin was trying to say to Pete on the ship-shore phone – Meyers had done a gypsy switch on them."

"Gypsy switch?"

"You buy a gold watch and they pull a switch on you; you open the package and it's made of tin. Or you buy a gram of coke and find out it's icing sugar."

"Or you buy some grass," she said, smiling. "And you find out it really *is* grass. The kind the cows feed on."

O'Doull looked at her quickly. She began to laugh.

"Suckers," she said. "I *told* Mitchell he should call it Operation Crackpot." She was laughing so hard that tears were beginning to come. She had to pull over to the side of the road and wipe her eyes. O'Doull just stared at her.

"Fifty tons of alfalfa," she said, coughing, struggling to control herself. "So it took your brilliant police force this long to figure it out. God, I'd love to have seen Mitchell's face. The poor schmuck." She took a deep breath. "I hope you guys haven't paid Meyers yet. Well, I guess you haven't. He's disappeared."

"You've known all along?" O'Doull shook his head as if trying to clear one of his daydreams from his mind. "Do you mean *you* guys did the switch on us?"

Flaherty tried to settle herself down, but broke out in giggles after a few seconds. "No, no. What do you think we are – crooks? Meyers was using you. Rudy Meyers – your own hired agent."

"And you were using us," O'Doull said slowly.

Flaherty started driving again, looking over her shoulder, pulling into the traffic. "Yep. You've been *double*-diddled. Hell, I'm sorry, but it was a perfect scam for us. When Mitchell came to me for help in finding a double agent, a

355

drug mole, I figured: this is perfect – the best possible way to keep an eye on Meyers. I knew Meyers was looking for a skilled crew to carry a big crop owned by Paez. And I figured this was the best way to keep a watch on him. A controlled delivery, as we say. And, Christ, for Meyers, it seemed perfect, too. He could get his dope into the States under the protection of the Royal Canadian Mounties. The shipment of alfalfa hay would be seized and burned. Paez would be none the wiser."

O'Doull slid back into his seat. He felt he was becoming unstuck.

"Meyers was the big fish that we were trying to catch. Kerrivan and his band – they were just bait. Small fry wiggling on the hook."

"And what were we?"

Flaherty glanced at O'Doull. Was he just squinting at her, or was he glaring? "You were his delivery service. The RCMP sea express."

"Holy fuck," O'Doull whispered softly to himself. After a while he asked, "How did Meyers do the switch?"

She avoided the question at first. "Ever been out to the Glades? It's a pretty drive." She turned west into Florida City, then continued along the highway to the National Park.

"The Sat-Track device," she said. "That was Meyers' excuse for pulling the ship into Miami. The transmitter probably could have been installed while the ship was still in Colombia, but Meyers needed a way to get the pot into the States. So he convinced Mitchell to go along with all the bullshit – the arrest on the high seas, the phoney courtroom act."

She looked at him, wondering how he was taking this. She felt a little badly – he was a nice guy.

"How do we know all this?" she said. "I had a man on the inside, code name Alfredo J., who was keeping me posted. Told me about Paez's big crop. Told me Meyers planned to do the switch in Miami. His Cuban guerrillas, the guys from the April Seventeen Movement, picked up a crop of hay somewhere, bagged it up in the standard sisal-wrapped *bultos*. They did the switch while Kerrivan's ship was sitting in the marina getting a paint job." She shook her head. "We missed it. Meyers is so quick, I can't believe it."

"And how was the switch made?"

"Remember the rusted old trawlers that were sitting beside the *Alta Mar* when it was in the ship-hangar? When we guessed what had happened and went out there, we found the trawlers had been towed away. Yep, all that fancy electronic equipment, the new paint job—all that was just a smokescreen while Meyers' men worked all night moving bales from the *Alta Mar* to the holds of the trawlers."

"Jess, I was on board the next day, checking out the Sat-Track, making sure it was functional. There was a bag of marijuana on the deck, open, spilling all over the place. It *wasn't* alfalfa."

"Oh, yeah, well they left that one bale on board the *Alta Mar*. A Coast Guard guy had ripped it open with a knife. They left it there so Kerrivan wouldn't get suspicious."

Flaherty pulled into a picnic area and killed the engine. She picked up a handful of cassette tapes from under the dashboard. "What kind of music do you like? Streisand? Willie Nelson? Rolling Stones? Everything for every taste. I've got Johnny Mathis singing 'Smoke Gets In Your Eyes.'"

"I don't care. I'm not interested in music."

"Something a little erotic? Here's something, like the disc jockey says, that I *know* you're going to enjoy." She plugged a tape in.

There was nothing for a minute, just some rustling. Then a male speaking Spanish in a husky voice.

"Translated," Flaherty said in a flat tone, "it means: 'No, my darling, take everything off. My God, how beautiful you are.' Let's move it ahead to the juicy parts." She pushed the fast forward.

A heavy male groan. A woman's voice: "*Come inside me. Oh, please come inside me.*" It was Marianne Larochelle. O'Doull's stomach turned over.

Again the man spoke in Spanish. Flaherty translated tonelessly, like a grade one pupil reading from a primer: "'Let me kiss it first. Let me reach inside you with my tongue.'" Flaherty's voice then became inflected with anger. "That bastard! That handsome, beautiful bastard! Here I am, sitting in a dark room, staring outside at a glorious moon, recording all of this, listening to it."

Then her voice became mournful. "You know, I really liked him."

Heavy groans of sexual hunger from the cassette. O'Doull wanted to scream at Flaherty to turn it off.

"Got to assume she isn't carrying the test tube of coke in there right now," Flaherty said. "I imagine they'd been snorting it earlier."

Larochelle's voice rose rapidly in pitch: "*Oh yes, oh yes. Oh please God, please don't stop. Mon Dieu! My God!*"

O'Doull was swamped by an ugly wave of *déjà vu.*

"*Dios!*" the man shrieked.

Larochelle's voice: "*Oh, Augustin, what have you done to me? I feel so strange. It's never been like this. Oh, God, I think I'm falling in love with you.*"

Flaherty loudly clapped her hands in mock applause. "Bravo! What a powerful performance."

"*Hold me,*" Larochelle's voice said. "*Stay inside me.*"

"*Forever,*" said the voice of Escarlata.

Flaherty took no notice of the fact that O'Doull's face had turned white. She merely sighed and sped the tape again. "Gets you right in the balls, doesn't it? We had enough wire in that penthouse to stretch a line to L.A. All legal, too." She pushed stop. "Okay, next scene: Kevin Kelly comes to the door about ten minutes later. He had been out getting stoned with some hippies in the park. Marianne and

Augustin scramble out of bed. There's some awkward conversation among the three of them. Then Colonel Escarlata blurts out to Larochelle: 'Don't go back to Canada. It's dangerous.'"

Flaherty found the right place on the tape after some switching back and forth.

"*Mi vida, don't go back to Canada. Stay with me. It's dangerous, and you can be arrested.*"

"*What do you mean?*"

"*You have been — how do you say? — set up.*"

Flaherty said, "She's really done a number on him and he is out to save her skin from the Mounties — and her friends' skins, too, for that matter."

"*I will go back to Cuba. Please come with me.*"

"*What in the name of the good Lord is going on?*" Kelly's voice.

"*There is a transmitter on the ship which Rudy and the police have put there. It is to track the ship by satellite.*"

"This is where Kelly goes to the phone," Flaherty said. "He raised the marine operator to try to warn Kerrivan."

"*Kevin, what are you doing?*" Larochelle's voice sounded anxious and confused.

"*I got to get ahold of Pete. I told him Meyers was a narc.*"

"*We have removed all the marijuana but a little bit.*" Escarlata's voice. "*Tell him to sink the ship, Kevin, and take the small boat in. It is the safe way. I do not want to see your friends arrested, my darling. I tell you this as a token of my love.*"

"He's got stardust in his eyes," Flaherty said. "Poor, sweet, beautiful guy." She sighed.

"*This is the marine operator speaking.*"

"We were hooked into the phones, too, of course," said Flaherty.

"*Kevin, I don't think you should.*" Larochelle's voice.

"*Now*, would you like to hear a little music?" Flaherty said, pushing the stop button. "Let's take a break. I can save the rest for later. The best part. Where Meyers comes waltzing in, right in the middle of Kelly's phone call to Kerrivan."

O'Doull's head was pounding with confused rhythms. "You listened to Kevin and Escarlata die." He spoke bitterly. "Were their deaths all part of the DEA master plan, too?"

"No, Theo, that's the last thing we wanted. I called the police right away. It was me who phoned the hotel desk, by the way, not Larochelle. I'm sorry about Kelly, of course. But Augustin – that really *was* a bummer. If he hadn't been killed, Meyers would be in the clink right now."

"Augustin Escarlata," O'Doull said slowly. A light began to flicker in his head. "He was your inside man. He was your . . . Alfredo, you called him?"

"Code name Alfredo J. I still don't know what his real name was. He was a find – God, he was a find."

"How *did* you find him?"

"Actually, he kind of found us. He wouldn't take any money. He was working *with* us, really, not for us."

"Who was he working for?"

"Cuba. Castro. They sent spies on the boatlift. Tent City was crawling with them. But Augustin was class, he was their number one. Probably actually *was* a Cuban colonel. Jeez, he was *so* good. You know, I think I could have fallen in love with him. Those romantic evenings on the park bench. But the subject was usually Meyers, though. Not love. Or we talked politics. He kept asking me if I was interested in politics. Ultimately, he took a chance on me, told me he trusted me, told me he was working for Fidel. He was a Red, Theo."

She sighed. "He took a *real* chance on me. If I had snitched on him to the CIA, those boys would have bumped him. Poor Augustin. He might have survived this and gotten back to Cuba if he hadn't fallen for that bitch Larochelle. What's she got, anyway? As if I don't know."

O'Doull tried to censor thoughts of Larochelle, tried to clear his mind of her and concentrate on Colonel Escarlata. "So he was sent here to infiltrate the anti-Castro terrorists," he said. "And he found his way into the April Seventeen Movement." Things were coming together as he spoke. "He met Meyers. And after he met Meyers, he came to you. He found out Meyers was going to finance the movement with three hundred million dollars' worth of dope money." He smiled crookedly at Flaherty. "He used you the same way you used us."

"Yeah, I guess. Meyers was going to finance a goddamn invasion of Cuba – that's what Augustin was worried about. The CIA – maybe they were getting the word from the State Department – didn't want me to touch Meyers. But I got my job to do, and I don't buy their crap."

She looked sad. "I wonder if Augustin was married? Anyway, I was supposed to meet with him one last time. In the park. At two o'clock in the morning. He was going to tell me where Meyers planned to stash the grass."

"And where *is* the grass?"

"I don't know. Augustin never made it to the park. And now we've lost Meyers." She shook her head sadly. "We blew a great scenario, Theo. Augustin was going to give us the word, and we were going to scoop Meyers sitting on top of a mountain of marijuana. And we were going to watch his crafty grin disappear from off his face."

O'Doull felt a little thrill of revenge over it all. He felt his police force had been badly used. "So you're up shit creek without a witness," he said. "Meyers has got away with it."

"We scoured their camp – the April Seventeen camp – the barracks, everywhere. We've had Meyers' office staked out for the last ten days. We ran a few test calls through his office, so we know he picks up his messages by pager. He calls from pay phones – local calls, not long distance. In the meantime, he's selling off the pot a few hundred pounds at a time. Just enough to keep the prices high without glutting the market. When it's all gone, he'll surface again – maybe in Cuba with three thousand mercenaries armed to the teeth and ready to start World War Three."

"Jessica, you ended up suckering everybody – even yourselves."

"The joke, hah-hah, is on us."

"Funny as hell," said O'Doull, "funny as hell. Well, I'll tell you something even funnier. I can find Meyers."

"I beg your pardon?"

"I can find that son of a bitch. I put together a little thing for Operation Crackpot, as you call it. I figured we'd slip it into Pete's watch. But it turned out Pete doesn't carry a watch. So I planted it on Meyers, instead. I had a hunch Rudy might try to disappear."

"Are you kidding, Theo?"

"A little bird-dog transmitter, no bigger than a match-head. While Meyers was taking a shower at the DAS camp, I slipped it inside his pager and wired it up to the antenna. Operates off the batteries."

Flaherty's mouth and eyes were all wide open.

"I'll need a large-scale chart of Miami," O'Doull said, "and a high-gain preamp to tie into a transmitter-receiver. Then we just crystal it to the right frequency and drive around Miami. The receiver will tell us when we're getting warmer or colder. It's like pin the tail on the donkey."

Flaherty leaned over and bussed O'Doull lightly on the cheek. "I think it's time you heard the rest of the tape, Theo." She pushed the play button.

CHAPTER FORTY-NINE

Johnny Nighthawk

I have lost track now. I forget what I numbered the last few tapes. This is Nine or Ten. I have got to get out of here soon. I have a living to make.

Okay. Miami.

The fix-it man is out of the country on business – this is what we learn from the woman who answers his office phone. She does not know when he is due back, but if it is urgent, she will take a message. She is not at liberty to say where he is.

Pete has the whole story about Kelly's murder, because Sergeant O'Doull spent some time filling him in and Marianne added some facts in a long note she kited to Pete in the St. John's lockup. And now Meyers has vanished. We ask ourselves: is he on the run from the police?

But, no. When Billy Lee phones the cop shop (he is a reporter from the Miami *Herald* catching up on old murders) he is told that the file has been closed. Murder-heart attack. What we expected.

These cops sure are pigs, I am thinking. Kelly has just been written off by them.

Pete is not fazed. He is prepared to wait Meyers out. Our guess is that he is still calmly playing both ends, and has gone off to Cartagena to report the disaster to Senator Paez.

"He'll be back," says Pete. "I will get him." That is how he puts it: I will get him. What does "get" mean?

Billy Lee tries to lighten things by showing us a good time in Miami, which he knows well, it having been a main staging area for many of his operations. We take a rented car to Lauderdale, to a smoke-easy he frequents there. He promises us European beer, girls, laughs, various varieties of hemp and other organic and chemical compounds, and not exactly under the table.

The front door operates on the Joe-sent-me principle. There is a glass fisheye in it so the manager and bouncers can look you over.

"Private club," a guy yells. "We don't know you."

"Just say Billy Lee Tinker."

After a second the door swooshes open and a big happy black guy, decked out in feathers and velvet, explodes out of there and wraps his arms around Billy Lee like a TV wrestler.

"Hey, White Trash, how you doin', baby?"

"Hey, Jake, give me some of them nigger fingers."

And so on. "Couple of my friends up north from the National Honkie League," Billy Lee says introducing us.

"*Hey*, man!" Skin is given, and we are ushered inside. Billy Lee is *known* in here. There is back-slapping and yahooing, as if Terry Bradshaw or Ferguson Jenkins had just walked in. In fact it is something like a Miller Beer commercial: "Hey, ain't you Pete Kerrivan? Hey, fellas, Pete Kerrivan! What a pleasure to meet you, man."

The Hawk is content to warm himself in the glow. Somebody thrusts a beer in my hand and I drop it back and grab another. I feel I deserve a few.

A hundred people are crowded into this room which is sweet and spicy with smoke. We have pushers, rounders, grifters, and wheelers with money to spend. Across the way a couple of guys are marking numbers with chalk on a board, taking down orders being called to them by the customers.

Jake shoves at us a little black fellow with a goatee. "This here is Brother Moses. He will get you what you want, when you want it, however you like it. Your credit's good, Billy Lee." Jake wanders off to tend to some other favourite customers.

Moses seems a little shy in front of The Presence. "How is it, Billy Lee?"

"Moses, how are y'all? Thought you was shovin' weed up north."

"Jus' about to go. Now, Billy Lee, you and your friends should try a little of this here." He pulls a pinch of weed from a beaded leather pouch and tamps it into a small-bowled pipe.

"Wal, I don't mind," says Billy Lee.

"Jus' take a half a lung of this, man. It will knock you on your butt. Ain't bin nothin' like this around here, ever. Like, *ever*. Baddest dope you ever taste, man."

When Billy Lee is in mid-toke, his eyes pop out. He takes the pipe from his mouth and pokes around in the bowl with his little finger, as if he is looking for some kind of strange bug he has seen in there.

"Where did this come from?" he says. He passes the pipe to Pete, who takes a taste. Pete looks at Billy Lee, frowning.

Billy Lee jabs a finger at Moses' jacket pocket. "Gimme, gimme." Moses hands the pouch over, and we rummage around inside it, rub the buds, smell our fingers. I take a little toke, a tester. It is definitely *punta roja*, all female flower. It has a very pungent, familiar bite. With his perfect palate, Kevin would have known for sure.

"Where did you get this?" Billy Lee repeats.

"It's yours, Billy Lee. There's three-quarters of a lid in there." Moses is proud of his generosity. "It go a hundred and eighty a ounce. *Here*. In Miami. Be two-fifty in New

York. Man, this is going to be a *boring* trip north." Boring? I guess that means the opposite. A guy has to keep up with the words.

"Now, Moses," Billy Lee says, "maybe you're a little whacked or somethin', 'cause you don't hear me so good, and I want you to listen real careful, 'cause I'm askin' you agin to tell me where you got this flowertop from, man."

"Yer talkin' near twenty-five hunnert a pound for quantity." Moses has a sly look. He is thinking: maybe Moses the Goatee will make a score off Billy Lee Tinker himself.

"Who connected you, Moses?"

"Man, I cain't make nothin' if I gives away my businessman." His eyes dance from Billy Lee's to mine to Pete's. Finally Pete, who manages our shrinking supply of dollars, peels five hundreds off the roll in his pocket, fans them out for Moses to see, then tucks them into his leather pouch and hands that back to Moses.

The little man peers around the room until his eyes settle on a skinny Latin type sitting at a table doing some business. Moses bobs his head in that direction.

"How much of this is there around?" Pete asks.

"Steady stream," Moses says. "Twenty, thirty pounds a day around here. Lotsa folks movin' it north."

We had never counted the bales when we unloaded at Captain Pike's in Judas Bight. It could be that as many as fifteen, twenty bales had been lifted from us here in Miami. By the guys who were working on the ship when we got out of the slammer here, I am thinking. Meyers' boys.

"That guy, he a Colombian?" Pete asks.

"No, Cuban."

Pete says in a low voice, "Maybe we can recoup some of our losses, boys." Louder. "Moses, go and tell him we are friends. Big buyers. Tell him to meet us outside."

Moses does that. He lets the man know we are good people, and the Cuban looks around the room, spots us, flashes us a smile and a wink. We wait a while, have another beer, then go out.

We can tell he is carrying a heater. He extends his hand. "Jorge," he says.

Billy Lee introduces us around. "I'm Chopper. This is Duke and Jack." I am Jack. Billy Lee will later amend it to Mad Dog Jack.

"My friends and me, we're big buyers from Texas," Billy Lee says, putting his arm about Jorge's shoulders. "I do Houston, Duke does Dallas-Fort Worth, and Jack does San Antone and west. You're gonna be a rich man, Jorge. Now how much of this *sinsemilla* you got?"

Jorge takes us to an old red Cutlass convertible and opens the trunk. Three pounds, bagged up.

"No, Jorge," Billy Lee says, "don't fuck us around." He switches to Spanish. "We are interested in hundred-pound lots."

Jorge shakes his head. "I can get fifty pounds at one time. I sell fifty pounds, I get another fifty pounds." His eyes look beady with concern. We are close enough for him to feel our hot breath. "I can see you tomorrow," he says.

Pete nods to me, and I twist him over the car with his arm bent behind his back. Pete pulls a loaded Saturday-night special from the Cuban's inside jacket pocket and pushes it against the man's ribs. "We are going for a ride," Billy Lee says. "We'll use our car."

We cruise a while, little rain-squalls hitting us from time to time. Finally, we park near a golf course, where it is dark. Billy Lee does the talking.

"The big guy on your left. They call him Mad Dog Jack in San Antone. Duke, on the other side, he got his brains scrambled when he O.D.'d on acid. All he can think of is killing. He *likes* to kill. We got to watch him close, Jorge." Billy Lee smiles. "What happened, man, is we got ripped off. And we think your front end are the guys that ripped us off. We lost millions and we're really mad about it. And Duke back there, he's so mad he's gonna cut your nuts out with a shiv if you don't tell us where this comes from." Real Al Capone. Billy Lee looks it with his dark glasses and five days' growth of beard. The cast on my hand helps me look heavy, too, although basically I am a natural for the part.

After more cajolery, Jorge guides us to Little Havana, down an alley off Flagler Street, to the back entrance of a little real estate business — a screen, probably, a *pantalla*. Billy Lee gets out and peeks into a window. There is light coming from behind a curtain.

"Can't see it, but you can smell it," he tells us. We leave Jorge and follow Billy Lee to the door. Jorge will run away, but he will be just one less fellow for us to handle.

I am able to take the door off with two hits from the heel of my boot.

"Miami police!" Billy Lee yells as he strides in. "Freeze!"

Who can tell these days who is a cop? We make a pretty good job of it, school of Starsky and Hutch.

There are two guys in here, weighing and bagging up about a hundred pounds of our *sinsemilla*. They are not carrying, which is a good thing, because there might have been blood spilled. But there is an automatic rifle sitting on a chair.

"There's enough here to send you to Raiford for twenty years," Billy Lee yells. "You fuckin' *chiciteros*! Scum! Poisoning people's minds!" He is shouting at them hysterically in two languages and has one of them against the wall, holding his shoulders with his big basketball hands.

"Calm down, calm down," Pete is going.

Billy Lee continues to rant, says we should "let the cocksuckers have it here and now."

"Easy, sergeant, easy," Pete says. "It's not *these* guys we want. We want the pushers who're supplying them."

This looks like the back end of the operation. There is

more where the hundred pounds has come from.

We pretend to have a little conference, and they can hear us arguing.

"Come on, let's just take them in, lootenant," Billy Lee says. "And maybe take a couple of rounds out of them on the way."

"No, I think we can make a deal," Pete says. He talks to the Cubans in Spanish. "I'll tell you what we're going to do. You show us where the stuff is, we'll let you go, we won't lay charges. But if you don't, my friends, we are going to beat the shit out of you, we are going to charge you with assaulting a police officer, possession of an illegal firearm, possession of narcotics with intent, and you guys are going to be stamping out licence plates for the rest of your lives."

CHAPTER FIFTY

The warehouse was on the Halifax waterfront and it was full of damp.

Peddigrew switched on the lights and locked the door behind him. There were evil smells from the stuff that had been on the *Alta Mar*: a mix of mildew and marijuana and salt and the disinfectant spray that health authorities had covered everything with.

But it was all here, the radios, Omega, depth sounder, radar – all the gear that Meyers had paid for.

"Well?" Peddigrew said.

"Well what, James?" said Larochelle, suppressing a smile.

There was no suppressing the smile of Senor Felix Juares, the proprietor of Maritimas Manejos del Atlantico, S.A. of Barranquilla, Colombia. Juares smiled until his gums showed. Finally he said, "Hokay, Senor James, we show you."

Juares and Larochelle waded into the jungle of gear and began hauling out all the orange plastic-covered lifejackets they could find, throwing them into a pile.

She counted them out. "Twelve of them, that's right. Thank God, we didn't have to use these. They'd have taken us straight to the bottom."

"Each wan seven kilo, Senor James." With his jack-knife, Juares slashed one of the vests open, slitting through both the fabric and the cellophane wrap inside. Several grams of uncut cocaine spilled onto the warehouse floor.

Juares scooped a thousand dollars' worth of snow into his hands and smeared it on his face and grinned. He looked like a kid caught in his mother's flour bin.

Each gram of this cocaine when cut twice with procaine would yield three hundred dollars, street price.

"You may not win all your cases, James," said Larochelle, "but somehow you always end up on top."

"Let's get these into the car," said Peddigrew. "It's a long, long drive to Toronto."

●

Johnny Nighthawk

It is a modern mansion near the ocean, secluded, surrounded by mangrove trees. There are maybe two or three acres inside a high spiked fence. From behind the fence, five Dobermans are snarling at us.

The gate can probably be unlocked only by electronic signal from inside the house. There is a buzzer outside it, but of course we do not try to announce ourselves.

The Cubans whom we arrested are still in Little Havana, still in the back of the real estate store. They are safe there, in the mop closet, their hands tied with good fisherman's knots, their Colt AR-15 rifle in the trunk of our car. If they yell out, their rescuers will find the hundred pounds of pot, so we do not expect them to yell out.

Pete has Jorge's loaded .22 in his pocket. "I am going over the fence," he says.

I say I will go with him but he says no. "I'll get the gate open from inside the house. Then you guys can drive in."

"Aw, Pete."

"Just keep the dogs off my ass. Occupy them."

He walks down the fence line while Billy Lee and I make

friends with the dogs. Billy Lee has a good country way with dogs and after a few minutes they are licking his hands.

Pete has disappeared. . . .

•

The fence took a right-angle turn, and he turned with it, keeping close to it, away from the swamp. He stopped where he could get a good view of the house from between the trees. It was an overpowering fruit salad: part Tudor manse and part Spanish hacienda, with wide arches, deep balconies, red-tile rooftops cascading down three levels. There were yard lights at back and front. Stained and leaded-glass windows on the ground floor glowed from a light inside. A young but sturdy banyan tree shaded the east wing.

Kerrivan went over the fence, sprinted across the lawn, climbed the banyan tree, and swung down from a branch, softly, onto a balcony.

A sudden rain shower muffled his sounds as he peeled the lead strip away from a pane of glass, reached inside, unlocked the door, and entered. He was in a bedroom. In the dim light he saw that the furniture was hidden by canvas dust covers.

The air reeked of marijuana.

He stepped into the hallway onto an inner balustrade, which looked down into a Spanish-style court. The furniture there, too, wore dust covers. There was light from a wall fixture near a covered bookcase.

Kerrivan was staring down at a hill of *bultos* – hundreds of them. Some were opened.

He crept down the great, curving staircase and went to one of the open bales. Scooping a handful of marijuana flower from one of them, he went to the light, and held the *sinsemilla* to his nose.

It took a minute or two for the full effect of Meyers' enormous sting to penetrate through him. He closed his eyes and took a few deep breaths.

It was a premonition, perhaps an extrasensory message, that caused him to whirl and duck suddenly as a hand flashed by with the speed and strength of an executioner's axe and cleaved through the fabric covering the bookcase, splitting canvas and wood and bringing down a hailstorm of old first editions.

Meyers' second blow was blocked by a collection of eighteenth-century poetry, and Kerrivan was quickly out of reach, pulling his gun as he scrambled away, pointing it at Meyers.

"I am not alone," Meyers said. "There are armed men in the guest house in the back." He was in a dressing gown, in bare feet.

"If you wake them up, I'll shoot you."

Meyers' face took on an expression of relief.

"Oh, it's *you*, Peter. God, I thought it was a thief. Or even worse, the cops." He smiled his flat unsmiling smile and took a few steps to the wall. Kerrivan kept the gun trained on him.

Meyers casually lifted a canvas-covered painting from its hook and set it on the floor. He began dialling the combination of the wall safe.

"This modest little *casa* was the safest place I could think of," he said. "Our company has been guarding it for a rather rich fellow who has gone on a four-month sailing cruise. A *very* rich fellow. Not a bad little hideout, is it?"

He brought out four thick bundles of currency. "I can't give you your full share right now. We're trying to sell it in small lots to keep the price up." He threw the four bundles at Kerrivan's feet. "That's four hundred thousand dollars."

Kerrivan knelt down, keeping his eyes fixed on Meyers, and picked up one of the bundles and stuffed it into his jacket pocket. "This will be for Merrie and the two kids," he said. "The rest I think I'll leave for the police. For when they come to bust you. Because I'm calling them, Meyers. Where's the phone?"

"Oh, come off it. I knew they wouldn't be able to keep you in jail when they found out it was only alfalfa. I've been waiting for you to show up so I could get some money into your hands. I thought you'd be *congratulating* me for having pulled this off so well. Take the money. It's yours. Hell, you can even take my car. I'll even see you to the door – and if you're going to be nervous about it, keep the gun on me."

"I suppose Senator Paez will be coming around soon, looking for *his* share."

Meyers grinned. "Come on, you and I both know he can grow lots more where this came from. What he doesn't know . . . ." He shrugged.

"Won't kill him," Kerrivan said. "But he'll kill you, won't he? You'll be number-one target for some jailhouse hit man when they put you in the joint." Kerrivan half-smiled. "That suits me just fine."

Meyers became animated. "Oh, for goodness' sake, Peter, let's stop fooling around. It was a scam; of course it was a scam. We're both in the business and we both know what it's all about. If you can get away with it, you're a winner; if you don't, you pay. You'd do the same thing in my shoes, Peter, the same thing. So I didn't get away with it. I pay. You know you can grind it out of me, and darn it, I'll pay. I don't wish to get arrested, and there's absolutely nothing in it for you if I do get arrested."

"Where's the phone?"

"Half of it. Half of every dollar I make from it. You've talked to Paez, and you've heard his little speech about trust. So I know you're going to squeeze me. Come on, Peter, you'll be a multi-multi-millionaire. Four hundred thousand now, and two hundred thousand week after week after week."

Kerrivan looked through the sliding aluminum doors that led out back to the swimming pool. Under a canopy was a poolside extension phone. He moved slowly to the sliding doors and rolled one of them open.

"Two hundred million dollars, Peter! No taxes to pay off that to the bandits in Washington. You love the sea – buy yourself a luxury sailing yacht. Heck, buy yourself a South Pacific Island. Buy yourself a New York chorus line for the night." He was a man pushing the keys, looking for the right one.

"How much will it take to buy back Kevin Kelly?" Kerrivan asked. He motioned with the gun for Meyers to follow him outside.

"*Oh*, no, you're not going to blame me for that one. Not for that one. Now, Peter, I didn't kill him. I promise you that. My word of honour. That's all been cleared." He was talking rapidly.

Kerrivan picked up the receiver and dialled the operator. His eyes were off Meyers for less than a second, but Meyers was flying at him by the time he released his index finger from the dial. Again, instinctively, he pulled his head back.

Meyers' foot was aimed not at his head but at the hand holding the gun. He seemed to put all his strength and leverage into the one lunging roundhouse snapkick, and it was on target. Kerrivan felt the bones of his fingers crack; his arm went numb. The gun whirled through the air and splashed into the water.

Kerrivan's street instincts took over. Meyers' lunge had been a desperate one, and he had saved nothing for a counter-strike. Out of control, he was unable to dodge Kerrivan's blow. The crashing left hook hit him square on the ear, and he sprawled. But he somersaulted as he did, and was on his feet again, centring, calming himself, his hands forward in the *zenkutsu-dachi* front stance.

Kerrivan didn't know any better than to come straight at

him. Meyers caught his forward arm in an upper rising block, took him off balance with a leg sweep, and swung him lightly over his hip. As Kerrivan fell head-forward, Meyers kicked away the arms that he had extended to ward off the fall, and Kerrivan's head hit the tile, landing with a crack. He grunted and lay limp, one arm dangling over the edge of the pool in the water.

Rudy Meyers breathed out slowly. His mind ordered his body to relax, and his body obeyed.

It was necessary now to be very calm.

None of his soldiers in the guest house had stirred from their sleep. Meyers was thankful for that. Witnesses would add complications. Simplicity – that was the key element of any good operation.

Where were the dogs? Had Kerrivan poisoned them?

He could see that the man was still breathing. A concussion, that was all.

Meyers wondered why he had not killed him at the outset. Kerrivan had come at him clumsily, an incompetent brawler. Meyers could easily have cleaved his face in with a right-handed knife edge. That he had not done so made him wonder at his will and resolution in future combat situations.

His weakness made him angry, and he reached down and slipped Kerrivan's glasses off, crushing the metal frames in a balled fist.

No, he told himself. Be calm. Again he stilled his body.

He picked Kerrivan's head up by the hair and searched with his fingers for a nerve point at the base of the ear. One squeeze there, then convulsion, then death.

But he hesitated. He thought. And he realized now that his earlier instinct in avoiding a quick karate kill had been the correct one. The injury would have told a tale. As would, he now realized, a bruise behind the base of the ear – or upon any of the killing points on the body.

Think, he told himself. Don't act quickly. But think quickly. Remember your training. The temptation is to be too clever, to indulge oneself in the brilliancy of one's skill and craft. . . .

Kerrivan groaned, and Meyers watched him, his mind racing. It would be easy to end his life – in so many ways. An eye-socket gouge. Or, better, a quick two-handed slap upon both ears. But that, too, would tell a story to a skilled investigator. Only a master could accomplish such a death. And Meyers would be the first suspect.

It must look like an accident. The body would have to be removed from the house – perhaps wrapped up in one of the empty marijuana bags. He smiled inwardly at the irony of a dope pusher's body being carried away in old marijuana sacking. Yes, that was the plan. They would have to move all the bales out, anyway. If Kerrivan had found him, others might.

Well, it was obvious: a skull fracture. A fatal brain injury. After all, there was contusion to the scalp already. The body could be found at the bottom of a cliff far away from southern Florida. The bottom of a rocky cliff.

The best strategies are the simple strategies. He had always believed that. But time was wasting. Bending down, he grabbed Kerrivan by the hair, lifting his head, then smashing it on the poolside tile. Meyers felt the cracking of bone, but the skull didn't cave in. The man had a head like a granite boulder.

There was a distant, tinny voice coming from somewhere. Was a radio on? Then he saw the telephone dangling off the hook. "Hello, sir, are you there?" An aggravation. Unsettling. Meyers could not abide open telephone lines – a private detective's paranoia. He went to it, rubbed the receiver with the velour fabric of his dressing gown, then settled the receiver on the cradle.

He returned to the poolside to attend to Kerrivan who still, amazingly, was breathing. This time he took a firm grip with both hands, one on each of Kerrivan's ears, and raised him up three feet off the tile, took a deep breath, and began to bring his head down towards the edge of the pool with all his force.

CHAPTER FIFTY-ONE

Johnny Nighthawk

I saw a blurred picture as I ran by the front of the house, a picture framed first by a pane of leaded glass, and second by the open doorway to the swimming pool. This was the picture: Rudy Meyers, with one hand holding Pete's head by the hair, smashing it onto the edge of the pool. A stark still-life that visits me yet, sometimes in my sleep, sometimes when I am awake.

It is worse in my sleep. I am running by the side of a house, a house as long as the Wall of China, and, oh God, I am running so slowly. I am encased in sludge, in a molasses bath, my thigh muscles aching, straining, pulling, and I am moving a few feet, and Meyers is bringing Pete's head down, and Pete's eyes are open and he is staring into mine, and I will never get there because I am pulling a thousand-pound weight behind me, and my mouth is open but no sound comes out . . .

(Although once, at night, a sound did come out. My senorita told me that I lurched from bed in the darkness and screamed, "I'll kill him!" She was in a state of terror.)

In reality, I suppose I was going like a cannonball, churning through flower beds, past the garage, across a patch of lawn, and out into the open behind the swimming pool. I

379

remember that it did not seem to make sense that Meyers, with his back to me, had just hung up the phone. Then I saw him going back to Pete, grabbing him by the ears, pulling his head up, bringing it down. . . .

I explode into Meyers like a runaway locomotive.

All I know next is that he and I are in the deep end of the pool, and he is thrashing crazily, like a speared crocodile. I lose my grip and his head comes up, and he screams: "I can't swim!"

And I get him under the surface again. He is a powerful man.

And I keep his head down. He is a wild windmill of arms and legs.

I remember hitting him with the cast on my hand.

And I keep him under. I keep him under. I cannot remember what I was feeling. Loss. Pain. Hatred.

He is tugging, pulling, biting, fighting with the strength of the gods. But slower, and slower, and slower. Then he stops moving. And I keep him down, pushing him deeper, deeper.

I can hear voices trickling through the great dam of anger and hate that has cut me off from the world.

"Johnny! Johnny, let him up!"

Whose voice is that? A voice I know. Yes, it is the voice of Billy Lee Tinker. A man who is a friend.

And other voices:

"Nighthawk, stop! Stop! Lord, I'm going in there."

A woman's voice: "It's too late. He's crazy."

Billy Lee again: "Johnny, Pete's *alive!*"

I bring Meyers up and watch his blue moonface bob to the surface, its eyes closed. I stare dully at this face, studying it with awe and puzzlement. A man begins to hoist him by the armpits up over the edge of the pool.

I recognize the man. He is the cop from Newfoundland. O'Doull, Kelly's friend. The woman is the DEA lady from Miami. I make out Billy Lee. He is squatting, with the

Dobermans beside him, and he is stroking them, cooling them out, and with his free hand he is holding the AR-15 rifle. He has it pointed at a group of men standing nervously near a guest house.

I take all this in as I scramble from the pool. I go to Pete. A trickle of blood is seeping from his mouth. I hold my ear to his mouth and I can feel and hear his sweet breath upon it.

O'Doull is kneading Meyers, pumping water from him. He turns him over and gives him mouth-to-mouth. Meyers starts sputtering and coughing.

But I am still in a blind, hysterical rage. "If Pete dies, I'll *kill* the son of a bitch! Get an ambulance. Get a doctor! If he dies, I *will* kill him. I *will* kill him!". . . .

•

O'Doull walked slowly from the emergency door of the hospital to Flaherty's car. She was behind the wheel, butting a half-smoked cigarette into the ashtray.

When O'Doull sat beside her, he hunched his head down, and pressed his hands to his face, beating back the waves of tension.

"Did they let you speak to him?" Flaherty asked. She lit another cigarette.

"A few minutes, that was all. He gave me the missing link." His voice sounded raw.

Flaherty wanted to reach out to him, to cradle him, soothe him. She made a tentative half-start, then reached a hand to him, touched the back of his neck, and began gently to massage the muscles there.

"When are you going back?" she said.

"Right away."

"Oh."

That was all she said. A nice man was Theophile O'Doull. Another nice man leaving her life. She felt suddenly lonely, vulnerable. But she was a cop, she told herself. Tough.

CHAPTER FIFTY-TWO

Peddigrew stumbled up to the door of his townhouse, swung five lifejackets in front of him and, panting, found his key and unlocked the door. That surge of power one feels with a few lines of pure cocaine did not speak falsely to him about the real condition his body was in. He had been neglecting the racquetball court. Juares, in no better shape, wheezed up the steps to join him.

But Larochelle looked as if she were carrying bags of feathers. She had stubbornly continued to do her exercises during every one of those mind-scrambling days since Miami. This morning, in her motel room – they had stopped overnight then continued their long drive from Halifax – Larochelle had danced around for two hours, high on cocaine. She liked the shape she was in.

Lara Peddigrew, hearing the commotion and the laughter at the front door, fluttered into the living room and greeted her husband. Peddigrew laid a delicate touch of a kiss on her forehead, then heaved the orange lifejackets, one by one, through the corridor, into a pile on the living-room floor.

For their seven years of marriage Lara Peddigrew had maintained, in Peddigrew's view, an innocence that verged on empty-headedness, and he preferred it that way. He never discussed with her, and refused to involve her in, his varied matters of law and business. She was beautiful, she was upper crust, and when they had guests she was a marvellous entertainer.

And what's more, she loved him – the sexual encounter with Kerrivan notwithstanding. She was the perfect wife.

His perfect wife fixed a trained eye on Larochelle, offering a smile that was expertly feigned. Larochelle was not her favourite person in the world. Entertaining her husband *and* his mistress was too much. Plus they add in this smelly Colombian.

"James," she said, "there's someone here to see you. I told him that you had just called from Port Hope to say you'd be here in an hour and a half, and I suggested he might have some tea while I made dinner for you and our guests. Was that all right?"

Peddigrew was so scared he felt his testicles rolling. "What do you mean, someone is here?" he said in a low voice. "I told you not to talk to anyone while I was gone. Who is it?"

"A Mr. . . . Dooley?"

Peddigrew put his head around the corner of the vestibule. Beside the pile of lifejackets there was an armchair and in that armchair was Theophile O'Doull, a briefcase on his lap. He looked sad.

"Lara," said Peddigrew, "would you go into the kitchen and prepare some hors-d'oeuvres?"

She went without a word to the kitchen.

Peddigrew assumed a haughty bluster. "Sergeant, I don't receive business visitors at my home at seven o'clock in the evening. You may call my secretary and make an appointment for tomorrow in my office."

O'Doull ignored him. He was looking at Larochelle.

"Hello," he said.

"Hello, Theo," she said. That was all. That, and her quiet smile.

O'Doull felt pain beat through him. It was a pain that had

never been there in his daydreams, where the hero felt no pain, no hurt, where the hero, the brave Detective O'Doull, was a man emotionless, controlled, capable of any special assignment.

"Would you please leave," Peddigrew said. "I don't wish to seem rude or inhospitable, but I am entertaining friends for dinner, and we are tired and we need a chance to clean up." With a gesture of his arm, he showed O'Doull where the door was.

O'Doull looked wearily at the door, looked at Peddigrew, and said in a soft voice, "You're under arrest, Mr. Peddigrew. The fellow who is standing behind you – I take it that is Juares? Mr. Juares, you are also under arrest."

He cleared his throat. "And so are you, Marianne."

He watched their faces change.

"The charge is importing cocaine into Canada."

"Cocaine?" Peddigrew engineered an expression of astonishment.

"Is it in the lifejackets?" O'Doull asked. "Oh, don't answer yet. It is my duty to warn you that you need not say anything but anything you do say may be used as evidence at your trial. Now you can answer. Is the coke in the lifejackets?"

The only sound was heavy breathing. O'Doull shrugged. He opened his briefcase, removed a cassette tape, plugged it into Peddigrew's stereo system, and turned it on.

"I have your party, ma'am."

"James, it's me, again."

"Yes."

"They've let us go!"

"What?"

"With the ship. With everything. I'm going to lay low. I'll be up in a few days. Pete is taking the ship up, but with the way this trip is going, they're sure to be caught."

"Did you unload the ship?"

"No, it's all there."

384

"I mean the . . ."

There was the sound of him blowing into the receiver. "That's your charade for blow, I think, Mr. Peddigrew," O'Doull said. "Blow, snow, cocaine."

Larochelle's voice: *"I know what you mean, the Hoagy Carmichael. It's still on the ship."*

"Stardust," O'Doull said. "So I have heard it called."

Peddigrew's voice: *"Telephone down to our friend. He is to meet us here in two weeks. Don't worry. Even if the ship gets busted, everything will be all right."*

"That is so," said O'Doull, "because even if we did arrest and seize the ship, you intended to get its contents released to you. That was your plan all along. In fact, it was just as easy for you if Pete actually did get busted. Then you could make a deal: the ship's gear in exchange for a guilty plea from your client. And indeed that's what you did. Like an Arab slave trader, you bartered him for the cocaine. And for Marianne's freedom."

He advanced the tape.

Peddigrew had turned white, and staggered as he made for a chair. His hell seemed to be expanding like square numbers multiplied. There is no feeling worse in the kingdom of the mind than that produced by a rush of cocaine terror.

Juares was still standing, uncertain, rubbing his hands. Larochelle had her eyes closed and seemed lost in space.

"Juares? Como esta?"

"Senorita Marianne! How are you, my pretty princess?"

"It will be up in two weeks. Come to Toronto then."

"Si."

"Call our friend at his office. Do you have that? Entiendes?"

"Si. Sure."

"Goodbye."

"Very brusque and businesslike," O'Doull said.

Lara Peddigrew arrived with a tray of canapes. Her husband waved her away with an angry sweep of his hand, not looking at her. "This is business, dear. Leave us."

She took a sense of the room, left the tray on the table, and stepped quietly out.

O'Doull ran the tape forward. "A few minutes later, Augustin Escarlata comes back from the sauna, and there is an erotic, if not exactly touching, love scene. *Joy of Sex* on tape. I'll spare you that. You should have accepted his invitation to go to Cuba, Marianne." She had her eyes shut tight, seemed to be struggling against phantoms in the recesses of her mind.

O'Doull continued. "Kelly comes in and Escarlata, as a gesture of love for Marianne, blows Operation Potship, tells them about the Sat-Track. And Kevin calls the marine operator in an effort to raise Pete."

"Jesus! Yeah, this is the Alta Mar."

"Pete. Pete. Can you hear me? I can hardly hear you, boy. Can you hear me?"

"Jesus ... world can hear. What the hell ..."

"Pete, listen careful. The ship is bugged. They got a tracker wired up to a satellite –"

" ... can't –"

"Meyers is working for –"

" – read you ... can't ..."

" – the narcs. It's a set-up."

"Repeat, I can't read you!"

"Just a minute. Stay with me. Hang on. I'll be back to you."

"Meyers has just knocked on the door," O'Doull said. "Kelly lets him in. I assume that Marianne and Augustin are hiding in the bedroom. Is that right, Marianne?"

"Don't say anything," Peddigrew mumbled.

"I'm sorry, I was hoping that Augustin would be here. Who are you phoning? I don't want you using the phone."

"Just making a plane reservation."

"Okay, now Meyers leaves. That sound is the door closing."

"Kev? You there?"

"Deep-six it, boy. Deep-six the cargo."

"Get off . . . and . . . off the fucking phone!"

"It's almost all alfalfa, Pete. Alfalfa. Meyers did a gypsy switch on us."

"I can't read!"

"Jettison the cargo, Pete! Sink the fucker and take the longboats in. It's a con. Scuttle the ship, Pete!"

"Those are the last words Kevin ever spoke," O'Doull said.

"I've got to stop him!"

"That's your voice, Marianne. There was a mike in the bedroom. You were thinking: scuttle the ship, and the cocaine goes to the bottom, too. You had lost the pot, and now you were going to lose the coke."

From the tape came the sound of a grunt, and a clattering noise, the kind a phone makes when it falls on its cord and bangs against a piece of furniture. O'Doull pushed the stop button.

"I didn't know until Pete told me at the hospital that you have a black belt in Tae Kwon-Do. It is among your many other accomplishments. Of course, the Miami police knew all along the murderer was you. That's why they were playing with me, secretly laughing at me while I was insisting that you saw blood on Meyers' shirt sleeve. Jessica Flaherty, who was taping all this, called the police up to the penthouse. She made a deal with Detective Braithwaite, Miami homicide. The Miami police agreed to follow you, but not bust you right away, so Jessica wouldn't risk compromising the investigation against Meyers."

O'Doull shook his head ruefully. "Problem is, you slipped away from them. Out of Miami. With my help."

"It was an accident, Theo."

"Marianne!" Peddigrew shouted.

"Too much coke in me. I went snow-crazy. And . . . and it gives you extra strength. You forget to measure your force. I meant to pull. I . . . I just wanted him to stop talking to Pete.

I didn't *mean* to kill him. Please believe me!"

"Uh-huh. Well, we have Kevin lying there dead, now. Dead of the heart attack you caused. Then you placed the phone back on the hook. And then we have this." O'Doull pushed play.

"Mother of God, Marianne! What have you done?"

"Oh, my God, I don't know."

"He's not breathing!"

"Augustin, please, come here. Hold me. I love you and I'm afraid."

O'Doull cut the tape in the middle of a terrifying shriek.

"And then there were no witnesses," he said.

He began passing around arrest warrants. There was an extra one for Larochelle, for her extradition to the State of Florida.

Larochelle wept. "How can you do this to me?"

"It isn't very easy, Marianne."

From her front window, Lara Peddigrew watched with dry eyes as O'Doull and two other policemen walked the three prisoners across the street to the squad cars that had been sitting in the shadows, waiting for Peddigrew and his friends to return from Halifax.

She had mixed feelings. She was glad to see Larochelle get hers. But she felt sorry for her husband. This was a hell of a price to pay for getting yourself hooked into a female spider like Larochelle. Greed and infatuation make a poor mix.

But Lara Peddigrew wasn't all that unhappy to have her freedom from the man. As she had him figured out, he was basically an asshole.

Johnny Nighthawk

Last tape. This is really a postscript.

I will be going back to Colombia in a few days. I have half a ton of high-grade *mona*, blonde, which is on its way down from the mountains. I will be hanging out by the Guaviare River waiting for the *canoas* to come. Sometimes it seems they take forever to bring it to you. But of course I am a gringo, and for gringos it is always rush, rush, rush. The Latins do not understand what the point of the hurry is.

I will probably still be sitting on the banks of the Guaviare when your book gets published. With my luck.

Send me a copy. That is all I want. No money. (I know writers are poorly paid. You have explained that to me.)

As I say, this is a postscript. The aftermath won't be of interest to you for your story. But let me fill you in on everybody just for your own curiosity.

As far as Johnny Nighthawk is concerned, he cannot get out of the smuggling business. Hell, I am not even trying. It is my work. It is what I do well.

Same with Billy Lee. He is still flying stoned. When I last saw him he was heading for Thailand. Different people, different scenery. He says he is going for the big one this time.

A four-ton cargo of Thai stick. I wish him well.

I met O'Doull when we both happened to be visiting Pete's farm at the same time. He is all right. He was thinking of quitting the force, but it looks like he is staying in, waiting for a transfer to come through to CID. He is a cop, that is what he is. I do not mean pig. I mean cop. He says he believes in the system. In the long run, as he puts it.

The Bullet, though, has quit the RCMP. I hear he is executive manager of the Canadian subsidiary of a U.S. home burglar alarm company.

The only person the courts are through with so far is Juares. He got fifteen. There was twenty million dollars' worth of coke involved, I hear.

Peddigrew is out on bail fighting some technicality – a writ of prohibition? – to the Supreme Court of Canada. I understand that that old lawyer Knowlton Bishop is prosecuting him. I would sure like to sit in on that one. I *can* go back to Canada. They dropped my charge, of course, and quashed Pete's conviction.

Marianne finally got extradited to Florida. She has some hotshot Texas lawyer working for her. He is probably working for nothing, having, doubtless, fallen in love with her. She had me going, too. I am not ashamed. The female of the species is more deadly than the male. True of hemp, true of humans.

Meyers is sitting in a federal prison writing detective novels. I am told he is appealing a ten-year sentence on the basis that the marijuana was seized illegally on the high seas. They say he has raised a convoluted argument about entrapment. But they got him for trafficking, for sure.

As far as Captain Jackpot is concerned, he has thirty-five acres in New Brunswick, an old lady, some farm animals. Sometimes I think he is okay. Sometimes I am not sure if he has permanent head damage. Mostly he sits out on his rowboat on a lake, fishing. He *seems* happy. He smiles. He does not talk much. I note that he does not smoke much grass any more. It is like he is stoned anyway, without it.

I hope Kevin Kelly is somewhere around, too. Enjoying an altered state of consciousness.